WOMEN v. RELIGION

"This book gathers together some heartfelt writings of women who give overwhelming evidence of the multiple ways in which religion has betrayed and abused the female sex. To read these writings is to realize that religion has been far more cruel than kind to women; and this is particularly reprehensible in view of the fact that it is based on lies, concocted for profit and for the benefit of men. A thoroughly enlightening work."

—Barbara G. Walker, author of *The Woman's Encyclopedia of Myths and Secrets* and *The Woman's Dictionary of Symbols and Sacred Objects*

"As someone who was raised in the Methodist church in the Midwest, I didn't meet another self-identifying atheist until I was in college and I didn't know any female atheists until law school. If I had been able to read Karen Garst's book then, my journey out of religion would have been easier. These essays about dealing with the socially ingrained biases against those who identify as female reveal how religion instigates and perpetuates those biases. All people will benefit from reading this comprehensive collection that explains the obstacles and struggles women face in and out of religion."

—Amanda Knief, Former National Legal Director, American Atheists and author of *The Citizen Lobbyist*

"Ever since the woman who went from talking to me on Skype to adopting me as her daughter after hearing my story, I've been in constant awe of her ability to empathize and stand up with others for what's right and good in this world. This book is no exception, as she takes stories from so many different experiences of women, and catalogues them here to give them voices. Karen Garst is one of the most caring, motivated individuals I've ever had the pleasure of meeting, and this book does a phenomenal job of not only displaying that, but backing up what she means when she says she wants to include the lives and experiences of others. She literally brings them together."

—Marissa McCool, author of *Silent Dreams: A Series of Essays and Poems from a Public Transgirl* and podcaster at The Inciting Incident

"In this collection of powerful essays—both personal and academic—Karen Garst thoughtfully and comprehensively tackles the subjugation of women by the Abrahamic religions. The book provides compelling arguments to back the proposition that these religions continue to assign second-class status to women around the world. The wide range of expertise offered by the anthology makes it an important addition to the growing pantheon of contemporary religious critiques—this book should serve as a clarion call to feminists everywhere to discard the psychological chains that religion imposes."

—Monica L. Miller, Senior Counsel, American Humanist Association

"Reading *Women v. Religion* is truly a journey through the minds and lives of women who have experienced the oppression and intimidation of the Abrahamic religions. They often lay their inner struggles bare as they take you through the journey of being in search of validation and wholeness. The essays clearly show that as one attempts to meet the constrictions of religious 'rightness' and 'goodness' they become lost to themselves. Shame, guilt, sin prevail until religion's grip is released allowing for the full expression of the individual."

—Rebecca (Becky) Hale, President, American Humanist Association and board member of the International Humanist and Ethical Union

"Despite the patriarchal and misogynist origins of many world religions, women of all ethnicities have the highest rates of religious participation across the globe. What accounts for this seeming contradiction? What social and cultural factors can address this disparity? The multi-faceted essays of Karen Garst's *Women v. Religion* provide an insightful historical critique of the dominance of organized religion and how it undermines gender equality, women's self-determination, and the agency of women of color. The book is a valuable resource for secular and religious scholars seeking an alternative to the thesis that organized religion and faith are necessary moral and social forces in women's lives."

—Sikivu Hutchinson, author of *Moral Combat: Black Atheists, Gender Politics and the Values Wars* and *Godless Americana: Race and Religious Rebels*

"Abrahamic religions infantilize all people, with their father figures and supplication demands. But women are especially subordinated. How? Karen Garst explains, in a book that provides a valuable compendium of smart, thoughtful critiques of religion's treatment of women. This tightly edited collection of essays by an array of accomplished women writers will enlighten and entertain even as it infuriates you with its deep dive into the patriarchy that is religion."

—Robyn E. Blumner, President & CEO, Center for Inquiry and Executive Director, Richard Dawkins Foundation for Reason & Science

"If you ever wondered about women's roles in religion through the ages, *Women v. Religion* will thoroughly educate you. If you ever doubted that religion has systematically subjugated women, this book will dispel those doubts. This set of essays is clearly written by 13 secular women and carefully edited by Karen Garst, but it's not exactly an easy read. It's a serious, revelatory, sometimes revolting and always carefully portrayed collection of women's trials with religion."

—Linda LaScola, co-author with Daniel C. Dennett of *Caught in the Pulpit: Leaving Belief Behind*

"This is an important and timely book, at a time when Islam is being labelled as a "feminist religion" by ignorant feminists who know little of its bloodied past. It is important to look at the time before Islam, at the lives of women erased during early Islam, so this myth of an equal religion cannot be popularized."

—Sadia Hameed, Spokesperson, Council of Ex-Muslims of Britain

WOMEN v. RELIGION

The Case Against Faith—and for Freedom

Edited by Karen L. Garst, PhD

PITCHSTONE PUBLISHING
Durham, North Carolina

Pitchstone Publishing
Durham, North Carolina
www.pitchstonepublishing.com

10 9 8 7 6 5 4 3 2 1

Library of Congress Cataloging-in-Publication Data

Names: Garst, Karen L., editor.
Title: Women v. religion : the case against faith—and for freedom / edited
  by Karen L. Garst, PhD.
Description: Durham, North Carolina : Pitchstone Publishing, 2018. | Includes
  bibliographical references.
Identifiers: LCCN 2017058147 (print) | LCCN 2018007940 (ebook) | ISBN
  9781634311717 (epub) | ISBN 9781634311724 (ePDF) | ISBN 9781634311731 (
  mobi) | ISBN 9781634311700 (pbk. : alk. paper)
Subjects: LCSH: Women and religion. | Sexism in religion.
Classification: LCC BL458 (ebook) | LCC BL458 .W655 2018 (print) | DDC
  200.82—dc23
LC record available at https://lccn.loc.gov/2017058147

To Elizabeth Cady Stanton

Take the snake, the fruit-tree and the woman from the tableau, and we have no fall, nor frowning Judge, no Inferno, no everlasting punishment—hence no need of a Savior. Thus the bottom falls out of the whole Christian theology. Here is the reason why in all the Biblical researches and high criticisms, the scholars never touch the position of women.

—Elizabeth Cady Stanton, in defense of *The Woman's Bible*

Contents

Introduction

My involvement in the issue of atheism began when the US Supreme Court issued its decision in *Burwell v. Hobby Lobby Stores, Inc*. In this case, a privately held corporation was allowed to avoid paying for certain forms of birth control for its female employees based upon its religious views. As a woman who grew up in second-wave feminism in the sixties and seventies, I couldn't just sit idle as women's rights were again jeopardized. As I believe religion is the last cultural barrier to gender equality, I write to inform women of its historical subjugation and degradation of women.

Prior to publishing my first book, *Women Beyond Belief: Discovering Life Without Religion*, I read extensively about the origins of religion, early worship of a female divine or goddess, the presence of pantheons of gods and goddesses across several cultures, and the development of monotheism in the Abrahamic religions. In addition, I built upon my doctoral studies on cultural reproduction to learn about the role of culture in the propagation of religion. My first book was composed of personal stories of twenty-two women who had left religion. This book focuses on how religion affects women from the perspectives of psychology and science as well as how women of different races and sexual orientations have been adversely affected by religion. As the title indicates, the case will be made that religion is against women. The verdict is in your hands.

After the tragedy of the September 11, 2001 attacks, four writers became synonymous with the New Atheism movement. They were called the Four Horsemen in reference to a term in the New Testament's book of Revelation. One of them, Daniel Dennett, states the following three purposes that religion serves: "to *comfort* us in our suffering and allay our fear of death, to *explain* things we can't otherwise explain, to encourage group *cooperation* in the face of trials and enemies."[1] His claim makes sense in the context of ancient history, when most religions began. Fifty thousand years ago, there was no science to explain the cycles of the moon or the natural disasters of volcanic eruptions or floods. A belief in a supernatural being or force helped early humans explain these phenomena. Gradually, the notion of specific deities developed across virtually all cultures, eventually resulting in what we call the practice of religion. Today, religion has permeated every aspect of our beliefs about who we are, where we came from, or where we go after we die. It has influenced our music, our language, our rituals, our communities, our political systems, and everything else that can be called culture since that time.

Its legacy, unfortunately, has not had a benign effect on women. All of the Abrahamic religions originally subjugated women, making them less worthy than men, unable to participate in religious leadership, and even responsible for original sin. Women were considered property and could be bought and sold like slaves and killed for committing adultery or for not being virgins when they married. They couldn't own property and were considered unclean. Women have made progress in terms of equal rights with men, at least in Western democracies, but even these gains have been fairly recent. Women in the United States have held the right to vote for less than a hundred years. It was not until 1960 that the first effective contraceptive was approved by the Federal Drug Administration. In 1972, Title IX prohibited educational programs, including sports, from discriminating on the basis of sex. In 1973 abortion became legal in the United States in the Supreme Court's decision in *Roe v. Wade.*

Yet even in the United States, women still face barriers. Why have we never had a woman president? Why don't we have more women as head of Fortune 500 companies? Why has the United States not signed the UN's Convention on the Elimination of all Forms of Discrimination Against Women? Why don't we have paid maternity and paternity leave like other countries in Western civilization? Why does there continue to be an attack on women's reproductive rights? Of course, the rights of women outside of Western democracies, particularly in countries with highly religious

---

1. Daniel Dennett, *Breaking the Spell: Religion as a Natural Phenomenon* (New York: Viking Penguin, 2006), 102–3.

populations following the Abrahamic tradition, are far more restricted. Practices like female genital mutilation, veiling, requiring a male escort, prohibition of driving a car, and no access to certain reproductive rights, to name just a few, still subjugate women today.

When examining the causes of the unequal status of women anywhere in the world, it would be hard to find a bigger culprit than religion, particularly monotheism and the Abrahamic traditions that form the basis for Judaism, Christianity, and Islam. Together, these three religions are embraced by 55 percent of the global population.[2] The next largest group, at only 15 percent, is identified as Hindu. Because the Abrahamic religions make up such a large portion of the population and therefore influence society so heavily, these three will be the focus of this book.

There is a tendency, especially on the part of religious apologists, to justify this subordination in religious texts and practices by stating, "It was just the way it was back then." However, this is not accurate. In the last sixty years, many books have been written that show reverence for a supernatural being may well have begun with a feminine divine. In the various caves dating from the Paleolithic era (from 2.6 million to 10,000 years ago), hundreds of figurines have been found, the majority of which represent females. Often referred to as "Venus" figurines, these images are carved out of soft stone, bone, or ivory. It is impossible to know exactly why these figurines were carved or how they were used. Did a woman clutch one as she was giving birth? Did a man carve one in reverence for the birth of a child? Most of them are found in the front of the caves where the hearth was, not in the back of the cave where the men and shamans painted bison on the walls and prepared young men for the hunt. What we do know is the making of these figurines was not an isolated event and the practice continued for tens of thousands of years.

Riane Eisler, in *The Chalice and the Blade*, states that these figurines were "all expressions of our forebears' attempts to understand their world, attempts to answer such universal human questions as where we come from when we are born and where we go after we die."[3] Steven Brutus, in *Religion, Culture and History*, refers to the work of Eisler and others who

---

2. Pew Research Center, "The Global Religious Landscape," December 18, 2012, http://www.pewforum.org/2012/12/18/global-religious-landscape-exec/.

3. Riane Eisler, *The Chalice and the Blade: Our History, Our Future* (New York: HarperOne, 1988), 6.

have linked ancient worship to female cult figures when he states that "the most important finding of all this work goes to the root concept of religion itself —*religare*, to tie or bind, to be tied to something, to belong—that the mother-child bond stands at the origin of worship."[4] Some of these carvings show a relationship between the cycles of nature and women. On one carving, entitled *Venus of Laussel*, a woman holds a bull's horn with thirteen slashes. Joseph Campbell, a master of mythology, hypothesizes that this number might relate to the number of nights between the first crescent and the full moon and the number of cycles of menstruation the average woman experiences in a year.[5] Imagine the questions that arose when early humans saw the correlation between these cycles.

Fast-forward to the Neolithic era (10,000 to 3,000 BCE) particularly in Crete, an island in the Mediterranean, and we see an advanced culture (viaducts, paved roads, indoor plumbing, and a flourishing trade). Yet the art contains no scenes of war, there are no massive fortifications around the cities, and certain frescos clearly contain figures of a woman to be revered—a goddess? a queen? What we do know of this period and beyond, from studying civilizations in the Middle East and around the Mediterranean Sea, is that most societies eventually developed a pantheon of gods and goddesses that were revered and worshipped in tandem. Many of us remember that class in high school where we tried to learn all the names of the Greek pantheon. The Romans simply adopted the Greek pantheon but gave them each a new name. What happened to these female deities? Why were they eliminated? How did monotheism arise and why? Reading the literature reveals several theories: the invasion of warrior clans, the need for militaries, the advent of private property for agriculture and herding, and the consolidation of power and religion in the hands of male leaders.

One of the earliest civilizations to rid itself of the female deities was the Babylonians. In their epic myth *Enuma Elish*, Marduk, the top male god, makes a deal with his fellow gods. If they will support him as supreme god, he will kill Tiamat, the goddess. The Hebrews, exiled in Babylon in 598 BCE for several decades, were exposed to this myth. This exposure likely

---

4. Steven Brutus, *Religion, Culture, History* (Portland, OR: Daimonion Press, 2012), 94.

5. Joseph Campbell, *Goddesses: Mysteries of the Feminine Divine* (Novato, CA: New World Library, 2013), 67.

firmed up their support for a single male deity even though references to worship of a female divine and multiple gods still remain in their writings from that time. There is even a creature in the Bible that is similar to the sea goddess Tiamat called a Leviathan. This sea serpent gets cut up into pieces in Isaiah 27:1 just like Tiamat was in the Babylonian myth.

And it continues on into what would become today's Abrahamic religions. What we see from the early biblical writers is a constant effort to put down the worship of Asherah, a female goddess worshipped by members of their tribes. These verses from Jeremiah 44:17–19 show the struggle the Israelites went through to enforce the worship of a single male deity when a group rebels and wants to return to the worship of a female divine, the Queen of Heaven.

> "Instead, we will do everything that we have vowed, make offerings to the queen of heaven and pour out libations to her, just as we and our ancestors, our kings and our officials, used to do in the towns of Judah and in the streets of Jerusalem. We used to have plenty of food, and prospered, and saw no misfortune. But from the time we stopped making offerings to the queen of heaven and pouring out libations to her, we have lacked everything and have perished by the sword and by famine." And the women said, "Indeed we will go on making offerings to the queen of heaven and pouring out libations to her; do you think that we made cakes for her, marked with her image, and poured out libations to her without our husbands' being involved?"

Furthermore, it is not a coincidence that the images of the female goddess in Canaan—both a snake and a tree—figure prominently in the Genesis story of Adam and Eve.

It is hard to overemphasize the importance of scriptural writings codified in a single book in each of the Abrahamic religions. These books formed the centerpiece of each religion and allowed the leaders to spread their message far and wide. The manuscripts or scrolls of the Old Testament are referred to as the Tanakh in the Jewish tradition. The early Christian communities had a myriad of documents which were codified as the New Testament in various councils as early as 393 CE in North Africa. When Islam developed, it too codified its teachings in a book called the Kuran, or Qur'an, in 609 CE. By this time, a book was essential if it was going to compete with Judaism and Christianity. The Church of the Latter Day Saints, which identifies as a sect of Christianity, also adopted a book claimed to be revealed to Joseph Smith in nineteenth-century America called the Book of Mormon.

Each of the essays in this book examines one aspect of the impact of these three Abrahamic religions on women. In the first essay, licensed professional mental health counselor Candace Gorham, author of *The Ebony Exodus Project*, dives deep into the impact of religion on our psyche. She outlines the basics of mental illness that can be caused by religion, including depression, anxiety, shame, and guilt. Gorham also discusses the ineffective religious treatment for mental health problems such as pastoral counseling, conversion theory, and faith healing.

Lauri Weissman, a professor of communications at a top-ranked American university, gives an overview of the first in the three Abrahamic traditions, Judaism, and its proscriptive roles for women. As "an oppressed and isolated minority within an oppressed and isolated minority," Jewish women have endured millennia of religiously justified misogyny. Scriptural disgust for female bodies and demand for ritual purity enforce an essential "otherness" by which women are excluded from leadership roles and core practices of many Jewish communities. These earliest attitudes are replicated by Islam and Christianity, which hold some of the same core texts to be sacred.

Alexis Record, frequent book reviewer and blog contributor, expands Gorham's discussion by focusing on the impact of childhood indoctrination. Record was raised in a fundamentalist household and was educated using Accelerated Christian Education. In 2001, Norway banned the curriculum for violating their Gender Equality Act.[6] A mother's roles are discussed as "helper, cook, cleans house, washes and irons clothes."[7] Record concludes with an action plan to help children know what is true and to give them the tools they need to distinguish facts from beliefs.

Dr. Valerie Tarico, author of *Trusting Doubt* and blogger at www.valerietarico.com, gives an insightful analysis of the treatment of women

---

6. Jonny Scaramanga, "Norway Banned ACE. Could the UK Follow?" *Patheos*, August 4, 2014, http://www.patheos.com/blogs/leavingfundamentalism/2014/08/04/norway-banned-ace-could-the-uk-follow/.

7. http://faithlessfeminist.com/blog-posts/exposing-accelerated-christian-education/

in the Bible and early Christianity. Her work outlines the tendency of Bible writers and subsequent Christian leaders to eliminate any notion of a feminine divine and to paint women as unclean, dirty—literally property to be owned, given away, sold, or claimed as spoils of war by powerful men. Christian apologists like to ignore the Old Testament and focus on the New Testament. Yet as Tarico outlines so well, it is hard to ignore the statements of early Christian fathers or the roots of their disdain for women in the Bible itself.

The third Abrahamic religion, Islam, is explored by Hibah Ch. Ch is a Syrian expatriate born and raised in Aleppo in a conservative Muslim family. She left Islam in her twenties and now studies chemistry and mathematics in the United States. Ch reveals that female deities in the Arabian Peninsula were initially revered but subsequently destroyed by Islam. In addition, there were successful business women and female rulers prior to Islam. Inspired by the patriarchal norms of Judeo-Christianity, the founder of Islam, Muhammad, adopted many of their negative proscriptions regarding women.

Aruna Papp, author of *Unworthy Creature: A Punjabi Daughter's Memoir of Honour, Shame and Love*, was born and raised in India. The oldest of seven, Aruna's formative years were governed by her father's pastoral service, the culture of honor, and her yearning for an education that eluded her. In an abusive arranged marriage, Aruna immigrated to Canada with two small daughters. There she learned about the rights and protections Canada offers to women. She embarked on a frightening but empowering journey that lead to two master's degrees, and a second, loving, and mutually respectful marriage. In her pioneering career counselling immigrant women, Aruna has been the recipient of dozens of awards, including the Toronto Women of Distinction. Aruna facilitates training on how honor-based violence differs from domestic violence. As a Canadian delegate at the 57th Session of the United Nations, Aruna spoke on honor killing in the West.

The next two essays, written by Valerie Wade and Deanna Adams, outline the impact of religion on African American women. Wade is a historian at Lynnfield Historical Consulting, where she assists families with genealogical research and conducts workshops on preservation and other history-related topics. Adams is the author of the blog *Musings on a Limb*, where she expresses her views as an African American atheist, professional, and mom on subjects related to the intersectionality of racism and skepticism. She currently serves on the board of the Humanists of Houston. Wade describes the culture in Africa prior to the Middle Passage of the slave trade. In many societies in Africa, there was a strong influence of female goddesses like Mawu, Yemoja, and Ala. The advent of Christianity, with its rampant misogyny, however, put African American women in a double bind: they were disadvantaged because of their race and because of their sex. Adams continues this history and states that during the civil rights era, Christian churches held back and many avoided involvement. Just like in the churches, women's involvement in civil rights was more as workhorses. After this era, the prosperity gospel phenomenon took much of the women's hard-earned dollars. Other impacts such as the prevalence of domestic violence and the lack of psychologically sound support also contribute to the struggle of African American women today.

Marilyn Deleija, born in Guatemala and raised in Central California, gives a unique prospective on what it means to be an Atheist Latin immigrant. She has worked hard to be politically active in her community and has also helped to improve political information access to them. She is a local volunteer in Central California and has helped in moving her community progressively forward. In her essay, her experiences reflect what she sees needs to be changed with regards to religion and how it can affect local communities, but more specifically, Hispanic prominent communities, like places she grew up in.

Hypatia Alexandria introduces herself as a multi-faceted individual, dedicated to promoting secular values as well as social, political, and business interests in the US Latino community. She completed her education in an all-girls Catholic school. Thus, she is well aware of the huge impact of religion, particularly Catholicism, on the US Hispanic population. She writes and discusses the influence religion has on Latino women and the multiple barriers they face in achieving true gender equality. Hypatia cofounded Hispanic American Freethinkers (HAFREE), a non-profit organization that encourages critical thinking in the United States. She is currently a PhD student at Virginia Tech.

Kayley Margarite Whalen, digital strategies and social media manager at the National LGBTQ Task Force, adds yet another dimension to the subjugation of women by religion—that of a transgender woman. In her essay, she weaves her personal journey both as a transgender woman and as an atheist along with current research on gender identity. It is an issue that virtually all religions have not yet come to terms with.

Dr. Abby Hafer, author of *The Not-So-Intelligent Designer*, takes up the discussion of evolution in her essay. She points out that evolutionarily speaking, females are the first, original sex. She contradicts the argument from nature by showing the many different gender roles and forms of sexual expression that exist in the animal kingdom, and points out numerous fallacies in the idea of intelligent design, in particular with regard to women's reproductive systems. She shows how the Abrahamic religions go out of their way to trap women, and reveals that the natural rate of spontaneous abortions makes the evangelicals' God by far the world's busiest abortionist.

Gretta Vosper, author of *With or Without God* and *Amen: What Prayer Can Mean in a World Beyond Belief*, leads a congregation in Canada's largest Protestant denomination, the United Church of Canada. She is in the middle of a controversy and may lose or leave her position because she is an atheist. She explores how her congregation developed around her after her declaration of atheism and how she has attracted congregants who want the community that a church provides but none of the doctrine.

I hope you enjoy these essays as much as I have. If you would like to enter your verdict in the case of *Women v. Religion*, please go to www.faithlessfeminist.com.

Karen L. Garst, PhD

1

Guilt, Shame, and Psychological Pain

Candace Gorham, LPC

We look for peace, but find no good,
for a time of healing, but there is terror instead.

—Jeremiah 8:15

Guilt and *shame* are two words that are often used interchangeably. A response like "You ought to be ashamed of yourself. I hope you feel guilty" shows how the words can often be used in ways that seem to mean the same thing. However, the two words actually have significantly different definitions. Shame involves how one feels about oneself. It is painfully intense embarrassment and humiliation that arises from having done something wrong. People full of shame have done something wrong, and they feel bad about themselves for having done it. Guilt, on the other hand, is about feeling responsible for something wrong. Guilt involves feeling remorseful and deserving of blame. When observing the psychological impact of religion, we must start with guilt and shame, as many religious traditions thrive by playing upon them to manipulate the minds and prey upon the emotions of their followers.

The Bible introduces readers to concepts of guilt and shame as early as the third chapter of the first book of the Bible. Genesis chapter 3 is the story of Adam and Eve eating the forbidden fruit, becoming aware and ashamed of their bodies, and being banished from the garden after they are found guilty of defying god's orders. The stage is then set for a relentlessly recurring theme that becomes painfully entrenched in the hearts and minds of followers. Not surprisingly then, in my clinical practice, I find that clients who struggle with guilt and shame are quite frequently influenced by beliefs and traditions based on religions that include the Adam and Eve story in its lore, Christianity among them. Since my personal and professional experiences primarily involve Christian traditions, this essay speaks specifically to the impact of Christian beliefs and practices.

People feel guilt and shame for a wide range of reasons, and some people have more shame- or guilt-inducing triggers than others. In addition to what I've learned about religious triggers from my clinical practice, in my book, *The Ebony Exodus Project: Why Some Black Women are Walking Out on Religion—and Others Should Too*, I share first-person accounts of Black women's experiences abandoning their religious beliefs. All of these women reported struggling with these emotions during their time as believers. Quite often we find that those who come from highly conservative religious traditions are likely to experience more guilt and shame than liberal believers and nonbelievers. In Christianity, this is because the Bible lists literally hundreds of actions or events that would be deemed illegal, immoral, or detrimental to one's relationship with god. The Bible sometimes goes into great detail about these laws and mores so that when believers commit a violation—and they most certainly will violate something—they are aware of the crime and guaranteed to feel guilty.

While a Christian who breaks a law, also known as committing a sin, might publically wear guilt like a scarlet letter, when the violation is damaging to one's relationship with god, the person is much more likely to struggle with shame. Since shame is such a deeply felt embarrassment, it's quite common for believers to be more ashamed of secret sins than for ones of which everyone is aware. When god is disappointed in us, we are ashamed of ourselves. Since religion is often deeply tied to one's personal and cultural identities, the psychological impact of its precepts can run deeper than those of any other influence, including family.

Christianity taps into a childlike urge to please our parents, hence god being referred to as a father throughout the Bible. We learn to value our parents when we are small children and depend on them for everything. We quickly understand that doing things that make them happy helps us feel more bonded and connected to them. When we do something wrong and they punish us, I'd dare say that it is the sense of disconnection and fear that they will stop loving us that terrifies us the most. So it is for many people when it comes to their relationships with god the father.

Depression and Anxiety

By far, the most common mental disorders are depression and anxiety. These two disorders often go hand in hand and can occur as a single episode with a specific trigger or be part of a chronic, lifelong cycle of recurring episodes with no clear triggers. Depression involves experiencing daily life in a variety of unpleasant ways, such as increased irritability, generally low mood, lack of enjoyment, weight or appetite changes, changes in sleep patterns, decreased energy, decreased concentration, thoughts of death, and suicidal urges. Isolation, increased substance use, or interpersonal problems are often observed in depressed people as well. To do a quick self-check for depression, look up the Patient Health Questionnaire (PHQ-9) online.[1] It is a short screening tool consisting of nine common depression symptoms.

Anxiety, like depression, is a common experience. Worry, fear, and anticipation are everyday experiences for nearly everyone, and acknowledging this is often much more socially acceptable than talking about depression. However, once anxiety becomes disruptive to a person's life, it too can rise to the level of being a diagnosable disorder. There are a variety of types of anxiety including phobias, trauma responses, panic, obsessions, compulsions, and generalized anxiety. Thankfully, study after study show that a combination of basic talk therapy and medication are 70 percent, 80 percent, and sometimes even more effective at alleviating depression and anxiety and facilitating long-term recovery.

Religious traditions exploit our natural tendencies by tapping into

---

1. "Patient Health Questionnaire (PHQ-9)," *Patient*, https://patient.info/doctor/patient-health-questionnaire-phq-9.

primal parts of who we are as individuals and as a collective. Upon gaining access to those parts of our psyche, religion can implant all manner of unrealistic expectations for ourselves and others, landing us in situations where we've violated a law or expectation, or damaged our relationship with someone. For example, it is natural to want to feel special, uniquely valuable to those we love, and Jeremiah 1:5 is often invoked to do just that: "Before I formed you in the womb I knew you, and before you were born I consecrated you." However, that feeling comes at a cost. The believer is also subject to unrealistic expectations of perfection. "Be perfect, therefore, as your heavenly Father is perfect" (Matthew 5:48). Since no one is perfect, Christians can often find themselves feeling guilty that they've violated a law, and they worry that their imperfection will damage their relationship with god the father.

These experiences inevitability lead to depression and anxiety. It is a common occurrence for me to have clients who talk quite a bit about their religious beliefs. They talk about their religious upbringing, their desire to live according to sound religious doctrine or spiritual guidance, and their dependence on their faith as a coping mechanism. Unfortunately, what they don't realize—or are unwilling to consider—is that it might be that very faith that is at the root of the oftentimes contrived or artificial dilemmas that create the guilt and shame that fuel the depression and anxiety with which they are struggling.

Treating Mental Illnesses

When it comes to treatment for mental illness, some people who belong to church communities suffer because of explicit and implicit messages that tell them their psychological distress is merely a crisis of faith. Perhaps people's faith is being tested by god the way he tested Job in the Bible. Maybe people are going through a tough time because they are being punished for committing a sin. Even more sinister is the suggestion that some people are struggling with psychological distress because of direct demonic influence in their lives. When people are closely tied to an organization, they are at an increased risk of being plagued by shame because of the community's tendencies to assume guilt when people are going through hard times.

The first place many people in these communities turn to for help is their pastors. Even those who decide they want to seek professional counseling, outside of the pastors from their church, enjoy the great privilege of knowing that any given counselor in the United States is quite likely to be a Christian or to believe in a higher power simply due to the fact that we live in a Christian- or spiritual-majority country. Nonetheless, formal pastoral counseling programs and mental health training programs at religious institutions offering graduate level degrees from accredited colleges and universities have proliferated within the past decade or so. Schools such as Liberty University and Oral Roberts University produce thousands of clinicians each year who are trained to let their spirituality guide their practice.

While I have no doubt that there are high-quality training programs for licensed professional pastoral counselors who are just as prepared to handle mental health issues as any other clinician, I am more concerned about the concepts they draw from to inform their practice, namely the Bible and Christian doctrine, than I am about how well the counselor is trained. Supervision and continuing education can address clinical skills deficiencies, but it won't ensure that one trained in a religious program will use evidence-based treatment models over spiritual practices such as praying and reading the Bible.

I have worked with and supervised a number of graduates of the Liberty University counseling program, and I can attest to the fact that their religiosity is reflected in their work, even when they don't mean it to be. In fact, the Secular Therapist Project,[2] of which I am a member, was founded specifically because it can be so difficult to find even traditional mental health workers who do not let spirituality slip into their practice one way or another. The demand is so great that over eleven thousand clients have registered on the website to connect to one of the over three hundred therapists who have listed themselves as committed to providing only secular, evidence-based psychotherapy.

Another more extreme form of Christian mental health "treatment" is called deliverance, a protestant variation of exorcism. It is the process of breaking the influence of demons from a person's life and is common among the Pentecostal, charismatic, holiness, and evangelical sects. Some believe that there are demons physically inside of the body that have to be forced out, and others teach that demons can become energetically attached

2. https://www.seculartherapy.org/

to a person or an object and cause problems in a person's life by way of influence. In both cases, this casting-out process involves a minister with spiritual gifts from god necessary for successfully casting out a demon, a Bible reading, and frequently some talisman such as anointing oil or holy water. If you've ever been to a "shouting church," you'll know just how disconcerting it can be to see a person running around, screaming, flailing about on the floor out of control, supposedly the result of either a demon resisting being exorcised or the Holy Spirit overpowering the physical body as it cleanses. I've had many people tell me that merely observing such a scene was traumatizing. Despite that fact that these manic outbursts supposedly indicated that a person was being blessed, healed, or delivered, they saw it as proof that their problems could be caused by demonic influence in their lives, up to and including being possessed themselves.

The overall theme of the Bible is that you should put all of your trust in this supernatural power and worship him. In exchange for that worship and adoration, Christians who believe in faith healing often expect that god will keep them happy, healthy, wealthy, and wise as long as they trust, worship, and adore him. The converse is that if they waver in their trust and faith in god, they may find that when they need him the most, he isn't there. Perhaps that is why some Christians place such heavy importance on the practice of faith healing. In their minds, there is no better way to demonstrate the depth of their faith than by forgoing (or at least minimizing the use of) scientifically based treatment and risking their lives.

Because recovery is believed to be the result of divine intervention, followers of faith healing traditions sometimes teach that believers should not even consult with professionals for a diagnosis or medical advice. In these traditions, physical or psychological illnesses are believed to be curable by praying, reading the Bible, worshipping, and fasting. The problem with this approach is that life is full of adversity. Some problems are solvable, and some aren't. When the adversity someone experiences is believed to be directly tied to how well they follow spiritual laws, they are at a heightened risk for experiencing guilt and shame—they must have brought the adversity on through lack of faith.

The reasoning goes that sick people will be healed if they have enough faith and that they won't be healed if they do not have enough faith. So, as time goes on—it might be hours, days, months, or years depending on the illness—if they aren't healed, they begin to consider that maybe it is not simply a matter of being patient; maybe they are not getting healed because they are disappointing god in some way, either by committing a sin or by failing to trust in him completely. At this point, these people are not only ill, but they are also riddled with guilt and shame. Imagine how much worse the intensity of depression, anxiety, or any other mental illness would get if your hope is to be healed from a mental illness but no healing comes.

Beyond depression and anxiety, strict Christian doctrines can lead to numerous other mental illnesses and disadvantageous situations that negatively affect church members, particularly women, including posttraumatic stress disorder, abuse, loss of identity, and financial and medical danger.

Posttraumatic Stress Disorder

Decades ago, the public knew very little about posttraumatic stress disorder. It was typically referred to as shell shock and believed to affect only men coming home from fighting in a war. Today, posttraumatic stress disorder (PTSD) is getting increasingly more attention and media coverage, especially in response to the rise in PTSD-related suicides of military veterans, but it can affect many people without military experience too. Simply put, PTSD is an extreme anxiety reaction to a life-threatening event, whether real or perceived. Common causes of PTSD include fighting in a battle, catastrophic events such as natural disasters, car accidents, rape, and victimization from a violent offense. It is key to keep in mind that sufferers do not have to have been victims themselves in order to develop PTSD—the threat only has to be *perceived* as life-threatening regardless of whether it was or not.

People suffering through untreated PTSD episodes might experience periods of hypervigilance, hyperawareness, being easily startled, paranoia, angry outbursts and rages, or fear of leaving the house. Sufferers often also battle with intense flashbacks, nightmares, and sometimes even hallucinations. If the trauma can be linked to a specific person, place, or thing, PTSD sufferers will often avoid those trauma triggers by refusing to physically put themselves in such situations, refusing to talk about the event, and trying not to even think about the traumatic event. Luckily, there are a number of empirically proven treatments for PTSD.

In truth, PTSD is difficult to treat because of the complexity of its etiology, the specific traumatic situation itself, the progression of symptoms, and related physiological changes. Because of brain imagining, scientists can pinpoint the areas of the brain with abnormal levels of brain activity and note neurochemical changes typical of PTSD sufferers. As with many of the most common mental and psychological disorders, there are quite a few psychotropic medications that are highly effective at treating PTSD. Since PTSD is essentially an intense combination of debilitating anxiety and endless mood instability, anti-anxiety medications, mood stabilizers, and antidepressants reduce reactivity, nervousness, insomnia, low mood, and suicidal ideations.

Because of the difficulty in treating the disorder, many specialized and alternative therapies have been used either as primary treatments or to augment a traditional course of psychotherapy and medication. One such treatment process is called exposure therapy, in which patients slowly increase their exposure to an anxiety trigger and learn to eliminate the anxiety by pairing the exposure with relaxation exercises. Exposure therapy is a very slow and deliberate process and absolutely should not be tried by an untrained professional because of the risk of re-traumatizing a person during the exposure portions of treatment.

There is significant research that supports therapies that incorporate mindfulness and meditation techniques and philosophies into treatment. Also, a rising star in the realm of respected PTSD treatments is the use of cannabis. Weed can help people with PTSD function in their everyday life by calming anxiety and lifting the mood. Smoked or ingested just prior to a counseling session, marijuana can relax clients enough so that they can talk more deeply about their traumas without being re-traumatized by the discussion.

Hell-Induced PTSD

I am of the opinion that religions and many of the threatening stories, concepts, and philosophies that accompany them are powerful generators of PTSD. Remember that in order to develop PTSD, a person's life does not have to literally be in danger. One only needs to believe that one's life is in danger.

According to the Bible, a Christian's life is constantly in danger either from demonic forces, the wrath of god, or eternal damnation. The concept of hell is, undoubtedly, one of the most pernicious of all Christian tenets. The idea that god has prepared a place of fiery torment to which he will banish men, women, and children for an eternity is not just terrifying—it is unfathomable. I have heard many stories of people cowering in their beds at night contemplating hell and eternity, praying that the flashes of horrific scenes would not haunt their dreams that night—scenes of flesh that burns for eternity but is never consumed.

In the Old Testament, terms that translate to our modern-day word *hell* typically refer to either cultural beliefs or physical places that have nothing to do with torment. For example, there's a word that refers to the place where all dead people were believed to go and a word for the garbage dump outside of town. It is not until we get to the New Testament that hell transforms into what we know it as today, a place of torment and eternal punishment for unrepentant sinners. The book of Revelation truly reflects the modern image of hell as portrayed in classic and contemporary art, TV and movies, and literature. While things may be shifting, the historical ubiquity enjoyed by Christian traditions, stories, values, and laws suggests Christians likely perceive and receive regular warnings about the endless list of sins that could land them in hell. This, combined with images of what hell supposedly looks like, appearing in our culture all around us intensifies the fear that their lives are under constant threat.

Review the eight-part diagnostic criteria for PTSD[3] and you might be startled at just how many of the twenty-seven symptoms a Christian with hell-related PTSD might have. What deeply disturbs me is that the group most vulnerable and susceptible to hell-related PTSD is children whose minds can become so easily overwhelmed by the imagery. Preteens, too, are at risk. Their cognitive abilities are developing to the point that they are able to contemplate what hell would be like with all of its endless, intense fire. In fact, such images and deeper comprehension can be so overwhelming, some might argue that it is nothing short of emotional and psychological abuse to teach children about hell.

I, for one, recall what it was like for me around the ages of twelve and thirteen when I was most terrified. I experienced quite a few of the PTSD symptoms myself, including:

3. Diagnostic and Statistical Manual of Mental Disorders 5 (DSM-5), http://dsm. psychiatryonline.org/doi/book/10.1176/appi.books.9780890425596

- Having been threatened with death (I took the threat of going to hell to heart.)

- Exposure that was:
  - Direct (I read the Bible for myself.)
  - Indirect (I listened to preachers, overheard family members talk about it, and saw it in movies and on TV.)
  - Repeated (I attended church for years and loved watching movies and TV.)

- Intrusive thoughts or memories (I recall two specific family conversations that haunted me until I left Christianity altogether.)

- Nightmares related to the traumatic event (I counted any dream related to hell as a nightmare.)

- Flashbacks (Images from pop culture or descriptions in the Bible would frequently appear suddenly in my mind.)

- Psychological and physical reactivity to reminders of the traumatic event (I felt significant anxiety for years, even as an adult, at the thought of specific stories I had heard as a child.)

- Avoiding thoughts connected to the traumatic event (I tried not to think about the stories.)

- Avoiding situations connected to the traumatic event (I eventually stopped watching movies with demons or ghosts, reading scary stories, or participating in conversations on the topics.)

- Distorted sense of blame for one's self (When something bad happened to me, I frequently blamed myself and worried that I must have committed a sin and therefore was at risk for going to hell.)

- Negative thoughts or beliefs about one's self (I worried that no matter how hard I tried, I would always be an unforgiveable sinner deserving of an eternity in hell.)

- Being stuck in severe emotions (Horror! Terror! Dread! Anxiety!)

- Difficulty falling or staying asleep (Sometimes I couldn't sleep because I was afraid of hell itself, sometimes because I was afraid of going there, and sometimes I'd cry because of friends or family members who were not Christians and who were sure to go to hell.)

It seems unbelievable that people would repeatedly put themselves and others through the drama of terrorizing each other. To what end? Fear and other emotions that trigger survival instincts often have more influence on our decisions than other emotions. If power and control are what one desires, sometimes there is no role in a community more powerful than that of the spiritual leader. If a leader can tap into fear, that leader can command obedience and submission. Thus, countless Christian leaders through the centuries have benefitted from the terror created by these images.

Spanking-Induced PTSD

In addition to the stories of hell, Christianity and the Bible endorse ways of interacting with and disciplining children that can be quite traumatizing. One particularly traumatizing action that comes highly recommended by the Bible is corporal punishment—using physical pain in an attempt to eliminate unwanted behaviors. I prefer to call it what it is: physical violence against children. Numerous verses endorse this method, including:

> Folly is bound up in the heart of a boy,
> but the rod of discipline drives it far away.
> (Proverbs 22:15)

> Do not withhold discipline from your children;
> if you beat them with a rod, they will not die.
> (Proverbs 23:13)

> The rod and reproof give wisdom,
> but a mother is disgraced by a neglected child.
> (Proverbs 29:15)

With scriptures like that, it will probably come as no surprise that four out of five born-again Christians support the use of spanking to discipline their children.[4] For Christians, the notion that loving parents discipline their children in ways that are sometimes painful is not unpalatable because they have already internalized another similar message—that god

---

4. Harry Enten, "Americans' Opinions on Spanking Very by Party, Race, Region and Religion," *FiveThirtyEight*, September 15, 2014, https://fivethirtyeight.com/datalab/americans-opinions-on-spanking-vary-by-party-race-region-and-religion/.

the father disciplines his children, Christians, in ways that are not always pleasant. While there are a great many people who use physical violence against children irrespective of any particular religious belief, it is especially disheartening when parents who, in every other area of their lives decry the use of violence, feel compelled to do so against their children out of the belief that it is what their all-loving god expects them to do.

Unfortunately for young Christians who commit sins, being traumatized by images of eternal punishment, riddled with guilt, and cloaked in shame will not be the end of their suffering. Physical discipline is believed to be an essential part of the process of becoming a better person, a more faithful follower, and a model citizen. Proverbs 20:30 makes a rather brutal and explicit link between this form of physical violence and its purported spiritual benefits: "Blows that wound cleanse away evil; beatings make clean the innermost parts." Anyone who thinks that the god of the Bible would not endorse violence against children needs to read again, particularly these two key passages:

> How happy is the one whom God reproves; therefore do
> not despise the discipline of the Almighty. For he wounds,
> but he binds up; he strikes, but his hands heal.
> (Job 5:17–18)

> Now, discipline always seems painful rather than pleasant at
> the time, but later it yields the peaceful fruit of righteousness
> to those who have been trained by it.
> (Hebrews 12:11)

God, the father, then, is a great discipliner. He uses everything from psychologically abusive tactics such as fearmongering to physically abusive practices with the intent to cause injury as ways to teach, guide, encourage, and strengthen his followers. The truth of the matter is that physical violence as discipline is never effective, neither for children nor for adults, but when discussing the use of physical violence, we must pay extra care to the vulnerable ones—children. As much as Bible literalists try to cover their eyes and ears and ignore the research, it's clear: spanking and all manner of physical violence as discipline do not increase long-term positive behavioral changes.[5] Instead, the opposite is true. The connection between being spanked as a child and dysfunction in life as an adult is strong and evident. Spanked children and teens have higher rates of aggression, delinquency, mental health issues—such as PTSD—and even less brain gray matter! These children then grow up to be adults at higher risk for legal trouble, substance abuse, and mental and physical health problems.

Physical and Sexual Violence

Women are more prone to depression, anxiety, and PTSD than men. In fact, they are twice as likely as men to develop any one of these three disorders.[6] Considering the female experience, it makes sense that women are at a higher risk for many of these illnesses. Women are more likely than men to experience many types of traumas—sexual assault, sexual abuse as children, domestic violence, and physical abuse as children. Then there are the traumas that can occur related to childbirth, miscarriage, and abortion. Unfortunately, many traumatic events have the power to cause psychological damage while simultaneously creating an emotional breeding ground for guilt and shame, as if the victim is to blame. The connection between religion and trauma and between trauma, guilt, and shame is especially pronounced for women.

Christianity is exceedingly paternalistic and misogynistic. The authority that men hold over women traces its roots to the very beginning of the Bible, where god creates Eve from Adam and deems Eve to be Adam's "help-meet" or helper (Genesis 2:18). Right away, we see that woman is intended to play a supporting role to man. Rather than have a unique purpose in life independent of anyone else's needs or expectations, according to the Bible, a woman should be prepared to spend her days sacrificing herself in order to help the men in her life, namely her husband but also her father and pastor, meet their personal goals and god-given purposes. As we have discussed before, many women succumb to the

5. Tracie O. Afifi et al., "Physical Punishment and Mental Disorders: Results from a Nationally Representative US Sample," *Pediatrics* 130, no. 2 (August 2012), http://pediatrics.aapublications.org/content/pediatrics/early/2012/06/27/peds.2011-2947.full.pdf.

6. Laura A. Pratt and Debra J. Brody, "Depression in the U.S. Household Population, 2009–2012," *NCHS Data Brief*, no. 172 (December 2014), https://www.cdc.gov/nchs/data/databriefs/db172.pdf.

psychological war that wages inside of them because of messages about sin, death, and hell, but it is also true that women frequently fall prey to the might of religious oppression because of physical aggression.

To return to our previous discussion on spanking and the use of physical violence as a form of discipline, there is a concurrent message regarding adult life—and it does immensely more harm to women than to men. The message is that love hurts. Physical pain is an indication of love. The Bible speaks of the "blows that wound," (Proverbs 20:30), "beatings" (Proverbs 20:30), and "the rod of discipline" (Proverbs 22:15) as tools that god and parents can use to prove their love for their children. Is it no wonder then that, consciously or subconsciously, some men easily extend this to justify beating their wives, lending credence to the belief that domestic violence is acceptable if the woman "deserves" it? There is even a website whose primary mission is to support Christian couples who seek to use biblical lessons about discipline in their marriage. Christian Domestic Discipline (CDD) involves a variety of discipline strategies, which can include spanking, built upon the premise that the husband is the authority figure in the marriage and the wife owes total obedience and submission to the husband.[7] While the CDD website says that men are neither to be dictators nor women doormats, it is not hard to see how quickly a marriage could degrade into such a situation in which the husband has the right to engage in what essentially amounts to physical assault because the Bible says so.

The Bible is also supremely brutal to women when it comes to sex. The Old Testament endorses explicitly violent treatment of women and female children who are not Israelites. For example, there are a multitude of stories about the Israelites attacking cities and, once the cities are defeated, being given permission to take all of the women and female children for concubines. Essentially, the god of the Old Testament encouraged sex slavery and trafficking.

The Bible can be inhumanely cruel in response to sexual traumas as well. The Old Testament has uniquely disturbing stances on rape and sexual violence, how they are defined, and how they should be handled legally. For example, the laws in Deuteronomy 22 explain the various ways judgment could be passed on a rapist and his victim: death of the victim and the assailant, the death of the assailant only, or the marriage of the

7. https://www.yumpu.com/en/document/view/45110017/the-learning-domestic-discipline-beginners-packet-freethought-

victim and the assailant—the determining factors being the location of the rape (city versus country) and the marital status of the woman. Countless women have been compelled to continue life as usual with lovers, ministers, fathers, uncles, brothers, coworkers, and caregivers who have sexually violated them. They have been compelled explicitly by people around them who urge them to let go of their feeling of victimization, convince them that they deserved it, or frighten them into silence and keeping the truth hidden. Even more heartbreaking is when these women never tell their stories due to a sense of guilt. I've collected dozens of stories from women who never revealed their experience specifically because the guilt they felt came from their beliefs about god's expectations. What a powerful degree of shame and self-blame it must be to keep a victim of such a traumatic experience silent! It is a degree exponentially multiplied under the incalculable influence of religious misogyny and hegemony.

Christian women are also traumatized by religious doctrines and church policies that mandate strict obedience and submission to husbands and fathers, stunt their natural growth toward self-determination and self-actualization, and deprive them of bodily autonomy and reproductive rights. Messages about how a woman caused the downfall of all of humanity, preaching about sexual activity that focuses disproportionately on a woman's "sin," and expectations that women be the homemakers who do all of the primary childrearing put women in positions where they end up full of guilt and shame when they inevitability do not meet the unrealistic standards set by the Bible and championed by the men in their lives. As a mechanism for social control, religion wields disproportionate power over women. Building upon society's tendency toward patriarchy and millennia-old concepts of the roles of women in society, Christianity is free to justify the physical and psychological oppression of women through the use of doctrine crafted from a holy book full of barbarity, depravity, and psychopathy.

When women are forced into full submission, something ugly and terrible is guaranteed to be playing the authoritarian role. We women for whom the concept of submission was once (or still is) an integral part of what it meant to be a faithful Christian can see it in each other's eyes. The Bible teaches that all people should be able to see the joy, glory, and blessings of god practically emanating from a woman who is a faithful Christian. Instead, when we truly sit with other such women and really look into their eyes, we recognize sadness, exhaustion, and hollowness. Full submission can only occur in the context of completely giving up oneself as an individual. In the church from which I learned these strong submission lessons, the women frequently talked about how difficult it was to be truly submissive precisely because we felt like we were losing our personal identities. We often felt like we were mourning our own deaths as we were no longer ourselves, but rather our husbands' wives and our children's mothers.

When it comes to human development, in addition to the influence of primary family roles (mother, sister, daughter), our identities are shaped through self-actualization—that process by which a person learns to recognize, access, and utilize her own skills, talents, and potentials in a way that is personally fulfilling and meaningful. The fully submissive Christian woman will find it difficult to complete the self-actualization process. Not only might she feel like she has lost her identity as an individual, she might also mourn the loss of versions of herself she had hoped to be. For example, for many twenty-first-century American women, self-actualization involves completing college or some other advanced education and establishing a career; however, a submissive Christian woman might have to forgo college at her pastor's urging, her father's refusal to pay, or her husband's insistence that she stay home with the kids. As life moves on and she reflects on what kind of person she could have been if only she had gone to college, a common initial emotional reaction is resentment toward those for whom she sacrificed. Deeper still, she might find intense shame and embarrassment, especially if she is surrounded by women who are well ahead in their self-actualization processes.

Religious submission frequently results in people not being able to fulfill their personal goals—career, education, unique experiences, and the like. Personally, what I find equally as troublesome is when people actually achieve some of those goals but the value of the accomplishment is minimized. Christians are warned not to be too proud of their personal accomplishments because *pride goes before a fall*. At other times, the value is minimized indirectly because they have to give god all the glory. The lesson, then, is that Christians are incapable of accomplishing anything noteworthy without god's intervention and support. But somehow women receive this message much louder and much more often than men. They have more people to submit to than men and are expected to do so much more deeply. This is psychological robbery, depriving each woman of opportunities for self-actualization.

The list of ways in which submissive Christian women might lose their identities, miss out on opportunities to reach their goals, and fail to self-actualize is endless. In essence, when a woman is deprived of the things she needs in order to become the ideal version of herself, she will fail to self-actualize. Submission theologies not only deprive women of these necessities, but sometimes these women even lose their very ability to recognize, let alone articulate, who their ideal self would be. Full submission requires that they swap out all of who they are as individuals for all that everyone else needs them to be. Depression and anxiety almost always accompany the struggle to feel like oneself again and, interestingly enough, depersonalization—a sense of separation from self—is also a marker of PTSD. If a woman is living with either of these illnesses, how much more devastating is it to her overall well-being when she is required to give up the last vestiges of who she is as a person in submission to a man, a religion, and a god?

Demonstrations of Faith

Also harmful to the psyche are some of the methods by which Christians are supposed to demonstrate their faith. The concept of Christian faith is complicated at best. At its worst, it breeds gross negligence and can be downright life-threatening. Rather innocuous but sometimes burdensome demonstrations of faith can include attending church regularly or praying and reading the Bible regularly. However, those actions can cause psychological harm when Christians are made to feel guilty if life makes it difficult for them to attend regularly or when they prefer to watch TV one evening rather than read the Bible.

Paying tithes and offerings is another way in which Christians can show god how much they trust him. Again, on the one hand, if people are financially stable enough that giving away 10 percent of the family's income or making regular offerings doesn't create a burden, then there is no problem. It is analogous to donating to any other nonprofit organization (a status which I and many of my secularist friends believe is unconstitutional for a church to have). However, tithing and offering become harmful when people feel the conviction to give money to the church while neglecting to pay bills or attend to other basic needs. Families have been financially devastated after literally giving away their life savings either to show god just how much they trust him to take care of them or to keep guilt and shame away by obeying god's word.

Attempting to demonstrate faith becomes even more dangerous when we move into the territory of faith healing. Just like with monetary giving, the belief that god can miraculously heal Christians is not in and of itself immediately harmful. A person can go to the doctor and take their medication all while praying that god will also work a miracle, speed recovery, or minimize complications. Unfortunately, just as with mental health treatment, there is a contingency of Christians who do not go to the doctor and do not take medication. Not only do they forgo the medication, opting to depend on god, some of them believe that doing otherwise would suggest that they lack faith in god to heal them. In other words, some Christians believe that the only way to be healed is to put 100 percent faith in god, and the only way to prove that they have unwavering trust in him is to refuse medication and, at times, all professional medical consultation.

I've witnessed Christians attempt to prove their faith in god through everything from suffering with a headache, despite having Tylenol and Advil readily available, to ignoring medical directives to be on bed rest while pregnant despite a history of miscarriages. When my friend allowed himself to be miserable for a few hours by refusing to take a pain reliever, that was harmless enough, but imagine the guilt and depression my fellow church member felt when she lost a second baby because the pastor told her that she could not stay in bed, that she was still expected to sing in the choir, and that she must submit to her husband's sexual desires despite the fact that her doctor expressly forbade it. But that is precisely what a faithful Christian woman will do when she believes that her faith in god will protect her from the consequences of failing to seek and heed medical advice.

The Intersection of Mental Illness and Christianity

Considering the high rates of religiosity and its socially crippling influence across all life domains in American society, it is completely fair and reasonable to ask how much religion accounts for violence, crime, and dysfunction. It's already clear that being a Christian doesn't automatically make you a better person, but how many people do bad things, using the Bible as their defense or believing it's what god wants? Spanking. Sexual abuse. Sickness and financial ruin. Why hasn't Christianity proven to be the societal prophylactic it promises?

We can further explore this conundrum Christianity faces by considering the quality of life of members of societies with lower levels of religiosity. For example, Scandinavian countries, known as secular societies due to their relatively low percentages of religious citizens, fare much better than Americans in almost every facet of society, from crime to poverty, from education to happiness.[8] America, with its majority Christian population, is a world leader in regard to our burgeoning prison population, increasing income inequality, and plummeting global academic rankings.[9] To be sure, there are innumerable variables impacting the functioning of a society and the health of its citizens, but let us not fool ourselves; religious doctrines are among that list. So far do the claws of Christian contempt for anything other than biblical "wisdom" reach that Christians routinely and willfully ignore research that could improve their lives emotionally and psychologically, interpersonally and sexually, physically and financially. Because of this willful ignorance, we may never fully grasp the extent of the damage Christianity has wrought on our society.

Considering the Consequences of Giving up the Faith

I have spent this entire essay talking about the known harm Christians experience as a result of manipulative and limiting Christian doctrines. Being a believer can have many psychological, emotional, and social consequences unseen to a new, moderate, or uncritical Christian. However, it is worth noting that walking away from one's faith also carries with it a significant amount of risk. One of the first things to examine when calculating risk of harm is why the person is leaving religion in the first place. In the same way a patient must weigh the risks and benefits of having a potentially life-saving medical procedure, a woman should carefully

---

8. https://www.usnews.com/news/best-countries/quality-of-life-rankings

9. https://www.washingtonpost.com/news/fact-checker/wp/2015/07/07/yes-u-s-locks-people-up-at-a-higher-rate-than-any-other-country/?utm_term=.b6030bf25138 and http://www.pewresearch.org/fact-tank/2017/02/15/u-s-students-internationally-math-science/

consider her reasons for leaving religion behind. The choice may seem obvious to nonbelievers, but it may not prove to be a positive experience if she is not 100 percent sure she is ready to leave.

It is not wise to make major decisions in emotionally charged states, and if a woman decides to abandon her religious convictions as a result of an emotional temper tantrum, when those emotions die down, she may find herself with a psychological trauma like no other. In a society in which Christianity is the majority religion practiced, such as the United States, the strength and volume of the narrative that Jesus is the only way to salvation can eventually overpower an ex-Christian's new religion or nonbelief, winning back her allegiance. Sadly, this return to one's original faith often comes with profound shame and guilt, as shown in the biblical story about the so-called prodigal son. The original departure was seen as an abandoning of absolute truth, and the human psyche has its own way of torturing us mercilessly when we betray the most foundational aspects of who we are. A woman should be just as emotionally sure as to why she's leaving her religion as she is cognitively sure.

Another issue to consider when deciding if leaving one's religion is the right decision at the time is the level of enmeshment between the person's religious practices and her social network. For example, if a woman is a member of an evangelical or charismatic ministry that places firm restrictions on fraternizing with people who are not as devout as she is, and therefore the vast majority of her primary social supports are likeminded, she may find herself in constant conflict when she decides to leave her religion. On the other hand, if she has friends who are either less conservative, not part of her specific tradition, or are completely nonreligious, it is more likely that she will not lose her entire support network. When the majority of a woman's support network consists primarily of highly devout men and women, her risk of emotional and psychological distress following her exit is going to be significantly higher than for a woman with a more diverse or liberal network. Is she prepared to face that distress? If she leaves then repents to return to her old community, she will probably be hurt, confused, angry, and ashamed by how much work it takes to feel like a legitimate member of the community again, if they even take her back at all.

Another source of psychological distress for women leaving religion is the fear of spiritual consequences. It was true for me and true for many women I have interviewed. Even though we were leaving because we had studied our way out of religion—not for emotional reasons or under the influence of others—the fear of hell, the devil, and curses had been so drilled into our hearts and minds that it was difficult to release. It was not easy to recover from PTSD, and even though we had coping skills, even though we knew the flashbacks were not real, even though we could use reality testing to know that we were safe, in the early days of our deconversions it was quite common for us to lie awake at night afraid of the shadows or to walk through the day fearing sudden death before getting the chance to reconnect with god were he real. Many people say resolving the fear of hell is the most intense and psychologically taxing aspect of the healing process. It certainly was for me.

The roles emotional reasoning and socioreligious enmeshment play in a woman's decision to leave religion produce psychological and social fallouts that vary in intensity from woman to woman. For example, an introvert who found frequent church gatherings stressful may fare better than the social butterfly who might slip into depression when she suddenly has nothing to do during the times when she would normally be at church. A woman who retained part of her personal identity during her tenure as a Christian will likely start to feel like herself significantly faster than the one whose only purpose in life was to serve others. The professional woman who can financially sustain herself will most certainly be spared a sizable portion of the stress pertaining to reestablishing independence, unlike the stay-at-home mom who was never afforded the opportunity to get the skills and education needed to survive without her husband's support. Is she prepared to survive by herself if financial supporters abandon her?

Although I believe all of the major religions are inherently harmful to the human psyche, I never advise women to leave their faiths. I suggest that they learn as much as they can about their religion, the case for it, and the case against it and to weigh the costs of remaining in that faith against the costs of leaving it. I am cautious because I know how profoundly personal the journey is, one full of dark moments of doubt and despair, a journey that each woman must embark on alone. However, I do hope that my story and those of other women like me will be comfort during the moments of private angst that will plague the process until she finds herself safely on the other side.

Finding Safety

As should be clear by now, once free from religion, many women may need to put in a considerable amount of work to feel emotionally and psychologically safe and well again. There are primarily two prongs to the healing process that I believe are necessary to find healing and to keep it. The first is to seek professional mental health support, and the second is self-education. As a licensed professional counselor, I might be a little bit biased, but I am of the mind that everyone could benefit from therapy. At its core, counseling is about nothing more than self-exploration. Who wouldn't benefit from knowing themselves better?

A woman who has lost a significant portion of her identity to a religion, an organization, or even her family and support network will reap immense rewards from engaging in such a process with the right therapist. In addition to traditional therapy, a woman may also benefit from wellness models such as mindfulness meditation in order to refocus on the self and the here and now, and to reduce worry about things outside of her control and the supposed hereafter. It is essential, at this stage of healing, that she select a licensed therapist with formal training and advanced education so that she receives effective treatment and compassionate care during such vulnerable times.

A woman might also consider psychotropic medication to support her through the deconversion process, especially if she has a specific trauma experience to address. Antidepressant, anti-anxiety, and even anti-psychotic medications are much more effective with significantly fewer side effects than mental health medications of days gone by. Many people worry that there are risks associated with taking these types of medications, but they are often no more risky than any other medication she might be taking. She should research it for herself because counseling and medication combined have been repeatedly proven to be highly effective in treating most mental health issues.

The second prong of the healing process I suggest is self-education. It is imperative that a woman leaving behind her religion have a firm grasp of why she is doing so, and the more entrenched the religious beliefs had been, the more studying she must do. Women who only attended church a few times a year will not find it nearly as difficult as the former minister suffering from PTSD. Having concrete arguments and counter-arguments for her stances will give her confidence to answer her friends' and family members' questions. Possessing even rudimentary education on the empirical evidence that shores up scientific explanations about how the natural world works—evidence pertaining to evolution, biology, and astrophysics for example—counteracts widely believed biblical and supernatural explanations. Being able to reference facts and research will guide her every day so that she might develop strong interpersonal relationships, make wise medical decisions, raise children to be critical thinkers, and meet her own basic needs with a much more clear-eyed and sober view of the world based in reality and verifiable facts.

Finding Healing in Leaving Religion

By now, the mental health benefits women would reap from leaving religion, especially patriarchal and misogynistic religions such as Christianity, should be obvious. Many of the women I interviewed for my first book, *The Ebony Exodus Project*, revealed that they felt significantly less depressed once they were completely free from their former religious lives. They were less depressed because they were less burdened by a host of other oppressive and profoundly unpleasant religious and social expectations. While it often took some time, they recovered from traumatic experiences such as being publicly embarrassed and shamed for natural behaviors, such as sex outside of marriage or in events outside of their control such as rape. Previously afraid of demons and hell, of committing sins and being alienated from god, of making mistakes and disappointing family, many of these women felt liberated from perpetual fear. The woman who frees herself from her oppressive religion is able to reconnect to her long-lost autonomy and identity. She discovers that the benefits of shedding commitments to organized religion outweigh the risks inherent in the deconversion process. She decides to shamelessly do what is best for herself. She will no longer merely hope for peace; she will find it. She will no longer live in terror; rather, she will live in her time of healing.

2

Half Human:
How Jewish Law Justifies the Exclusion and Exploitation of Women

Lauri Weissman

The impulse of men to own women would be there whether they believed in god or not. It's just that it might be a bit harder to persuade female babies that they should be owned by men, if they were not told that god wants it to be true.... So that getting rid of the idea of the supernatural is one step—only one, but a very important one, perhaps the first one, perhaps the biggest one—on the road to emancipation.

—Christopher Hitchens[1]

---

1. "Christopher Hitchens—Women and Religion," YouTube video, 2:30, from an interview by Elizabeth Carvalho on Milênio Brazilian television in November 2007, posted by "thescorpionking2020," January 11, 2011, https://www.youtube.com/watch?v=rmJDAzgvp6o&feature=youtu.be&t=90 at 2:30.

Jewish women are an oppressed and isolated minority within an oppressed and isolated minority, and have been so for thousands of years.[2] Like Islam and Christianity, Judaism is not only obviously man-made, as Christopher Hitchens was fond of saying, but distinctively male-made: religious teaching systematically distorts our perceptions to make people, particularly women, easier to control. Supernatural shackles on our minds have replaced iron shackles around our ankles, and through religious misogynistic indoctrination, women are taught to enslave themselves for men's benefit. The subjugation of women and children is not an unfortunate side effect of religion—it is religion's purpose.

Jewish law (including the Torah, the Talmud, the Mishnah Torah, and the Midrash as well as rabbinical tradition) governs all aspects of Jewish social and spiritual life, replicating the (outdated) values of its authors in succeeding generations. Misogyny and religion conspire through these strictures to subjugate women by prescribing to them a secondary (and sometimes subhuman) social role, perpetuating disgust for female bodies, and overvaluing traits that make women responsive to control: modesty, obedience, meekness, and purity. Through pervasive metaphors and ideological frames, cultural conditioning, and explicit religious instruction, we teach each young woman to tolerate being owned and to welcome suffering, priming women for lifelong exploitation.

To convince half of a population that they must be ruled, shame and guilt must be instilled, ever-present self-doubt created, and immense fear

---

2. To meet the needs of this collection, and because it is the tradition I followed and studied most recently, I emphasize the Jewish law and cultural observance throughout this essay. I will sometimes call on corollary examples from Christianity and Islam, which are both plagiarized from Judaism. I dove briefly but deeply into the sea of Talmud before the essays of Robert Green Ingersoll and the New Atheists threw me a lifeline of logic. The religious teachings I will identify as problematic and destructive are not unique to Judaism nor necessarily more prevalent in Judaism than in other systems. They are intrinsic to human institutions: rationalizations for the powerful to rule over other people. Lifelong "Jews by chance" may find my "Jew by choice" perspectives presumptuous, uncomfortable, or unsophisticated; I remind them that halakha forbids looking down on the convert or reminding her that she was once a non-Jew. I hope those who identify as Jewish will forgive my occasional oversimplifications of the breadth of Jewish belief and practice across communities and centuries, who exist on a spectrum from mostly agnostic, progressive reconstructionist feminist Jews, to insular Orthodox and Haredi communities of anti-modernity. To comment on the fundamentals of a religion, however, we look to its fundamentalists.

of disobedience cultivated. The pervasive sense of shame and worthlessness prevents us from trusting our own judgment,[3] from being honest about who and what we desire, and from developing intimate, honest relationships.

Regular attendance of religious services in hopes of achieving salvation actually exemplifies and perpetuates this fear and guilt, which keeps us returning to the abusive situation, where only more fear and guilt get piled upon us. The psychological strain of inevitably failing to meet the impossible standards instills the knowledge that we are fundamentally dirty and undeserving, and those broken scripts keep people coming back to the pews and *mikvahs* for absolution. The neural pathways of guilt are laid early and reinforced regularly. Only by first selling the disease of original sin can religion claim to be the cure.

The Torah and Talmud, as well as the Qur'an and the Christian Bible, teach that humans belong to god and were created for his pleasure. We owe unquestioning obedience and submission to our owner, who may "do with us according to his will." This power relationship is explicitly replicated in the father-daughter and husband-wife relationship: a woman is owned by someone who has absolute right to her, and who knows better than she does what is best for her. Personal boundaries are meaningless in a religious context.

In Jewish and Christian culture, the desire to control and restrict female sexuality is less overtly violent than in some other traditions, but a woman is powerfully brainwashed and psychologically manipulated from birth to imagine that her value is in preserving her virginity until her father has selected a husband and handed off ownership *by giving her away*. Innocent daughters tie their self-worth to the economic value that can be extracted by their fathers, and their ownership titles can be transferred in the sight of god and government.

Female children are not taught to try to better their circumstances, or their communities, or their societies. They are instructed to submit, allegedly to an imaginary friend, but more accurately to the priest or pastor or rabbi, guru, prophet, or sage, father or brother or husband who owns her and claims to rule her on behalf of the almighty.

Consensual, enjoyable human experiences result in shame and

---

3. "The heart is deceitful above all things, and desperately wicked: who can know it?" (Jeremiah 17:9). Torah quotations in this essay are taken from: http://www.jewishvirtuallibrary.org/.

dishonor against the person who owns her body—this is the essence of patriarchy, but it is the language of religion too. Consider the common purity mantra of a young woman "saving herself for her husband." The young woman does not own herself; someone she's never met owns her, and she is the temporary custodian of his property, her body. She is born owing an unpayable debt, and her choices are not her own; they are made for her by men: fathers, brothers, husbands, gods, prophets, and priests. Her own desires, safety, enjoyment, and self-determination are not even afterthoughts; they are to be actively distrusted. Consent, in other words, does not matter. What matters is submission. Humiliation, debasement, degradation, pain, and suffering are to be tolerated, even celebrated. This path and this partner have been preordained for her.

Religious teaching undermines women's rights to bodily autonomy and self-determination. By the time we have grown into women, we have practiced obedience and self-suppression so long that we are not able even to conceive of our own autonomy. We are overruled by god and men, our choices negated and our judgment devalued. Our hearts are wicked and uniquely susceptible to temptation *because* that heart is contained within a female body.

Judaism can never be made compatible with the empowerment of women, nor can any religion relying on its scriptures. The emotional, physical, and psychological energy women waste enacting ancient superstitions would be reason enough to rid ourselves of prescientific superstitions. But religion is not simply a waste; daily damage is inflicted on women and girls by those claiming god's authority. Even liberal interpretations of Abrahamic legend replicate and reinforce Iron Age misogyny, which dehumanizes and excludes women, and rituals that perpetuate disgust and fear of the female body and its functions. Only when we give up the twisted (im)morality of Hebrew scripture and renounce the worship of the Abrahamic god, can women be full and equal participants in civic, intellectual, or economic spheres.

Dehumanization and Exclusion of Women

Abrahamic explanations of creation explicitly have women created lesser, as the helpmate, the vessel for sons but never heroines themselves. Original sin explicitly indicts women, and our desire for knowledge above our station, as the literal root of all evil. Virtue is derived from obeying and satisfying the husband, and ignorance is a condition of that servitude. If the myth of female inferiority is to be maintained, woman must be prevented from receiving quality educations and holding certain jobs. If women were biologically incapable of performing a task, there would be no need for a formal restriction.

From the first chapter of the Torah, from the beginning of humanity, a woman's independence, feminine curiosity, is the literal source of evil. Men are undone by beguiling women, but via Eve's/Chavah's apple or Pandora's box, women are undone by desire for free will and knowledge, and by disobeying men.

Most of the vices of men are regarding their temptation by women: men are overcome with lust, or tempted by sinful sexual desires, or deceived into neglecting religious duties. Women's innate subversiveness and rebelliousness jeopardize not only her own character but also her husband's and children's.[4]

Man and woman, male and female bodies and behaviors, are understood to be both halves of a single whole, and also opposites. Jewish life depends heavily on compliance with the binary. Homosexual, transgender, and gender-nonconforming individuals are targeted for persecution because they are a direct threat to this understood binary and demonstrate a willingness to live outside the proscribed actions of masculinity. The first law against homosexuality appeared in 342 CE and set death as the punishment. About fifty years later, the emperors specified, "All persons who have the shameful custom of condemning a man's body, *acting the part of a woman's*…shall expiate a crime of this kind in avenging flames."[5] The religious obsession with homosexuality is at least partly about revulsion for a man who would voluntarily submit to the role of woman. Under Justinian I (527–565 CE), spiritual death is attached to homosexuality, and its consequences extended beyond the individual to threaten the entire community.[6]

---

4. The Talmud says that when a pious man marries a wicked woman, the man becomes wicked, but when a wicked man marries a pious woman, the man becomes pious (Rabbah 17:7).

5. The Theodosian Code and Novels, and the Sirmondian Constitutions 9.7.6 (emphasis added). trans. Clyde Pharr (Princeton: Princeton University Press, 1952).

6.. Justinian I, *Novel* 77 and 538, trans. in D.S. Bailey, *Homosexuality and the*

Judaism prescribes social roles intended to foreground women's reproductive and nurturing functions, usually by placing them under the control of a dominant husband. Women's fungibility—their use as currency between the men in their lives—is well illustrated by the pervasive metaphor, the cognitive master frame: the comparison of women's bodies, particularly their sexual "purity," to a valuable gem or jewel.[7]

Women who succeed in suppressing their sexual selves until the marital night often face significant psychosexual dysfunction, including crippling guilt and shame, feelings of worthlessness, and lack of enjoyment of sex. The conditioning that ties their personal and spiritual worth to virginity is not easy to overcome, and a complete absence of understanding of the mechanics of their bodies compromises their ability to enjoy pleasure and to pleasure a partner. Following the rules, according to purity teachings, will result in a joyous union of souls: kosher sex, the best sex. The sweet awkwardness of two virgins, because so much cultural meaning has been loaded onto the moment, can be disappointing, even terrifying. When even sexual fantasies are seen as adultery against the future husband, a young woman cannot gain much sexual self-awareness. When sex is not immediately excellent, many women perceive it as a personal failing, or feel broken or betrayed by what they were taught.

If those young women should become among the significant percentage of women who experience domestic violence and marital rape, they are unlikely to fully recognize, or ever recover from, the betrayal. On the other hand, many fantasize about nonconsensual sex, because the lack of female sexual agency makes those sexual encounters perversely safer, less sinful, less damaging to the soul. Purity culture places immense guilt and shame on young women who display sexual desire and sexual agency: when she is plundered, she is free. Writes feminist atheist blogger Libby Anne of her post-purity-pledge marriage:

> It was as though imagining and miming being coerced was the

---

Western Christian Tradition (London: Longmans, Green, 1955). "Because of such crimes, there are famines, earthquakes, and pestilences; We admonish men to abstain from the aforesaid unlawful acts, that they may not lose their souls...so that the city and the state may not come to harm by reason of such wicked deeds."

7.. George Lakoff and Mark Johnson, *Metaphors We Live By* (Chicago: University of Chicago Press, 1980).

only way I could truly let go, detach from myself, and give myself permission to feel sexual pleasure. Being an active sexual agent, even in my thoughts, had been a no-no for so long that this suppression had become hard-wired into my brain. It literally took us *years* to figure out a way for me to have orgasms without pretending that our sex was non-consensual.[8]

According to religious and cultural metaphors, women and their bodies are passive receivers of, and vessels for, male potency. This corresponds to prescientific understanding of female physiology within an exclusively male paradigm, namely that the male "seed" contains a complete child and the woman is merely its incubator. Jewish law places a positive commandment on men to "be fruitful and multiply" but no such commandment on women. Nevertheless, the Torah presents childless women as empty, forlorn, or under divine punishment. Motherhood and marriage are the entirety of a Jewish woman's role, her status, and her future. In traditionally observant sects, a woman not married off by age twenty-one is a shame to her family; a childless woman is a shame or curse upon her husband, an impediment to his duty and destiny. A wife-mother, by contrast, is subsumed into her roles of nurturing, her identity disappearing as we laud—think carefully about this "compliment"—her selflessness.

Whenever women do participate in Jewish public and religious life, they are marginalized, both symbolically and literally. The *mechitzah* (the screen or curtain separating men from women in synagogues, at weddings, and during prayer) enacts this separateness, which is beyond questioning, but social custom excludes and isolates women far more than the literal screen. Full community participation and complete personhood, and their accompanying rights, are overtly penis contingent.

When a minyan meets—a religious quota necessary to enact certain rites and to call down certain blessings—only adult men are counted. In some circumstances women may remain in the room, but they are not people, strictly speaking. Their prayers do not count toward community obligations. The morning prayer recited by a Jewish man articulates his gratitude to his creator for "not making me a woman," or a gentile,

---

8.. Libby Anne, "The Purity Culture and Sexual Dysfunction," *Love, Joy, Feminism* (blog), *Patheos*, November 2, 2011, http://www.patheos.com/blogs/lovejoyfeminism/2011/11/the-purity-culture-and-sexual-dysfunction.html.

or a slave. Women's optional prayer thanks the creator for making her "according to His will." Exclusion from prayer and practice is exclusion from full Jewishness. Significant events of the Jewish life cycle, and their sanctified observances—from the bris and bar mitzvah to the wedding night—are (sometimes literally) available only to possessors of a penis. Jewish feminist scholar Blu Greenberg notes, "[R]ituals that celebrate biological events unique to women (such as childbirth and the onset of menstruation) are conspicuously absent in the tradition."[9] Women may not hold leadership roles in conservative or orthodox synagogues, and Talmudic study (the central role of the Jewish community and the source of its shared identity) systematically excludes women. Exclusion, from birth to death, from defining public and community events, creates in young women a deep sense not of inferiority but of essential otherness, separateness of femaleness.

Because the responsibility to study and comply with Jewish laws (perform *mitzvot*) is considered both a privilege and an obligation, women's exemption from these laws is sometimes portrayed as providing a favorable position, a respectful deference, a relief from tiresome obligations. More accurately, a woman's duties under Jewish law are limited because her role is to be private and domestic rather than public or institutional, and honoring the full range of commandments (including those which must be performed at certain times of day) would disrupt wife-mothering. This was once dressed up for me by a rabbi who said, "See? Women are barred from study not because they are not pious but because they would be *too* pious and would remain at the synagogue all day." Our anticipated neglect of chores and wifely or motherly focus is considered adequate reason to restrict our mobility and educational prospects.

In highly observant communities, separation of the sexes permeates all spheres of life. Modesty is reverence for mystery, especially in Haredi sects in Israel and the United States. Even married men should not gaze on their wives' nakedness; to make love with the light on is forbidden. Women are to be beautiful but not draw attention: they do not wear loud shoes, or perfume, or the hair uncovered, in the street or even at home, in case of unannounced (male) visitors. Immodest women, whose ankles and clavicles might sometimes see sunlight, are loathed for tempting men,

---

9. Blu Greenberg, *On Women and Judaism: A View from Tradition* (Philadelphia: Jewish Publication Society, 1998), 9.

indulging male curiosity. Because women's singing voices can't be removed from television and movies, these diversions are forbidden.

Swedish furniture manufacturer Ikea produced a special version of its catalog for Orthodox Jews, featuring closets full of traditional clothes and depicting a world occupied exclusively by men and boys.[10] In the shops of Jerusalem's Orthodox neighborhoods, women pictured on product packaging are covered with stickers.[11]

Removing images of women from the public sphere, allegedly to protect their modesty, is the reactionary erasure of women and is just as problematic as the exploitation of female bodies in advertising. When Israel's National Transplant Center bought a series of bus ads to urge Israelis to become organ donors, they included the faces of both men and women. Observant Jews vandalized buses and threatened to set them on fire if the photographs of women were not removed.[12]

Neighborhoods that are densely populated by Haredi are bordered by signs that warn women not to enter dressed "immodestly," but many rabbis maintain that a woman's appearance is "immodest by nature."[13] Women are prevented from occupying the same public spaces as men: sidewalks and religious meeting places are segregated by sex, because the mere presence of women is a threat to men's holy duties.

In the guise of praising modesty or protecting men's character, women are induced to cover their bodies and sacrifice their individuality. The extremity of this obsession with erasing the female body is the Islamic burqa: women consigned to sacks of cloth are made—and made to feel—faceless and invisible.

10. Jeremy Sharon, "Ikea Creates Haredi Version of Catalogue, without Women," *Jerusalem Post*, February 16, 2017, http://www.jpost.com/Israel-News/IKEA-creates-haredi-version-of-catalogue-without-women-481779.

11. Elana Maryles Sztokman, *The War on Women in Israel: A Story of Religious Radicalism and the Women Fighting for Freedom* (Naperville, IL: Sourcebooks, 2014).

12. Dan Even, "Ultra-Orthodox Pressure Takes Women Off Ads for Jerusalem Organ Donor Campaign," *Haaretz*, November 8, 2011.

13. Pierre Klochendler, "Israeli Women Defy Disappearance of Female Images from Billboards," *Thomson Reuters Foundation News*, November 22, 2011, http://news.trust.org//item/?map=israeli-women-defy-disappearance-of-female-images-from-billboards/.

Disgust for Female Bodies

Religion's obsession with female anatomy is not incidental—it is definitional. The near-universal linguistic equivocation of the feminine and the vaginal with disease, dirt, and femininity is a topic for an essay all its own. Conversely, the sacred is made synonymous with virginity and cleanliness through the regular chanting equivocation of *holy, virgin, mother, child, infant,* and *immaculate.* The revulsion of the patriarchal leaders for the vagina and its issuance is perhaps best exemplified in the birth of mankind's redeemer to a virgin. In other ancient traditions, gods emerge from their mother's flanks (Buddhist), from skirts made of serpents (Aztec), or from their father's forehead (Greek)—making something holy involves denying its association with the vagina and that contaminating flow of blood. Arguably, the Christian nativity story is an upgrade for women in admitting that Mary did give vaginal birth, instead insisting she was not penetrated pre-pregnancy.

Nowhere is this revulsion clearer than for menstrual fluid and menstruating women. Menstruating Muslim women are prohibited from fasting, praying, reading the Qur'an, or entering a mosque. Jewish women are not permitted to sleep in the same bed as their husbands, nor sit in his chair, lest she pollute it and, by extension, him (Torah, Leviticus 18:19, 20:18). The ritualized shame is definitional to womanhood and is described in the language of both sin and filth, or often in the Qur'an, "harm," "illness," and "pollution."

Women in the Ethiopian Orthodox Tewahedo Church may not enter the temple during menstruation, and even a non-menstruating woman's impurity contaminates her husband, who may not enter the temple for a day after sexual contact.

Among the Kalash religious minority in Pakistan, menstruating and birthing women generate impurity that requires a special cleansing ritual, the same one used after contact with corpses and decomposing animals. Cultural stigma around menstruation, particularly when geography or poverty block access to menstrual sanitary products and private space in which to change and dispose of them, causes many pubescent girls to drop out of school.[14]

---

14. Sugata Roy, "Menstrual Hygiene Key to Keeping Girls in School," Unicef India, March 19, 2011, http://unicef.in/Story/122/Menstrual-Hygiene-Key-to-Keeping-

The equation of menstruation with sin and impurity has a profound cultural legacy. Current law around menstruation and ritual impurity (*niddah*, Leviticus 15:19) is derived from pre-Babylonian restrictions on temple-related ritual acts: either gender could lose the right to handle temple objects after seminal emission (Leviticus 15:13), skin disease, menstruation or irregular bleeding, childbirth, or miscarriage. Later rabbinic tradition disregards seminal emissions and skin disease, making ritual impurity an exclusively female condition.[15] After the fall of the second temple in 70 CE, the sanctification and purity practices were preserved as a method of controlling sexual interactions and sustaining socially useful taboos about the mysterious workings of the female body.

While the restrictions on male behavior disappeared in the absence of the temple, the restrictions associated with menstrual impurity actually expanded: later interpretations hold that spouses, nonsacred objects, furniture, even whole cities can be contaminated by a menstruating woman's touch.[16] In the scriptures, niddah is used to describe grave sexual sin and other abominable acts (Lamentations 1:8; Ezra 9:11; 2 Chronicles 29:5) and is spoken of as a contamination of the land itself (Ezekiel 7:19–20, 36:17).

A Jewish woman is "unclean" the week comprising her period and seven "clean" days after, during which time her husband may not touch her (orthodox married couples don't even pass objects, sit on the same sofa, or sleep in the same bed while the woman is niddah, to avoid accidental touches). Women who adhere to these guidelines are functionally excluded from work outside the home: for two weeks out of every four, a female doctor would contaminate every patient and instrument she touched. Businesswomen would be prohibited from shaking hands with clients and would contaminate her seat in the boardroom, the table, the telephone, the pens, the flipchart.

Each day the niddah inserts a ceremonial white linen cloth (edim) to inspect her vaginal secretions for their relative holiness, and if she is unsure about the color of the discharge, gives the cloth to her husband

---

Girls-in-School.

15. Judith Hauptman, *Rereading the Rabbis: A Woman's Voice* (Boulder, CO: Westview Press, 1998), 150.

16. Rachael Biale, *Women and Jewish Law: The Essential Texts, Their History, & Relevance for Today* (New York: Schocken Books, 1995), 153.

to take to the rabbi for his inspection.[17] Never the type to leave details to chance, halakha contains excruciating detail about what kinds of vaginal discharges make one unclean: "five kinds of blood in a woman are unclean: red, black, a color like bright crocus, or like earthy water or like diluted wine."[18]

Thirty-six transgressions in the Torah are punishable by death: the first is "when one has intercourse with his mother," and the fifteenth is "when one has intercourse with a menstruous woman." The level of fear and disgust regarding the shedding of the uterine lining must have been paralyzing once upon a time: on par, indeed, with incest. Fully half of the capital offenses involve forbidden sexual relations, and the rest command death for crimes as diverse as counterfeiting anointing oil, sacrificing your child to Moloch, working on the Sabbath, and eating bread on Passover. Notably absent from the prohibitions is rape or any mention of consent.

Menstruation isn't only a barrier to sexual relations, however. If a woman experiences spotting, she must begin the count again and wait seven clean days. During this time, she contaminates everything she touches. She remains niddah until she bathes in the communal bath, called a mikvah, and offers a redeeming sacrifice. If her husband has touched her garment, her bed, or her body, he also must wash his clothes and bathe in water— no small sacrifice in a desert-dwelling tribe. In most cities and towns, the mikvah is located in the basement of the synagogue, fed with natural rain water. The woman removes all her clothes, jewelry, even contact lenses— anything that would prevent the purifying water from touching every bit of her. She showers with soap first, which itself does not remove the niddah. After trimming back her nails, the woman descends the stairs of the stone mikvah. Between repeated chanted verses, she submerges herself

17. Tirzah Meacham (leBeit Yoreh), "Female Purity," *Jewish Women: A Comprehensive Historical Encyclopedia,* https://jwa.org/encyclopedia/article/female-purity-niddah.

18. Mishna. Niddah, 2:6. Other rabbinic classifications of menstrual discharge include "fenugreek water or the juice of roasted meat, yellow, red like the blood of a wound, black like the sediment from ink, bright crocus, and diluted wine." This level of detail has a certain prurience to it (not unlike the medieval witch-hunting councils stripping down a young woman to search for confirmatory satanic moles), but it would not be fair to claim the obsessive clarifying of these details reveals any sexual interest on the part of the rabbis. This level of detail is common in the mitzvot and is replicated for the preparation of food, washing of fabrics, cleaning of dishes, and disposing of waste.

completely, to the satisfaction of the mikvah lady, a trained witness who checks that not a fingertip or stray curl remains above the surface. Then:

> And on the eighth day she shall take unto her two turtle-doves, or two young pigeons, and bring them unto the priest, to the door of the tent of the meeting. And the priest shall offer the one for a sin-offering, and the other for a burnt-offering; and the priest shall make atonement for her before HaShem for the issue of her uncleanness. Thus shall ye separate the children of Israel from their uncleanness; that they die not in their uncleanness, when they defile My tabernacle that is in the midst of them. (Leviticus 15:19–31)

Menstruation was perceived by the rabbis in a biologically accurate (for the Iron Age) but socially problematic way—as the loss or passing of a potential life that was not realized. Because a woman is assumed to be always ready to conceive and bear a child, a period is regarded as the earliest possible miscarriage, and the woman incurs a small ritual death and debasement for *her failure* to bring forth the life with which she has been entrusted.

Even when a woman does conceive and give birth, presumably fulfilling the purpose god has bestowed upon her, she is still unclean. Jewish law dictates that after having given birth to a boy, a woman is ritually impure, spiritually void, *tumah*, for seven days. But the void, tumah, is twice as great after the birth of a female child, and the mother must wait fourteen days to remove this ritual impurity. From the moment of her birth, a Jewish girl-child is a liability to her family's holiness, twice the spiritual burden and ritual risk as her brothers. Even miscarriage of a female fetus doubles the risk, since a male fetus is thought to be fully fashioned after forty-one days, but a female only after eighty-one days (Mishnah, Niddah 3:7).

The status of tumah is sometimes explicitly distanced from notions of sinfulness, degradation, and inferiority in an attempt at benevolent sexism. Liberal interpretations sometimes attribute the "uncleanness" to some desirable vulnerability, a special weakness resulting from a woman's "godly potential" as origin of both life and loss.

Some third-wave feminist interpreters have tried to absolve Judaism of its revulsion for menstruation by identifying niddah as a protected state for women, during which they must connect to their husbands in nonphysical ways and be viewed as more than a sexual object. While cultural mores permit the sexual use of women with impunity, niddah limits when these attitudes can be acted on. Some interpretations indicate niddah may be a defense against marital boredom, "Because a man may become overly familiar with his wife, and thus repelled by her, the Torah said that she should be a *niddah*" (Niddah 31b). Even these less explicitly misogynist explanations put restrictions on the behavior of women for the benefit of men.

Exemptions to ritual impurity under specific conditions make it clear their intent is not to empower women or to prevent contamination, because the rules can be bent to ensure women are available for the sexual needs of men: in times of war, "women may always be assumed clean in readiness for their husbands. When men have come home from a journey their wives may be assumed clean in readiness for them" (Niddah 2:4).

Menstruation, and having a female reproductive system generally, is an impurity and an offense to god, for which women require redemption through regular intervention of male action. The funeral rite for the uterine lining and ritual immolation of animals to purify sin are thus explicitly intertwined: a twisted theology of blood sacrifice that makes menstruation and childbirth a blessing and a curse placed upon women, a unique burden to the soul and a threat to the entire community. What makes them female also makes them ritually impure: each woman is intrinsically dirty, and her inalienable filth can contaminate her loved ones and her land if she does not behave demurely.

Punishment of Female Sexual Agency

The assumption that a woman's value and access to the divine, as well as her greatest shame, are between her legs is an extension of the subordinated role of the female that pervades Judeo-Christian cultures and excuses and enables sexual abuse. This gross misconception of feminine worth perpetuates the view of women's sexualities as mediums of exchange between men, our sexuality consisting of what it can buy, our value preserved by our lack of agency.

The cultic obsession with virginity predates any one religious tradition. The Israelite tribal society, like nearly all Bronze Age civilizations and a tragic percentage since, treats female sexuality as a male possession and characterizes violation of a woman as a property crime against the woman's owner, the man with legal claim over her reproductive capacity.

In such an economy, men who have wealth and status are permitted to take on multiple wives and concubines, having as much sex as they wish.[19] Men who can take on bond servants and female slaves may have even more sex. The legal status of the children to inherit is limited to the offspring of the relationship recognized by the religion and/or state: a tactic for concentrating resources that is widely documented in Old Testament patriarchs, infanticidal apes, and the British monarchy. Married women and mothers are venerated in exactly the ways that desexualize them and place them off limits to other men. Adultery and unmarried sex become strictly taboo, and masturbation is discouraged.

In such patriarchal orders, the social scorn and punishment for abandoning a pregnant mother might fall on the father of that child, but it does not. In a patriarchy, the young woman's shame is absolute, and it contaminates the reputation of the family if virginity is compromised before ownership of the vagina has been transferred by a member of the (all-male) government or religious hierarchy. In ancient Israelite societies, a woman who voluntarily had sex without sanction from her father was worthless, ruined, devalued, a liability. If the man, whether rapist or lover, refused to marry and assume responsibility for her (a marriage he had a right to refuse, though she did not) she would be effectively excommunicated (or worse), as would the bastard child if she was pregnant. A woman who was raped, likewise, was not given a choice in the marriage to her rapist, but her bride price/virginity ransom of 50 shekels was still due to be paid to her father, because she had no sexual agency. Female sexual agency and consent actually worsened the crime and its consequences for all involved.

We might prefer to imagine this savagery is a part of our ancient history, and to some extent, civil society evolved facades and euphemisms to distance ourselves from the barbarity of such treatment. Between 1925 and 1960 in Ireland, Canada, and the United States, thousands of "fallen women" and their "illegitimate" children, many pregnant as a result of rape or exploitation by employers, were forcibly imprisoned in workhouses operated by Catholic nuns.[20] Forbidden to contact their families, these

19. The Torah permits a man to take a concubine, that is, a woman in a monogamous sexual relationship without a *ketubbah* (marriage contract) or the traditional *kiddushin* (Jewish marriage).

20. Stephen Ruggles, "Fallen Women: The Inmates of the Magdalen Society

prisoners were made to do both hard labor and harsh religious penance for their violation of the patriarchal order. The bleak life faced by these "penitents" can hardly be imagined: ongoing degradation and humiliation designed to break the spirit, endless days of uncompensated labor and meager rations, punctuated by violent beatings.

To protect the inheritances and reputations of the powerful, an enormous campaign of human trafficking and forced family displacement developed, giving rise to the worst kinds of abuse of power. Orphans and other undesirables were imprisoned in Catholic institutions, hidden behind walls or far out in the country where their existence wouldn't be a burden or an embarrassment. Sometimes young women were permitted to return to their families and towns after some years of "penance," but children almost never did.

In a tiny town in County Galway, Ireland, at least eight hundred of those illegitimate children were dumped unceremoniously into a septic chamber beneath the Bon Secours Mother and Baby Home.[21] The mass grave was filled mostly in the 1950s, and exclusively with the bodies of infants and toddlers. It's important to note that nuns were not going into the villages at night to kidnap young women; families were voluntarily sending away their daughters because the stigma of unsanctioned baby making was so crippling. Authoritarian, patriarchal control, wrapped in religious shame and secrecy, makes women and children disposable.

While we may understand the utilitarian origin of these customs, their subsequent enrobing in the guise of sanctity and sacredness has embellished their significance and offers the disguise of divine intention to the priority of owning other human beings. As women became less willing to be owned, elaborate symbolic ceremonies developed to subdue them. Indeed, the need to enact increasingly complicated rituals to signify the ownership of women and the proper transfer of reproductive capacity (weddings) is evidence of the *Homo sapiens'* storytelling and meaning making as a tool of cultural control. The particulars of these ceremonies (the setting, the ritual objects, the incantations, the vows) are tribal and arbitrary, mere pretense by which ownership of women is enacted and excused.

Asylum of Philadelphia, 1836–1908," *Journal of Social History*, 16, no. 4 (1983): 65–82.

21. Dalby Douglas, "Inquiry Urged on Site Called Mass Grave of Irish Babies," *The New York Times,* June 4, 2014.

Powerful men are in control of the commodity of female sexuality. To be commoditized, effectively, virginity must be preserved until economic value can be extracted from its recipient. Religious notions of purity and sanctity, and their contrasting metaphors of shame and uncleanness, deliberately bind each woman to a male guardian's control over her sexuality. Her value is in her obedience; she is worthy of protection only if she is pure. Her human sexuality (every bit as intrinsic to her humanity as to a man's) is sublimated through fear of eternal torture and an early, ingrained sense of worthlessness and shame. Only by pretending that women are less than fully human can men justify owning women and ruling over them by violence. Only by convincing a woman of her innate inferiority can men induce her to submit. In religious teaching, femaleness itself is a defect, a burden to be born, the result of divine punishment and disfavor, inherited guilt from the first woman's sinful search for knowledge above her station.

Psychological Priming for Sexual Abuse

The attitudes and beliefs intrinsic to religious patriarchy help to groom, shame, and silence victims of abuse; hide and perpetuate horrific abuses; prevent abusers from receiving help; and shield them from just consequences. By deliberately stripping children of their voice and agency and teaching them to distrust their own judgment, religious teachings prime children for abuse. Inculcated early with strict gender roles, traumatized by frequent assaults disguised as discipline, and forced to repeat mantras of humiliation and self-loathing, children develop entrenched neural pathways that become their defaults as adults.

When personal boundaries are violated, the recipient of this treatment feels demeaned, depersonalized, and devalued (boys are actually slightly more likely than girls to be abused in religious institutions, and less likely to disclose it[22], suggesting the stigma of homosexuality may be even stronger than that of femaleness or other sexual activity). Religious women are in the unenviable position of being doubly dispossessed of their own decision-making: both the male guardian and the perpetrator of sexual

---

22. Nina Spröber et al., "Child Sexual Abuse in Religiously Affiliated and Secular Institutions: A Retrospective Descriptive Analysis of Data Provided by Victims in a Government-Sponsored Reappraisal Program in Germany," *BMC Public Health* 14, no. 282 (2014), https://bmcpublichealth.biomedcentral.com/articles/10.1186/1471-2458-14-282.

abuse (not to mention a vindictive creator) have claimed the right to make decisions that supersede women's own judgment. One or both might claim to do so in the name of an all-powerful (male) god, but even if a god is not specifically invoked to excuse the abuse, the believing victim accepts that such treatment must be allowed in his "perfect plan."

Subservience and obedience are demanded as penance for the failing of being born a woman. Obedience is emphasized as a woman's primary role, in addition to protecting her virginity when her father and husband are not around. Righteous Muslim women are to be devoutly obedient (to Allah and to their husbands) and guard in their husband's absence what Allah orders them to guard, such as their honor and their husbands' property (Qur'an 4:34).[23] The Prophet Muhammad was asked, "Who are the best of women?" and replied, "The one who pleases (her husband) when he looks at her, obeys him when he gives a command."[24]

Priming-induced automatic behavior and recurrent thinking are well established in social science literature. Repeated neurological programming results in established channels that become unconscious defaults. Activating a concept in someone's mind not only makes us more likely to use that concept when judging others—it also makes us act in accordance with the stereotype and use it to contextualize our own thoughts and actions.

The use of conditioning behaviors to induce compliance is a primary focus of the religious service: the liturgy follows familiar patterns; we are soothed by submission, by being told what to do and knowing what is expected of us. We chant in unison, sit, stand, kneel without knowing exactly why other than that we have been told to obey. The neural pathways associated with words of self-debasement and surrender, paired with giving over control of the body, become increasingly strong, and we slip into them easily, trancelike, in times of trouble. Repeat that priming every Sunday, or each night before bed, or five times a day, and the programming begins to rival the more primal urges of our species. Indoctrinate yourself hard enough, and you can almost beat human drives: believe the impossible, abstain from sex, fast for extended periods, walk over fire, sacrifice your child, blow yourself up in a crowded café.

---

23. Qur'an quotations taken from https://quran.com.

24. Al-Tirmidhi 3272 quoted in "What Does Islam Teach About...a Woman's Place," *What Makes Islam So Different?*, 2017, https://www.thereligionofpeace.com/pages/quran/men-in-charge-of-women.aspx.

Labeling destructive and controlling behaviors as *loving* is a form of gaslighting necessary for religious indoctrination and long-term abusive relationships. Many religious individuals grow up without love connected to acceptance, honor, or individuality. When absolute submission is a condition of a relationship—whether to a deity or a husband—emotionally healthy boundaries, consent, and equality are functional impossibilities. The "free gift of grace" and "unconditional love" are promised to those willing to pay the steep price and obey the many conditions. This doublespeak about love and obedience is deeply damaging to the self-concept and distorts our understanding of healthy relationships.

Touch is central to many deeply meaningful experiences in believers' lives: baptism, ceremonial circumcision, laying on of hands, ritual submersion, foot washing. In each case, the predominant metaphors are of submission and abdication of self, and/or of purifying the body, usually while being ritually touched by another person, as a condition of being accepted by the community.

People conditioned to obey and turn their decisions over to powerful men are likely to be vulnerable for exploitation in other ways as well. Like all cults, religions prey on the vulnerable, the neglected, the desperate. Among the most vulnerable are children.

Religious Grooming in Childhood Sexual Abuse

Forensic psychologists have documented the behaviors of serial child molesters and have identified a predictable series of patterns by which abusers select and groom their victims. These stages of grooming involve engaging a child's trust, gradually expanding access to the child, and building a rapport with the child, who comes to believe that the relationship shared with the abuser is special, uniquely intimate, grown-up, or loving. If a child threatens to disclose the abuse or too actively resists the advances of an abuser, the abuser may frighten the child and threaten him/her with harm or loss of special privileges, including favored status. A cunning manipulator might abuse hundreds of children without being confronted.

Religious leaders occupy positions of moral authority. From the earliest ages, religious children are sent the message that the man in the holy vestments is in control. All the adults in a child's life stand when he tells them to stand, sit when he tells them to sit. He tells them what to eat (in ritual form) and what to drink. The finer points of priestly power in theology are lost to the child observer: the man speaks for god, and he controls the bodies within his vicinity, overriding their normal individuality with a divine mandate for conformity and obedience. This absolute power, and the reverence and deference given to the self-selected who claim to speak for god, is an inevitable draw for those who would abuse supplicants. Not only children are affected: between a quarter and half of all clergy members have illicit sexual contact with a parishioner (of any age) over whom they hold power, and as many as 6 percent habitually aggress against prepubescent and adolescent children.[25] Even those having sex with adults perpetuate the culture of secrecy and shame around sexual activity that protects sexual predators and offenders.

Similar research, including extensive interviews with confessed serial child abusers, has identified predictable circumstances that raise the likelihood of an opportunistic sexual offender to molest children.[26] Risk factors for opportunistic abusers are cultivated by the practices of some religions: the abject secrecy of the confessional, secrets kept from parents, the capacity of the abuser to speak for an almighty and ever-present power, to promise paradise or threaten unending torment. The routine invasions of privacy and bodily integrity, including ritualized touch, help to normalize and desensitize a child before touch turns sexual and makes the child less likely to recognize abuse as qualitatively different than the routine abuses

25. Teresa Watanabe, "Sex Abuse by Clerics—A Crisis of Many Faiths," *Los Angeles Times*, March 25, 2002, A1; Cal Thomas, "Their Sins Only Start with Abuse," *Baltimore Sun*, June 19, 2002, 9A; Mark Clayton, "Sex Abuse Spans Spectrum of Churches," *Christian Science Monitor*, April 5, 2002, 1; Philip Jenkins, *Pedophiles and Priests: Anatomy of a Contemporary Crisis* (Oxford: Oxford University Press, 2001).

26. I take the advice of experts here in consciously differentiating child abusers—perpetrators who commit assaults upon actual children, a crime with devastating consequences to child development—from the often loosely applied term *pedophile*. To my understanding, pedophilia is a paraphilia in which an individual is sexually aroused by thoughts or images of prepubescent children. Many pedophiles struggle their entire lives but succeed in never sexually touching a child because they understand intellectually how devastating this can be for the child. But I understand the power of sexual attraction and the complexities of secret compulsions: the same sympathy and social support should be extended to these individuals as greets alcoholics and people with self-harming behaviors or eating disorders. For the duration of this essay, unless noted otherwise, I will differentiate the complex, often-compulsive psychosocial attraction from the criminal action.

of power which are performed publicly and prescribed by god.

Nearly all controlling, abusive relationships begin subtly—such as demanding the right to judge the validity of another person's decisions, to overrule someone else's judgment or agency. Later, this demand might be enforced through threats of violent retribution, or compliance coerced through an elaborate system of public humiliation, shaming, and shunning. Boundaries are gradually eroded with consistent small overreaches. Preventing a clear understanding of, and sense of ownership over, the body from birth is a necessary component for securing compliance from victims and slaves. If we internalize a deep distrust of our bodies and their messages early enough, we will welcome a steady hand to guide us, even if it occasionally wields a weapon.

Religious rituals that emphasize secrecy, nudity, and cleansing give opportunistic offenders more opportunities to be alone with, and invade the personal space of, congregants in their care. The requirement for women to bathe in the mikvah offered the opportunity for a Washington, DC, rabbi to spy on his naked female congregants and for others in Brooklyn's Orthodox community to victimize young boys whose faith required them to be naked and often alone. The inclusion of sexual deviancy (like celibacy) as a job requirement made the Catholic Church particularly vulnerable: those willing to forgo consensual adult sexual connection may be preselected for stunted psychosexual development, compulsive sexual behaviors, and other risk factors for chronic abusers. Because the secrecy and sexual shaming of religious communities discourage disclosure and delay detection, sexual abusers within faith communities have more victims and younger victims than nonreligiously affiliated abusers.[27]

Religious Protection of Abusers

The secrecy and shame surrounding sexuality in Abrahamic religious traditions, combined with reverence for those claiming spiritual authority, makes the already traumatizing process of disclosing sexual abuse nearly impossible.

---

27. Nina Spröber et al., "Child Sexual Abuse in Religiously Affiliated and Secular Institutions: A Retrospective Descriptive Analysis of Data Provided by Victims in a Government-Sponsored Reappraisal Program in Germany," *BMC Public Health* 14, no. 282 (2014), https://bmcpublichealth.biomedcentral.com/articles/10.1186/1471-2458-14-282.

The extreme shame attached to many of the behaviors common in survivors of sexual trauma—including alcohol and drug abuse, compulsive consensual sexual activity, and withdrawal from loved ones—slows recovery. But more insidiously, religious teachings often shame the emotional experiences women attach to victimization: women are counseled not to feel anger, not to speak ill of others, not to put their own needs first. The further damage done by this pressure on the recovery process no doubt lengthens the years of suffering religious women experience.

If they do speak up, the tightly woven communities and social isolation of these religions raise the consequences of disclosure for victims and their families, who are often blamed for causing trouble and punished for speaking out. When the alleged perpetrator is a member of the same insular religious community, accusations may be met with open hostility. Retaliation against accusers and their families is common, and victims are often pressured to recant stories and excuse the behavior of religious leaders. The social consequences fall on the powerless, and the powerful close ranks. Families are often offered money, ostensibly for therapy but with the condition that charges be dropped or accusations recanted. Children reporting abuse have been expelled from religious schools and their families evicted from homes and neighborhoods. Their safety is threatened. Witnesses are intimidated.

The intimidation and punishment are not reserved for children, though. Rabbi Nuchem Rosenberg of Williamsburg, Brooklyn, was formally banned from synagogues by religious authorities, and religious judges published an order shunning him in a community newspaper: "'The public must beware, and stay away from him, and push him out of our camp, not speak to him, and even more, not to honor him or support him, and not allow him to set foot in any synagogue until he returns from his evil ways,' the order said in Hebrew."[28] This seems like justice for someone accused of coercive sex or molestation, but Rabbi Rosenberg's crime was starting a telephone hotline with information in Hebrew, Yiddish, and English, encouraging victims of rabbinic sexual abuse to call secular authorities. Religious communities obviously have methods and resources to punish

---

28. Sharon Otterman and Ray Rivera, "Ultra-Orthodox Shun Their Own for Reporting Child Sexual Abuse," *New York Times*, May 9, 2012, http://www.nytimes.com/2012/05/10/nyregion/ultra-orthodox-jews-shun-their-own-for-reporting-child-sexual-abuse.html?pagewanted=all.

abusers in their midst, but to protect the powerful, they aim those weapons at victims and victim advocates instead.

Lashon hara (literally "the evil tongue") is gossip, slander, or other disparaging speech, and it is typically prohibited in Orthodox Jewish communities, not only to be spoken, but to be heard or believed, because no harm could be done by gossip if no one listened to it. The Talmud claims lashon hara kills three: the person who speaks it, the person who hears it, and the person about whom it is told (Talmud, Arachin 15b). The prohibition is used to silence victims of abuse and their families. Abuse survivors are often afraid to commit a *shonda*, or to bring embarrassment upon their families and communities or defame the name of god (*a chillul Hashem*) by accusing a religious leader.

Because Jewish self-identity is tied to a higher moral standard, the incidence of such human failings as sexual abuse and assault is feared as a threat to the community's chosenness. If accusations are addressed at all, it is through insular rabbinical courts called Bet Din, which do not have the resources to investigate these crimes or properly treat traumatized victims. Even if convicted, abusers may be readmitted to a synagogue, the community, and the rabbinate. The religious obligation is on the victim to forgive.

In Defense of Feminist Judaism

Intellectual fairness requires we acknowledge the many ways modern Judaism is less misogynistic (if not necessarily less patriarchal) and kinder to women than its derivative and rival religions. Tragedies like widow burning, honor killing, and (female) genital mutilation have occurred rarely among Jews and, when they do happen, garner rabbinic condemnation. The Torah and Talmud often ascribe feminine character to god (*Shekinah*, or "dwelling presence"), particularly in the mystical teachings of Kabbalah, unlike other religions that allow for only a male god. Furthermore, many facets of a man's character are determined by how he treats the women he is responsible for, and the community expects leaders to treat their wives and children well.

Seven of the fifty-five recorded Hebrew scriptural prophets were women, and while 12 percent is low, the United States Congress did not reach that level of gender inclusion until the 1990s. The Qur'an, by comparison, cites only one woman by name (Mary) and references all others as the wives or mothers of certain leaders or prophets, accessories to masculine power. Modern Jews are often social activists and overwhelmingly choose to educate and empower their daughters as well as their sons. Many influential feminist activists, including Betty Friedan and Gloria Steinem, were educated and observant Jewish women who openly critiqued what they saw as anti-woman elements of Judaism without being disowned by their families.

The progress of human society, particularly in its treatment of women, has outstripped the ancient moralities to which Judaism traces its identity. We would not tolerate a rape victim sold to her captor for fifty shekels and a promise to never divorce her, a young widow inseminated by her deceased husband's brother, the adulteress stoned to death, the harem of a king kept caged for his pleasure, or the slaughtering of whole villages for the pillage of virgins. Even if Jewish law once offered above-average protection to women (for example, giving a social future to the rape victim and charity to the widow), we no longer rely on such Bronze Age barbarities to protect half our population from the other half.

Yet even liberal, modern Judaism is at odds with feminist progress, intelligence, and progress. Overall, and particularly in Orthodox communities, women are discouraged from pursuing higher education or religious leadership because these are distractions from their primary roles as wives, mothers, and caretakers of the home. To transcend these norms, or even to aspire to nonconformity, is viewed with suspicion and derision, engaging the religious tools of guilt and shame to keep women's minds in check.

Conclusion: Every Feminist Should Be an Atheist

Punishing female intelligence, independence, and insubordination (note that when ignorance and obedience are required, the former two become the latter) is intrinsic to the teachings of ancient Hebrew scripture. Judaism, and its runaway subsects of Christianity and Islam, is a tightly woven tapestry of ancient superstition, misunderstood biology, and simple, vicious misogyny. These threads cannot be untangled in pursuit of a gentler, more egalitarian worldview, no matter how sincere our hope to find a modern morality in revealed scripture. Religions are products of the *men* who made them, and any social order derived from those teachings will always exclude women, exploit us, or ignore us.

Patriarchal religion perpetuates and protects the systemic abuse of women, both in institutions and in religiously influenced families and marriages. Popular headlines reveal that hundreds of thousands of rapes and assaults are sometimes seen as "a black eye for religion," or even a serious flaw in rabbinical courts or Vatican policy. Abuse and the compulsive control of women are *not* flaws in an otherwise well-intentioned, functional religion. Abuse and control over women's bodies are *the intended functions* of religion. Religious indoctrination not only contributes to and conceals abuse—religious indoctrination is, in itself, abusive.

Religion excuses and normalizes the treatment of women as sexual objects by abusive men, all while perpetuating attitudes that shift the shame, self-loathing, and social stigma onto the victim. Otherwise loving relationships are poisoned by the gendered power imbalance and women's resulting vulnerability.

Religion and misogyny warp our self-perceptions and our relationships, our institutions and our civilizations. Powerful priming scripts and institutional power are being used to disastrous ends: sexual exploitation, religious violence, and defrauding the vulnerable.

So long as religion holds itself exempt from criticism, women will not be treated as equals, we will not be permitted to inspire and employ half the brilliant minds on this planet. We cannot afford to wait. Vocal feminism and atheism *now* are moral obligations: anything less makes us complicit in the dehumanization, commoditization, and sexual exploitation of women. To protect the defenseless and progress toward humanism, women must abandon religion.

3

Women v. Indoctrination

Alexis Record

Keep these words that I am commanding you today in your heart.
Recite them to your children and talk about them when you are at
home and when you are away, when you lie down and when you rise.

—Deuteronomy 6:6–7

Part I: Why Children Are Susceptible to Indoctrination

I grew up in a Christian home where the Bible was taught, service to the Lord was encouraged, and church attendance was mandatory. The bubble I grew up within was tightly controlled, and most of the influences on my thinking were limited to those that reinforced the conservative Christian worldview. Getting out of the house almost always meant going to church, Bible study, prayer meeting, or school. Of course, our "school" was on church grounds and used the infamous Accelerated Christian Education (ACE) curriculum. Every independent study ever conducted has shown ACE to be an inadequate or unacceptable education on academic grounds.[1]

---

1. Some examples include: Alberta Department of Education, *An Audit of Selected Private Schools Programs*, EDRS 256 022, 1985; Dan B. Fleming and Thomas

Instead of preparing students for higher learning, ACE prepares students to serve God: "We do not build Christian schools primarily to give a child the best education nor to teach him how to make a good living," claims ACE's founder. "Teaching him how to live and to love and serve God are our primary tasks."[2] This works unsurprisingly well at pounding religion into young minds by confusing facts with religious claims and teaching both as equally valid. At the time I was in the program, ACE advocated beating sinful children with a "rod of correction," so my understanding of the world was pressed into a small box and I was kept in line through constant positive, negative, and punitive reinforcements.

The prepackaged fundamental Christian worldview I was handed became the one I adopted: "We are like an unclean thing," I memorized in school. "All have sinned…the wages of sin is death." In my denomination, sin was not an act I did, but a state I was in.[3] This gave my parents, pastor, and other school staff the right to use violence against me to bring me to righteousness. My natural state *disgusted* our mercurial God and gave him the right to torture me in a place of eternal separation called Hell. But being faithful and good did not mean believers could avoid the kiln. Putting us in the "furnace of adversity" (Isaiah 48:10) was our deity's sadistic way of testing the faith of even the best, most moral followers. Fire is also promised to be used to test (1 Peter 1:7), save (1 Corinthians 3:15), and "salt" or improve (Mark 9:49) believers. Our denomination called this the refiner's fire, and it was used to remove daily sin—the leftovers that Jesus's death didn't quite clear out of our systems. The correct response to this guaranteed scorching, according to Romans, was to "present [our] bodies as living sacrifices," and "boast in our sufferings" (12:1, 5:3).

I often spoke about peace, love, and pleasing God when describing

C. Hunt, "The World as Seen by Students in Accelerated Christian Education Schools," *Phi Delta Kappan* 68, no. 7 (March 1987): 518–23; Carl Moser and Del Mueller, "Accelerated or Exaggerated? An Evaluation of Accelerated Christian Education," *Lutheran Education* 116, no. 1 (1980): 8–17, and Cathy Speck and David Prideaux, "Fundamentalist Education and Creation Science," *Australian Journal of Education* 37, no. 3 (November 1993): 279–95.

2. Jonathan Theodore Scaramanga, "Systems of Indoctrination: Accelerated Christian Education in England" (doctoral thesis, University College London, 2017), 28.

3. Many Christian denominations use Romans 5:12 to support the doctrines of original and hereditary sin.

my faith to those outside my religious bubble, but that was mere edifice built up from a foundation of self-loathing. My mom couldn't reassure me that I was a good girl who didn't deserve fiery torture, because that's not what biblical Christianity teaches. Nor could she tell me God wouldn't hurt me. "For the Lord disciplines those whom he loves," says Hebrews 12:6, "and chastises every child whom he accepts." She could only give me tangential assurances that Jesus would save me and vague ideas as to how I secured that salvation through faith. But belief was not something so concrete I could nail down what exactly constituted it. As a result, I was always worried my repeated mantras and multiple promises skyward were not enough. It took some time before these spiritual practices led me to feel the assurance that my faith was real and my salvation secure.

Targeting Children

My indoctrination was closer to the extreme end than most, but it is easily integrated into the larger narrative of worldwide belief systems and how they are propagated. A pyro God sounds horrific to outsiders, even to those in religions with their own questionable deities, and I have often wondered how I could have ever truly embraced a faith that would make any sane person recoil. The answer lies in the fact that I wasn't simply taught these lessons, I *inherited* them. They were my upbringing—repeated tirelessly by those who raised me. To reject them would have been to conjure the temerity to reject my family, my community, and my own identity. That is a lot to ask of anyone, but grossly unfair to ask of a child.

The process of teaching a set of assumptions that cannot be questioned is the definition of indoctrination. Unlike education, lessons taught through indoctrination are not critically evaluated and are often presented without the subject's full consent. In my case, religion was pressed upon me before my brain was developed enough to understand such concepts, competently weigh options, or reach independent conclusions.[4] I've found Proverbs 22:6 particularly true to my situation: "Train children in the right way, and when old, they will not stray." This idea is also mirrored

---

4. I accepted Christ as my savior at three years old and was baptized a few years after that. At that point, my brain had not yet developed enough for me to truly evaluate what I was doing. See H. T. Epstein, "Phrenoblysis: Special Brain and Mind Growth Periods; II. Human Mental Development," *Developmental Psychobiology* 7, no. 3 (May 1974): 217–224.

in the words attributed to Saint Francis Xavier, "Give me the child until he is seven, and I will give you the man."[5] I cannot tell you what I had for breakfast last week, or remember all of Freud's defense mechanisms I learned in college, but I can quote Bible verses and sing worship songs that I learned when I was five years old.

In Matthew 18:3, Jesus says, "Truly I tell you, unless you change and become like children, you will never enter the kingdom of heaven." Adults tend to have too many pesky critical thinking skills, and even the least learned among us can surpass the ability of small children. With what we know about children's cognitive development, and built-in trusting nature, it's no wonder indoctrination is so insidious. If children were only taught empirical, unassailable truths until the point of full brain maturation, how likely is it that they would fully embrace unsubstantiated religious claims?

Instruction Before the Age of Reason

At no time in my childhood was I given a chance to research for myself what to believe, nor was I informed about any alternative options. The evidence I was presented for my church's religious claims included Bible verses, smiling faces, authoritarian tones, or the reinforced echo chamber of a tight-knit community. It was implied that these things constituted lines of evidence, so my ability to evaluate ideas was limited to whoever happened to be in charge at the time. To say this failed to prepare me to be an adult in the world would be a gross understatement.

The dark side of indoctrination is that it's no less effective when it violates our innate sense of right and wrong, and no less difficult to escape when these lessons are shown to be ridiculous, illogical, or untrue. Thomas Jefferson noticed that "truth advances and error recedes step by step," yet with indoctrination, the reverse can also happen. I responded to the accumulated doctrines piled up inside me by distrusting my instincts, thinking of myself as bad, hating LGBTQIA people, fearing the world run by Satan, praying instead of helping others, being disgusted by my own sexuality, going without food to be closer to God, telling children they were going to burn, and truncating my educational prospects based on

---

5. James Thompson, "Give Me a Child Until He Is Seven, and I Will Give You the Man," *The Unz Review: An Alternative Media Selection*, May 20, 2013, http://www.unz.com/jthompson/give-me-child-until-he-is-seven-and-i_20/.

the mistrust my school gave me of "godless" scientists and academics. No amount of lovely doctrines that once inspired me can make up for that.

Hereditary religion was forced on me when I was little, and as I became an adult, I was encouraged to do the same to my children to "grow God's kingdom." When I was expecting my first baby, a pastor of the church we attended told me he was excited that I would "raise him up in service of the Lord." (We had a girl, but church talk tended to be androcentric.) When we were adopting our second child, many people encouraged it as a form of missionary work. After I was no longer convinced about Christianity, one person told me she regretted having supported my son's adoption. Apparently, it would have been better for him to die unloved in an orphanage and go into the arms of Jesus than be raised by an atheist and go to Hell. This person understood our next point about religion: Children become the religion of their parents in the majority of cases.[6]

Religion is generally a matter of geography. It's not a coincidence most Muslims come out of Muslim families or are born in Muslim countries. It's an observable fact that people are influenced by those who surround them, with parents being the primary source of influence on children.[7] Most of the religious adults I know discovered the "truth" just so happened to match the religion they had been taught growing up. That's certainly convenient. Some family friends of ours believe that God will choose who will go to Heaven and who will go to Hell, and there is nothing the individual person can do to change their necrodestination. Yet, to the shock of no one, these friends' children all happen to be God's elect. Imagine that!

One way parents can ensure their children follow in their religious footsteps is by framing their spiritual practices as part of membership in the family. "As for me and my house, we will serve the Lord" is a phrase from Joshua 24:15 that was quoted often while I was growing up. My house served the Lord; this service was predicated on family obligation. I had no choice, yet my pastor would argue I was given a choice to serve the

---

6. Tom W. Smith, "Counting Flocks and Lost Sheep: Trends in Religious Preference Since World War II," GSS Social Change Report 26, National Opinion Research Center, January 1991, http://gss.norc.org/Documents/reports/social-change-reports/SC26.pdf.

7. Phyllis Heath notes that younger children are primarily influenced by their parents, with community influence happening later. See *Parent-Child Relations: Context, Research, and Application,* 3rd ed. (London: Pearson, 2012).

Lord or not, and I just happened to choose correctly. It goes without saying that giving vulnerable children a so-called choice that comes with dire relational consequences is the same as making the choice for them. Let's not pretend differently. And this choice is almost always a binary option between accepting and rejecting their family's religion. No valid third option is realistically given. It was not until my early thirties that I got a taste of the fallout from leaving Christianity, and by then I was mature enough to emotionally survive it.

After I deconverted from my religion, only a few of my close relationships remained intact. I was uninvited to holiday gatherings, was unfriended on social media, lost babysitters, experienced strained interactions with once-close family members, and had to change my will since those who had previously been selected to inherit my children in the event of my death had disappeared entirely from our lives without a word. This hurt me very much, but I was a mature adult with coping skills at the time. I cannot imagine how a child would handle similar devastating losses.

The threat of losing a community can keep people from easily departing from their religion, but for true believers, fear of supernatural retribution is what glues them down. Victims of indoctrination are much less likely to seek out answers outside their authority or community, so the first time many of us become aware of the evidence (or lack of evidence) for our beliefs, those beliefs have already been deeply ingrained in us by people we trusted. Hell is one of those beliefs I didn't question for the first thirty years of my life. I felt so foolish as a grown adult using Google to look for any physical evidence of it, and not being sure of the answer I'd find. When my daughter was little, she asked me on the way home from church if I was going to Hell for being an atheist. She was just as incredulous as I had once been to learn there was absolutely zero credible evidence for Hell. We've never touched it, tasted it, smelled it, seen it, or felt it with our bodies, I informed her. This was in direct conflict with the brazen certainty in which she'd been taught that the land of torture was absolutely a real place—one she might have pointed to on a map. She asked why grown-ups in church would teach her it was real without knowing for sure. My husband was quick to inform her that the Bible made this claim, and it held religious authority over biblical Christians like himself. Still, Hell became firmly planted in the category of *belief* rather than *hard fact* in my daughter's mind. It was enough to calm her fears.

Why We Believed in the First Place

One point about religion that I wish more secular people would realize before making memes about its weirder practices is that the nuts and bolts of religious community tend to work. Many of the lessons I learned from my faith were backed up by the testimony of our congregation—anecdotal evidence that confirmed life was better when we obeyed God's word. When the Bible talks about human beings, it doesn't describe aliens. It says to be kind to one another, and when I did that, it led others to be kind back. It said to be a hard worker like the ant—that led me to succeed at my job. When lying was called an abomination to the Lord, I got a reputation for integrity by avoiding it. These practical teachings were effective, and because of that, I was more likely to accept the religious reasons of *why* they were effective.

People tend to gravitate to what benefits them over what's true, but that does not mean that the truth is unimportant to them. That friction between what we hold dear and what we suspect to be true can cause a great deal of cognitive dissonance. Doubt will always be a companion of faith due to faith's ethereal nature, and religions will always have myriad ways of overcoming it. Framing doubt as something to be battled, with succumbing to it seen as a personal failure, makes doubt an enemy rather than simply "your intellectual conscience pleading with you to be honest with yourself."[8]

Ideological Prison

If it were easy to objectively evaluate our most precious assumptions, everyone would do it. As an adult believer who wanted to explore the truth of her faith's claims, I knew I could not give my efforts an open mind out of fear. I instead settled for a half-opened mind, like a child watching a scary movie by peeking through her fingers. When the cracks in my worldview first began to appear, I reacted by building an exoskeleton around my deeply held beliefs by reading books that validated rather than evaluated my faith. I joined every Beth Moore Bible study I could find! Finding any flaws in my religion was incredibly difficult for me, so I allowed confirmation bias to permeate my search for truth. I became skilled at focusing only on the answers to prayer, the beauty of creation, or the love of my church, never

---

8. Peter Boghossian's definition of *doubt*, Twitter, January 18, 2016, https://twitter.com/peterboghossian/status/689261540906762240.

the ignored requests, the gruesomeness of the food chain, or the horrific teachings of the Bible. It was like someone going through a rainbow mosaic and chiseling out only the red pieces to prove the whole piece was red. Eventually, despite my best efforts, the other colors could no longer be ignored.

Digging into the Bible searching for truth was like putting my fingers deep into a sandcastle. It fell apart. Losing the Bible as a source of authority made me feel lost. I started to fear that everything I knew was wrong. When my foster daughter had learned Santa was not real, the realization messed with her world. "Is Justin Bieber real? Is Katy Perry real?" she demanded in a panic. I tried not to laugh at the time, but now here I was asking in a similar sweat: "Is God real? Is prayer real?"

A little while back, there was a bit of a stir when word got out that the astrological signs of around 86 percent of people had changed due to better information.[9] Those who relied upon horoscopes, admittedly a small percentage of people, had believed that they worked. Yet now most of those who had claimed their horoscopes were accurate had the wrong one! When we want something to work, our biased brains will make it work. That is part of the explanation behind why placebos are effective. From what we know about the flexibility of belief and the psychological tricks of the mind, we know the zodiac change will not devastate most believers. Many will simply ignore the new information. Some will downplay the accuracy of old horoscopes while being amazed at how much *more* accurate their new horoscope is. It's human nature.

Since my religion, unlike other versions of Christianity, was based on biblical inerrancy, and since the Bible included countless false or blatantly contradictory claims, I was forced to rework my beliefs until they were so thoroughly vague, or couched in enough rationalizations, they became unfalsifiable. Believers are not stupid; they simply have the human propensity to protect *a priori* beliefs. When confronted with direct evidence against a belief, believers can become more devout in response. Researchers at Dartmouth College have called this the backfire effect.[10] It's

---

9. "Don't Freak Out, but Your Star Sign Has Probably Changed, *Cosmopolitan*, September 15, 2016, http://www.cosmopolitan.com/uk/entertainment/news/a45943/star-sign-horoscope-change-2016.

10. Brendan Nyhan and Jason Reifler, "When Corrections Fail: The Persistence of Political Misperceptions," *Political Behavior* 32, no. 2 (June 2010): 303–330.

a normal part of how our brains protect us from uncomfortable truths. When my faith-based assumptions were questioned or corrected, I doubled down on them. I dismissed any evidence, no matter how clearly presented, as a test from God or a trick of Satan.

Hooked by the Hoodwink

After indoctrination takes hold, what a child is taught starts to feel true. As a believer, I could feel incredible giddiness or profound wonder when I told people about Jesus. My head and heart would absolutely sing. I may have used the Bible to form my beliefs, but I relied upon my feelings to support them. I assumed my internal convictions came from the Holy Spirit, at least in part. Yet my feelings seemed to follow my convictions. My former beliefs felt right, but then as an adult, so did my revised beliefs. Eventually even my rejection of beliefs felt right as well—or at least it did after the initial abuse to my psyche caused by the initial loss. It seems that feelings cannot be relied upon to help lead people to object truth.

In one attempt to confirm my faith, I opened all my old blog posts and prayer journals. Reading through the "answered prayers" left me stunned at how ordinary they were. Not one single miracle in my life lacked a completely natural explanation, even though I was sure I had remembered otherwise. My life generally worked out the same both before and after giving up prayer. This discovery should have been obvious, but it was devastating to me. This was the first of many epiphanies I had about the world.

There had been times I was certain the Holy Spirit had given me the exact right words that seemed to come out of nowhere when sharing my faith with others, but I had the exact same thing happen when answering questions about why I didn't believe in God. I even had an impulse afterwards to thank God for bringing examples to mind. I doubt the Holy Spirit was helping me sum up why the concept of God was improbable!

Even those "blessings" I was trained not to call coincidences kept happening after giving up God. The final straw was when I had gone $80 over budget and that same day I received an unexpected check for the exact amount I needed to cover the deficit. "You know this is only going to help me *atheist* more," I joked to the ceiling. My beliefs had changed, my feelings had changed, but reality hadn't changed at all.

Perhaps the most surprising discovery of all was when I experienced the same exact high I used to have during worship at church while singing "Sweet Caroline" in a group of around 150 at my local Sunday Assembly. Then of course there was the time I had the exact same sensation I used to get reading the Bible when reading the first Harry Potter book. I was invited to join a Harry Potter and the Sacred Text study group that developed at Harvard Divinity School. It had been inspired by the question: What would happen if we treated beloved books as sacred?[11] By treating the Harry Potter series as Christians do with the Bible, Jews do with the Torah, or Muslims do with the Qur'an, Harry Potter fans have been able to enjoy a sense of reverence, inspiration, and the ability to glean wisdom from the Wizarding World to apply to their daily lives. I was able to seamlessly transfer the exegetical skills I'd accumulated over fourteen years of religious education to J. K. Rowling's chapters. It turns out, my Bible wasn't special; it was simply the totem I used for channeling my intellectual curiosity, pursuit of wisdom, and transcendent feelings. Now I can re-create "spiritual" experiences in a secular context. It turns out they are part of a universal human phenomenon.

It Feels Right

Believers in extremely contradictory religions all report similar sensations when practicing their very different faiths. Again, it all feels right. Even when beliefs are not grounded in truth, the sensations created by those beliefs absolutely are. This may be why so many religions require belief before blessings, and acceptance before assurance. Former pastor Dan Barker, who preached from the Bible for almost two decades, agrees, "If the only way you can accept an assertion is by faith, then you are conceding that it can't be taken on its own merits."[12] If you are forced to believe something before it *feels* real, it's probably not real.

Brain scans performed by Dr. Andrew Newberg from the University of Pennsylvania School of Medicine showed that when sincere practitioners were engaged in religious activity—like Catholic nuns praying or Buddhist

---

11. You can listen to the podcasts at https://itunes.apple.com/us/podcast/harry-potter-and-the-sacred-text/id1096113994?mt=2.

12. Dan Barker, *Losing Faith in Faith: From Preacher to Atheist* (Madison, WI: Freedom from Religion Foundation, 1992), quoted from the Quotations Page, http://www.quotationspage.com/quote/26815.html.

monks meditating (perhaps even Harry Potter fans chanting the Sorting Hat's song)—they had increased activity in the frontal lobe and decreased activity in the parietal lobe.[13] To sum up those brain functions badly: They felt more and were aware of themselves less. Sacred rites physically affect the brain and change a person's perception of the world.

The brain's altered state during religious contemplation has positive and negative aspects. For example, religion has been criticized for making people less intelligent. A meta-analysis of sixty-three studies found "a significant negative association between intelligence and religiosity" in fifty-three of those studies, or 84 percent.[14] But religion's effect on the brain, namely lowering activity in it which affects intelligence, can also reduce stress. Many participants in a University of Toronto Scarborough study worried less about their mistakes in tasks after thinking about God due to reduced brain activity in the anterior cingulate cortex.[15] Of course this only worked for believers who had already accepted these concepts as true. While thinking God is in control can have negative consequences in situations where the stakes are higher, it does make believers less worried and more content. In my church we often said, "Let go and let God," as a cure for stress. These practical teachings work, and as previously stated, people tend to gravitate to what works over what's true.

All spiritual experiences are limited to the human cranium. While many scientific studies have looked into common supernatural claims, there has never been a single piece of evidence to support any of them, that is, outside of their very real effects on the brain. We already know there is a link between religion and the temporal lobe because those who suffer from temporal lobe epilepsy have been observed having profound spiritual experiences as a result. So, what would happen if we messed with the temporal lobe? Apparently, God happens.

Neuroscientists Stanley Koren and Michael Persinger created and

---

13. Miron Zuckerman, Jordan Silberman, and Judith A. Hall, "The Relation Between Intelligence and Religiosity: A Meta-Analysis and Some Proposed Explanations," *Personality and Social Psychology Review* 17, no. 4 (August 6, 2013), abstract.

14. Michael Inzlicht and Alexa M. Tullett, "Reflecting on God: Religious Primes Can Reduce Neurophysiological Response to Errors," *Psychological Science* 21, no. 8 (August 2010), 1184–90.

15. *Through the Wormhole with Morgan Freeman*, "The God Experience," Science Channel, video, 3:02, http://www.sciencechannel.com/tv-shows/through-the-wormhole/videos/the-god-experience.

developed, respectively, the God Helmet, which targets the temporal lope by altering its electromagnetic field. Most participants who have worn it reported a presence, like an intelligence or person, in the room when none was there.[16] When sincere people speak of communing with a supernatural being, they could be simply interpreting what their gray matter is physically experiencing. Since we experience reality through the filters of our minds, we rely on our perceptions to give us an accurate picture of reality. Yet the brain has so many quirks that we've had to develop an entire scientific method to protect us from errors in perception.

Transformed by the Renewing of Your Mind

Instead of calling religious indoctrination "brainwashing," we might rightly call it "brain changing." Religious practice can set off pleasure centers in the brain that are associated with sex, love, or drugs. The religious beliefs themselves do not have to be of intrinsic or universal value; what matters is what the believer has been brought up to think about them as true or valuable. This is why nonbelievers were not affected in the same way as believers in the University of Toronto Scarborough stress study. This is also why the famous atheist Richard Dawkins only felt dizzy and strange after wearing the God Helmet.

I once thought Aron Ra's words about religion were too abrasive, but the more I've studied, the more I've understood them: "Religion is increasingly seen as a matter of mental conditioning, emotional manipulation, and inculcation—a mild form of mind control via the auto hypnotic power of pretend."[17]

I have tried to present a sympathetic picture of religious practitioners, and help provide some understanding of the innate human programming that keeps people believing. But I want to be very clear that religious belief is far from innocuous. While the severity of the harm will depend on the severity of the belief, and believers have been known to do valid good deeds in the world, major religious belief systems do have a cumulative negative net effect.

---

16. Michael A. Ferguson et al., "Reward, Salience, and Attentional Networks Are Activated by Religious Experience in Devout Mormons," *Social Neuroscience*, November 29, 2016, 1–13.

17. Aron Ra, *Foundational Falsehoods of Creationism* (Durham, NC: Pitchstone Publishing, 2016), 131.

Part II: The Harm of Indoctrination

Religious indoctrination ruined parts of my childhood, left me unprepared for living outside the church, diminished my educational aspirations, pushed me into marriage at a young age, and almost destroyed my life. Indoctrination was the bullet wound I had to go through life with, and it keeps getting the credit for my own recovery from it.

Many of my loved ones see me as a good person who has a passion for helping others, especially orphaned children and homeless neighbors, but too often my religious upbringing gets the credit for my own morality and hard work. In reality, my religion subverted my natural inclination to help others by adding burdens and barriers to the process. I had to try to convert those I was helping, for one thing, which undermined my sincerity and added conditions for my assistance. For another thing, I had to "avoid the appearance of evil" (1 Thessalonians 5:22) which caused me to shun instead of support certain "sinners." Shedding Christianity made me a better person in these regards.

Today I'm an atheist, despite my ACE school's best efforts to produce a fundamentalist Christian, and because of this I've often had my indoctrination experience downplayed by those close to me. "Well, it didn't work on you," I was told when I complained to a family member about my children being indoctrinated by Sunday school teachers. I didn't want someone presenting something that was not demonstrably true as a fact to my children, but my family member was more concerned with my children learning values. What motivates putting kids in church is the belief that religion is good for them. But is it?

Religion is Bad for You

One study found that telling children about a loving supernatural being who rewarded them for good behavior was actually bad for the children's relationships with those caregivers.[18] Children felt betrayed when they discovered this being was not real. Researchers sympathized with parents who were simply repeating traditions that they themselves had been taught as children, yet they urged them to stop. The supernatural being in this case was not a god, but was Santa Claus.

---

18. Christopher Boyle and Kathy McKay, "A Wonderful Lie," *Lancet Psychiatry* 3, no. 12 (December 3, 2016), 1110–1.

While I do not know an intelligent adult who still believes in Santa, I know many intelligent adults who believe in equally improbable beings. Rachel Held Evans is one of my favorite Christian authors and got me to engage with epistemology for the very first time after reading her childhood apologetics for Santa. Epistemology is the study of knowledge that examines how we know what we know. As a child, Evans defended Santa the same way she had been taught to defend God. When asked if she'd ever seen him, she said, "No, I haven't. But Santa leaves enough evidence of his existence to prove it beyond a reasonable doubt. [Gifts and cookie crumbs] point to him as bending trees point to the existence of wind."[19] She went on to defend his supernatural strength and speed as similar to powers angelic beings have in Scripture, and his reindeer as similar to the talking donkey in the book of Numbers.

She had good points! This showed me the value of maintaining a high standard for evidentiary support when forming my own beliefs. I found that some of the beliefs in my wheelhouse had as much substantiated backing as Old Saint Nick. If I was going to rely on claims, such as eyewitness testimony, instead of demonstrable evidence, then what was the difference between a belief in Jesus's resurrection and ascension, a belief in Muhammad's ascension on a winged horse, or even a child's testimony of a fat man in a red suit ascending up the chimney?

Extraordinary claims require extraordinary evidence, and incredible claims require credible evidence, yet a lot of people do not believe this should apply to religion. Some members of my family, as well as my friends, considered my suspension of belief in all unsupported claims too severe, like throwing out the baby with the bathwater. They would have preferred I had merely found a better version of my faith as Evans or my husband did. Their reasoning? Faith was good, and as a result of it, I would have peace, comfort, and happiness. Of course, drunks can be happy or comforted with alcohol, but it doesn't mean alcohol is good for them. And ignorance is bliss, but we do not consider ignorance a virtue.

Faith Is Not a Pathway to Truth

Beliefs are not always fully based in reality, but people always are. An

---

19. Rachel Held Evans, *Evolving in Monkey Town* (Nashville: Zondervan, 2010), 32–33.

uncritical belief, no matter how good the intentions behind it, can be unhealthy because any logic placed upon it will not hold. If we think of truth as a set of rules that govern what happens to us, then beliefs that feel good but are not based on those rules will have negative consequences for us. Religion may preach that a believer's prayers change things, that God intervenes in a believer's health, or that angels watch out for believers to protect them from accidents. Yet if that were true we would expect the numbers to reflect this; the proportion of religious cancer patients or religious victims of car accidents would have to be less than the proportion of nonreligious ones. If, in fact, recovery from illness or injury depends a lot more on access to medical science than access to religious ceremony, then relying on a belief that contradicts this will lead to trouble. I had to learn this the hard way as I'll describe later.

I do not want to overstate the impact of religion by claiming it will ruin lives, because it doesn't always. But neither do I want to understate the impact of religion, because we know it can. Not all people who experience indoctrination are taught hateful doctrines that hurt people. Many times they are simply presented with nice-sounding ideas that have no anchor in anything solid. For example, some people are merely taught God is loving. This assumes there's a deity who takes up space in reality in some actionable way, and that its chief characteristic is something human beings would recognize as love. It seems innocent enough, inspiring even, yet I've sat with those grieving losses who think God has left them because there is nothing loving about their situation. I've also heard people disregard the suffering of others based on a belief that it could have been prevented if only they'd embraced this loving God before tragedy struck. So, this seemingly nice belief in a loving God can result in victim blaming or leaving the hard work of helping others in imaginary hands.

Sexism

It doesn't take a bunch of studies to see sexism in religion. All we have to do is look at the dearth of women in positions of authority within major religious institutions to get an idea of how they are viewed. My religion taught me that I belonged to my father and then later, to my husband. I have memorized a number of chattel passages from the Bible used to defend this view of women as property. Yet even religions that are kinder to women can practice what social psychology calls benevolent sexism. This flavor of sexism views women as less valuable than men in subtle ways. Compared to hostile sexism, which will insult or antagonize women outright, benevolent sexism will compliment them in a childlike or prejudiced way based on stereotypes. The Bible does this when it labels the wife the "weaker vessel" compared to the husband (1 Peter 3:7). Even when "weaker" was interpreted in my church as "more precious and valuable" it still meant women weren't equal to men and were kept away from responsibilities and leadership. It's this variety of sexism that leads men to undervalue women's contributions to the workforce. So it's no surprise that researchers have found a concrete connection between religion and cheating women out of wages.

The wage gap in the United States rises a measurable 0.3 percent for every 1 percent rise in religiosity in each US state.[20] If women are seen primarily as subordinate "keepers of the home" as Titus 2:5 says good women should be, then employers who subscribe to a religious view may subconsciously see women as less deserving of a paycheck. A man in my former church once told me that men were the breadwinners and women simply worked for fun money. He owned a business and employed both men and women. I doubt they had equal paychecks.

Othering

Religious identification can also create us-versus-them thinking out of deeply held, yet ultimately subjective ideas. Even a pastor's sermon about loving one's neighbor can carry a subliminal understanding that the church's God is the loving one, the church the correct one, and their loving practices the ideal ones. Following that logic, what does that make the neighbor they are called to love? Less loving, less correct, and with less-than-ideal practices by comparison. Being a member of my denomination worked to make me prejudiced against other denominations, even within Christianity, but especially those outside it. Will Gervais from the University of British Columbia found in a set of studies that believers did not trust those in other faiths (like Muslims), but especially not atheists whom they trusted as much as rapists.[21]

20. Travis Wiseman and Nabamita Dutta, "Religion and the Gender Wage Gap: A U.S. State-Level Study," February 26, 2016, https://papers.ssrn.com/sol3/papers.cfm?abstract_id=2738523.

21. W. M. Gervais, A. F. Shariff, and A. Norenzayan, "Do You Believe in Atheists?

Racism

Another major problem created by faith systems is racial prejudice. A meta-analysis of fifty-five major studies found a strong link between religion and racism.[22] Racism may also rely on the above in-group/out-group trust dynamic, which probably kept our ancient ancestors alive when they came upon strangers who could be a threat. Those in the in-group could be trusted, yet those outside of the group could attack us for our resources. People haven't always come with *believer* or *atheist* labels so our ancestors needed a quick way to determine who was friendly by instantly recognizing shared characteristics before getting too close. Yet that kind of automatic prejudice based on appearance holds no place in a modern society—in fact, it works to hold us back from greater collaboration and living peacefully together.

While we can get this in-group/out-group dynamic outside of religion, being part of a band or having membership in a mommy group does not seem to carry the same radical connection to racism as religious identification. Nonbelievers, referred to as "religious agnostics" in the meta-analysis on racism mentioned above, were found to be racially tolerant compared to the monotheistic believers.[23] That's probably because God is the ultimate trump card, like children winning a game by claiming infinity points. The claim may be empty, but it communicates dominance and supremacy. Religion makes the in-group God's favorite. My church used to assert our God was omniscient, omnipotent, and omnipresent. I grew up thinking I was on the side of the most powerful being in the universe. I imagine it's a similar heady feeling driving white supremacists like Hitler's followers when they call themselves the "master race." Human beings, especially those in power, have a tendency to think their own group or race or gender is best. If their church is run by straight white men, then the default thinking is that God's favorites are straight white men. Critical thinking is one of the best deterrents to prejudicial thinking, yet belief is the antithesis to it. In other words, the cure may be found in digging up the foundation.

Distrust Is Central to Anti-Atheist Prejudice," *Journal of Personality and Social Psychology* 101, no. 6 (December 2011), 1189–206.

22. Deborah L. Hall, David C. Matz, and Wendy Wood, "Why Don't We Practice What We Preach? A Meta-Analytic Review of Religious Racism," *Personality and Social Psychology Review* 14, no. 1 (February 2010), 126–39.

23. Ibid.

When the Fruits of the Spirit are Rotten

Sexism and racism are bad enough, but what about basic decency? Unfortunately for those who indoctrinate their children thinking it will provide good morals, researchers found a worldwide negative association between religion and altruism.[24] Religiousness was inversely predictive of children's altruism, or in other words, the more religious children were, the less charitable, kind, and generous they were. The study also confirmed that the longer children were exposed to religion, the worse they scored in these areas. Almost every religion has a version of the Golden Rule included in its doctrines. Christianity has fruits of the spirit such as love, kindness, and goodness that are supposed to be proof the Holy Spirit is working to make followers of Christ above average in these areas. Yet teaching these ideals to children, even claiming children will have supernatural help achieving them, has not shown to produce morally superior children. The Golden Rule seems to have its limits within religious settings.

The altruism study also included measuring children's inclination to harm others and found religion positively correlated with punitive tendencies. Religious children, especially Christian and Muslim ones, were not only less likely to be helpful, but they were also more likely to be hurtful. When shown a cartoon character bumping into someone, the religious children tended to want that character punished, even if the bump was presented as accidental. Both the Bible and Qur'an punish sin in extreme ways, so that may explain why children brought up learning those faiths were more likely to react more extremely to presumed offenses.

What made the secular children in the study more empathetic and giving? Causation is hard to pin down, but it could be as simple as not belonging to a "special people"—the in-group of God's favorites. If all people are the same, then how I feel when I get hurt must be how they feel. But if people are different based on a hierarchy of whom God likes better, then maybe others don't feel what I feel. This dehumanizes others and makes it easier to refuse them help.

When Dr. Vern Bengtson added secular families to his famous Longitudinal Study of Generations, he also noticed "empathetic reciprocity,"

---

24. Jean Decety et al., "The Negative Association between Religiousness and Children's Altruism across the World," *Current Biology* 25, no. 22 (November 16, 2015), 2951–55, http://www.cell.com/current-biology/abstract/S0960-9822(15)01167-7.

the ethos behind the Golden Rule, was a cornerstone of secular parenting.[25] Bengtson found high levels of family unity as well as strong ethics and morals in secular families, with many of them doing a better job of clearly communicating their moral principles coherently and passionately to their children than their religious counterparts. It seems that when divested from religion, the Golden Rule is more effective.

All of these finding go against the popular belief that religion is good for teaching children morals. However, 53 percent of Americans still think belief in God is required for morality, and that number jumps up to 62 percent when looking at white evangelical communities like the one I grew up in.[26] Yet in a study out of the University of Manchester, Dr. Ingrid Storm found that our society's decline in religion has not come with a corresponding decline in morality.[27] If morality were solely a religious concept, or had a strong correlation to religious belief, then we would expect to see some sort of hit to morality in the last several years as the percentage of nonbelievers has increased. Instead we see the exact opposite as the number of nonbelievers continues to rise in the developed world and crime rates continue to fall.

While belief can make people happier, as we saw in the stress study, secularism makes *societies* happier. In his comprehensive work on secularism and well-being, Phil Zuckerman points out that the more religious a society, the less happy and healthy its members:

> The most secular democracies in the world score very high on international indexes of happiness and well-being and they have among lowest violent crime and homicide rates. But there's more. A perusal of any recent United Nations World Development Report reveals that when

---

25 Secular families added in 2013. Bengtson's thoughts on secular families taken from Brougham, Rachel, "Studies Show Morals, Understanding Abundant in Secular Homes," *Petoskey News*, April 2, 2015, http://www.petoskeynews.com/featured-pnr/studies-show-morals-understanding-abundant-in-secular-homes/article_3d2d2c59-2a90-5302-8abc-06db05c6f119.html.

26. "Belief in God Essential to Morality?" Global Attitudes & Trends, Pew Research Center, May 27, 2014, http://www.pewglobal.org/2014/03/13/worldwide-many-see-belief-in-god-as-essential-to-morality/revised-report-images-1.

27. Ingrid Storm, "Morality in Context: A Multilevel Analysis of the Relationship between Religion and Values in Europe," *Cambridge University Press* 9, no. 1 (March 2016), 111–38.

it comes to such things as life expectancy, infant mortality, economic equality, economic competitiveness, health care, standard of living, and education, it is the most secular democracies on earth that fare the best, doing much better than the most religious nations in the world.[28]

It turns out I'm part of a whole group of people who do better without religion.

Knowledge Heals

The success of my indoctrination was directly proportionate to the failure of my education. I recognize my parents placed me in an ACE school out of love, but I continue to struggle with the abuse and educational neglect I experienced there. When institutions lend their weight to the indoctrination process of children, society suffers. William Jennings Bryan, an apologist for the Christian faith, once famously said, "If we have to give up either religion or education, we should give up education." His sentiments were praised by my ACE school, and were required reading as part of our English course. ACE's method of teaching facts about the physical world, many of which they get wrong,[29] while at the same time teaching equal "facts" from the Bible, blurs reality with religious concepts. I lacked the sagacity to always know which lesson was *belief* and which was *truth* because the same people who taught me how to do fractions also taught me an omnipotent being was reading my thoughts and causing earthquakes.

Upon graduation from ACE, I did not understand what constituted evidence, how to think critically, how to write a paper, the value of peer review, or anything about evolution other than it was a false conspiracy. I was, however, extremely knowledgeable on what was written in the Bible. I can tell you from personal experience this kind of vacuous curriculum hinders a child's ability to gather data and make informed decisions and discoveries. It leaves children vulnerable to being taken

---

28. Phil Zuckerman, "Atheism, Secularity, and Well-Being: How the Findings of Social Science Counter Negative Stereotypes and Assumptions," *Sociology Compass* 3, no. 6 (December 2009), 949–71.

29. Countless examples of ACE's bad science can be found in "Christianist Textbooks Revealed," *The Orbit*, https://the-orbit.net/entequilaesverdad/christianist-textbooks-revealed/.

advantage of by others. As a result, I fell victim to a lot of scams, false claims, and pseudoscience parading as medical advice. One time when I was a young mom, I tried to cure my baby daughter's high fever with prayer instead of medicine. I was unaware that intercessory prayer had already been debunked as completely ineffective in the largest, most expensive study of its kind the year before my daughter was born.[30] As a victim of indoctrination, I wouldn't have even searched for proof of the validity of prayer. My daughter was lucky; not all children of extremely religious parents survive the experience.

Survivors of Indoctrination

My friend Julie Reitz spent ten years in ACE, with the majority of those years spent at ACE headquarters where her father was a production manager. These days she spends her spare time reaching out to former and current students who have suffered from their ACE experience. Reitz remembers having to move out of her home before she could escape ACE.

"When I left home, I started reprogramming myself immediately," she wrote me about her experiences. "So now I am approaching 50. I am finally at peace, but my whole adult life was wasted in getting to that point."

Reitz and others are part of a support group called Survivors of Accelerated Christian Education started by Jonny Scaramanga. Dr. Scaramanga has researched ACE for years, exposing many of its alarming lessons in articles published online. Since 2013, he has conducted extensive interviews of former students from ten ACE schools in England for his qualitative study of their experiences. He noticed many of these adults spoke about forced faith:

> My participants almost universally agreed their schools had been centers of indoctrination. Many participants referred to indoctrination unprompted. Three called their parents "brainwashed" by the influence of the church-school. Nathan described "a degree of mind control." Mike accused his school of "brainwashing" him. Without being asked, four participants described what their schools did in general

30. Herbert Benson et al., "Study of the Therapeutic Effects of Intercessory Prayer (STEP) in Cardiac Bypass Patients: A Multicenter Randomized Trial of Uncertainty and Certainty of Receiving Intercessory Prayer," *American Heart Journal* 151, no. 4 (April 2006): 934–42.

as "indoctrination," and two more stated they had personally been indoctrinated. Other participants used words amounting to the same thing: Kaye, for example, said staff "forced you to be a Christian."[31]

One participant, Harry, had wholeheartedly embraced ACE's version of Christianity and was reluctant to call it indoctrination. "Maybe I downplay that in my own mind, y'know, cos I don't wanna feel that I was, you know, set on this inevitable course that has come to its fruition." Harry also stated his belief that all schools indoctrinate, including secular ones, betraying an ignorance of the difference between education and indoctrination common among those who have been indoctrinated. Unfortunately this indoctrination included convincing students they were dirty, sinful, deserving of horrific torture, and in need of salvation. A member of the Survivors of Accelerated Christian Education group posted this comment as a salve for those grieving their years absorbing such doctrine: "You are not messed up. You were messed *with*."

Consequences of Indoctrination

Religion is an accidental by-product of our cognitive abilities. Scientists have noticed that children starting around four years old tend to be naturally biased toward religious ideas. One study out of Boston University shows children are more likely to gravitate toward answers to life's questions that include purpose instead of randomness, implying there's a designer— whether a grown-up or a deity—behind the scenes.[32] From the countless times I heard "God did it" growing up, I know some people don't grow out of this thinking! ACE merely capitalizes on a child's natural tendency to order the chaos around them.

In a different Boston University study on children and their understanding of the world, child development experts found that five- and six-year-olds from religious backgrounds could not differentiate fact from fiction like their nonreligious peers.[33] From a brain development

---

31. Scaramanga, "Systems of Indoctrination," 224.

32. Deborah Kelemen, "Are Children 'Intuitive Theists'? Reasoning about Purpose and Design in Nature," *Psychological Science* 15, no. 5 (May 15, 2004), 295–301.

33. Kathleen H. Corriveau, Eva E. Chen, and Paul L. Harris, "Judgments about Fact and Fiction by Children from Religious and Nonreligious Backgrounds," *Cognitive Science* 39, no. 2 (March 2015), 353–82.

standpoint, this would be the age that children could discern such things, but religious indoctrination had delayed or impeded this stage.

A child's heuristic process takes advantage of contextual clues to discover how things work. Indoctrination often works to subvert the heuristic process by giving a wrong set of core facts, like someone typing on a keyboard with their fingers one row over from the correct starting position. When stories with supernatural elements were taught as truth, children incorporated them into their understanding of the laws of nature. Having those elements in a story then was not seen as a clue that the story was fictional.

So what happens when religious children grow up? Researchers at the University of Helsinki found that the religious believers in their study had a poor understanding of the world around them.[34] They found higher rates of religious belief corresponded to lower intuitive physics skills, lower mental rotation ability, lower math scores, and less knowledge of biological phenomenon. The part of this study that made headlines, however, was the discovery that religious participants tended to apply human characteristics to inanimate objects, such as believing rocks had feelings. As someone who once believed this about rocks, I know firsthand how awful it is when your sense of the world is altered by spiritual concepts. Jesus said rocks would cry out if his disciples remained silent, and John the Baptist said God could raise heirs to Abraham through stones. I did not completely shed this assumption that God sometimes gave rocks anthropomorphic characteristics until I started shining a hard light on those tucked-away assumptions as I deconstructed my faith's claims. I wonder how many people carry similarly bizarre beliefs into adulthood without really thinking about them. Those who deny the facts of science when they contradict the Bible fall into this trap when they claim "God works in mysterious ways."

Part III: The Cure for Indoctrination

We've seen how religious indoctrination has a real impact on the brain, altering how it functions, and affecting how people interact with reality. Several studies suggest that religion is positively correlated to racism,

---

34. Marjaana Lindeman and Annika M. Svedholm-Häkkinen, "Does Poor Understanding of Physical World Predict Religious and Paranormal Beliefs?" *Applied Cognitive Psychology* 30, no. 5 (September/October 2016), 736–42.

sexism, and punitive tendencies while being negatively correlated to altruism, morality, and intelligence. So how do we avoid indoctrinating our children into these systems?

When my daughter was around six, she saw a fortune-teller machine at an arcade and wanted to know what it did. When I explained it printed out a card with her fortune on it, she balked, "That's silly." Before I could praise her insight, she continued, "Don't people know they can get a fortune cookie? Then you have a fortune *and* a cookie!" Although there's no arguing with cookie logic, I was able to ask her questions and discovered she held an assumption about the world that was not based in reality. It turned out, she believed grown-ups knew everything, and if they knew everything, then they'd know the future too. Of course, this hypothesis could be tested. I asked her to think of a number between one and one hundred and I would guess it. Even though I was a grown-up, I never managed to guess her number. Instead of telling her, "Fortunes aren't real," which I easily could have done, I wanted to educate her about them so she could apply that information to similar claims later instead of having to ask me for the validity of each one.

Encourage the Quest for Truth

It's important to remember that education and indoctrination are separated by a huge chasm of intention. Lessons learned through indoctrination cannot be questioned, and those on the receiving end will be pressured to accept all tenets uncritically. Conversely, education requires questioning and investigating while encouraging critical thinking. Indoctrination leads to dependence on authority. Education will lead to independent thought. Indoctrination is much more likely to rely on threats. Telling children they will suffer God's wrath or hurt a teacher's feelings if the lesson is not accepted are both threats. Education should always be free of threats. Children should be encouraged to have doxastic openness—the ability and freedom to revise beliefs based on sufficient reasons. They should not feel so married to any idea that they could not revise their opinions when presented new evidence. We should embrace saying "I don't know," accept being wrong, and celebrate correction. Many of the greatest philosophers and most successful scientists do this.

Careful wording can distinguish beliefs from objective truths. My children have an atheist parent and a Christian one. I respect my husband very much, and the success of our co-parenting in the face of deistic differences has everything to do with two little words: "I believe." When their father teaches them about his religion, he deliberately says, "I believe" or "the Bible says" before stating a religious claim. When I teach my kids about other religions, I am careful to preface those worldviews by saying "they believe" or "their holy books say." This has alleviated any confusion the kids might have about what's real and what's religious.

People often ask why my husband is okay with his kids learning about religions this way. The reason is that both of us value truth. If Christian claims are true, they will be supported by facts. Scientific observations should not then, at least in theory, threaten any religion. If they do, then the religion is not compatible with observed truth, and it must be discarded or revised. If God is responsible for creating the world, why should his, her, their, or its religion fail so simple a test? A belief may cause a change in the brain, but it will not cause the universe to rearrange itself to conform to it. It's better to seek an inconvenient truth than preserve a convenient belief.

I have also been asked why I bring up religion at all around my kids. Why not ignore the topic entirely? Learning about religion is important because it affects so much of the world my kids will grow up in. David McAfee has written a couple of books teaching religious concepts to children and recommends the phenomenological approach to studying religion. This includes learning about how religions popped up, what they teach, and how they have progressed or evolved. McAfee found that a paucity of information on religion at home did not keep children from being curious about religion and seeking it out, often from biased sources. The funny thing is that when I was a believer, I would teach my kids about Jesus, and now that I'm an atheist, I am still teaching my kids about Jesus.

This type of education has led my oldest child, now ten, to independently conclude that religious beliefs come from the religious groups themselves. She noticed that any religion under study was often tied to the cultural values of the nation around it and limited to the scientific understanding at the time the religious texts were written. So exposing her to religious beliefs, a great deal of which were Christian ones, did not indoctrinate her. As the adage goes, "Teach them one religion, and you indoctrinate them. Teach them many religions, and you inoculate them." Or "Study one religion, and you'll be hooked for life. Study two religions, and you're done in an hour."

I can't think of a better way to show all religions have human rather than supernatural origins than systematically studying and comparing them.

Why Not Church?

I once allowed churches and Christian institutions to teach my children, but they were unable to do so completely honestly. One day my son came home from a Christian club horrified that there was a man in his heart. He was four. This interloping chest squatter didn't make my son feel protected or special, only violated. The nice lady who taught him his body was possessed after he closed his eyes and said a few words did so without any disclaimer. Now we try to avoid putting our kids in the care of anyone who may have a vested interest in their conversion.

Truth v. Indoctrination

Children should be given the tools they need to evaluate what is true. Anything less is not honest and will damage their understanding of the only world they have. While my indoctrination did not have the desired result of keeping me a Christian, it did redirect the course of my life in a negative way by severely limiting my options for three decades. Children have the right to have options for living outside of one mold. They should not be hobbled by beliefs that defy reality and result in hardships due to ignorance. They should get the best chance at a life free of prejudice and full of happiness, a life that values their intelligence. No one benefits from being indoctrinated.

4

Owned:
Slaves, Women, Children, and Livestock

Valerie Tarico, PhD

*Even if women wear themselves out or die from childbearing—
no harm done. Let them die from bearing. This is the purpose
for which they exist.*

—Martin Luther[1]

Christianity was born among the Iron Age cultures of the Ancient Near East, and for almost two thousand years it has carried forward parts of the worldview from that time and place. These ancient ideas so infuse our culture that we don't even notice them. Like the air we breathe, or the water that flows through pipes into our homes, or the soil under our garden, they are simply background for the complicated and ever-changing tapestry of modern life.

---

1. *Luther's Works* 45:44–45, as quoted in *Beggars All: Reformation & Apologetics* (blog), http://beggarsallreformation.blogspot.com/2010/04/luther-if-women-wear-themselves-out-in.htm.

Intellectually we know that air or water or soil can be contaminated and that this affects whether we thrive or become sick and stunted. But unless something goes dreadfully wrong, we usually are so busy with day-to-day life that we don't stop to analyze these background factors. The same can be said of certain ideas from the past that shape how we think about ourselves and each other.

One of the most fundamental—and I believe fundamentally toxic—Iron Age ideas that permeates the Bible is this: Powerful beings, including powerful people, have the right to own others and use them for their own purposes, with or without consent. In fact, *God made some kinds of people, along with nonhuman animals, to be owned and used by others.*

Gender roles in the Bible are built on top of this foundation. In most of the Bible's texts, women are literally possessions of men, as are livestock, children, and slaves. The legal term *chattel* refers to moveable personal property, economic assets that are not real estate. It has the same root as the word *cattle*. In the Iron Age world of the Bible writers, women were chattel.

This is a strong statement, and I will return to back it up with evidence, chapter and verse. But as the phrase *livestock, children, and slaves* suggests, male-female relationships are just one small part of a broader picture. You cannot understand the scripts for women and men in the Bible and derivative texts or Christian-dominated cultures without understanding how deeply and broadly the Bible endorses the idea that some humans have a God-given right to own others. This includes the right to their bodies and the fruit of their labor; the right to make demands and force compliance; the right to punish resistance, inflict pain, and even, under the proper circumstances, to kill.

The Very Beginning

The book of Genesis contains two creation stories. In the second of these, Yahweh makes the first man A'dam out of mud. He presents the newly created human with a parade of other animals as possible companions, but A'dam rejects them all. So Yahweh then forms woman from the mud-man's rib and gives her to him, with no consent on her part needed. Nor, by the way, do any of those other animals have the option to reject A'dam as a suitable companion.

Throughout the Hebrew and Christian Bibles, God does what he wants to the creatures he has created: blessing, deceiving, selectively favoring, infecting, healing, rescuing, pitting one against another, burning or drowning en masse...you name it. They belong to him, so normal moral constraints don't apply. The fact that they have minds and preferences of their own—the fact that they can feel pain or love or can yearn for life—doesn't really matter in the moral calculus. They are his; he can do what he wants.

With some limits, this divine entitlement, meaning the right to be above normal morality and do as you please to lesser or weaker beings, trickles down: God exercises dominion over humankind. He gives male humans, who have been made in God's image, dominion over women and other animals. He gives certain special men, the patriarchs, dominion over other men, especially their own clans and their neighbors. This includes their neighbors' possessions, including land and livestock and, again, women. All of this is based not on merit but on birthrights.

Later, he gives Hebrew warlords (all male, of course) dominion over tribes and groups of tribes and eventually small kingdoms. In time, European royalty will cite the Bible to shore up their God-given right to hereditary power, conquest, and colonialism. Powerful men will cite the Bible to justify both slavery and the virtual enslavement of women. Bible-based misogyny isn't just old history.

Christians disagree about how much the Old Testament—and even the whole Bible—should dictate how we live today. Some today see the Bible as an imperfect record of imperfect humanity's struggle to understand God and goodness. They say that we have a moral responsibility to sift through it, keeping nuggets of timeless wisdom and discarding the rest. Biblical literalists disagree and insist that the whole package, if properly understood, is literally perfect.

Battles about the Old Testament emerged even before the Gospels were written. Two early sects, Marcionites and Gnostics, saw the Old Testament god as an evil tyrant, a different being from the god of Jesus. By contrast, the author of Matthew, who wrote for a Jewish audience, put these words in the mouth of Jesus: "For truly I tell you, until heaven and earth pass away, not one letter, not one stroke of a letter, will pass from the law until all is accomplished" (Matthew 5:18). The Church of Rome would later side with the author of Matthew—and, as the saying goes, that has made all the difference. Through the Hebrew texts that became the Roman Catholic

Old Testament, the Iron Age concept of chattel got spread throughout Christendom and beyond. We see this throughout our history and Western culture, including in the following scenarios:

- **Fourth-century Catholic councils endorsed the Hebrew Scriptures as a package,** permanently binding them together with the assemblage of Christian letters and literature that became the New Testament. To this day, the Old Testament is literally bound with the New Testament in the most widely bought and sold book on the planet, which Christians call holy and declare to be uniquely God-breathed.

- **In the fifth century, the whole Bible, Old Testament included, inspired a derivative religion, Islam, based on a derivative book, the Qur'an,** which further cements the concept of human chattel, giving devout men the authority to take foreign sex slaves, trade female offspring for goods and favors, control the bodies and finances of women in their household, and commit acts of violence against those who fail to submit (all of which, by the way, are also endorsed in the Bible).

- **The Christian New Testament fails to repudiate the concept of slavery, or of women and children as chattel.** Today, many Christians dismiss the Old Testament and cling to the New Testament, which they see as endorsing love. However, the New Testament does not retract the concept of chattel from the Old Testament. Paul sends a slave back to his master (Philemon 1:10–12). Wives are told to submit to their husbands (Ephesians 5:22) and keep silent in church, with head coverings as tangible symbols of submission (1 Corinthians 14:34 and 11:2–16). In the central narrative of the New Testament, God the Father gives his only begotten son to be a human sacrifice (John 3:16), echoing the older stories of Abraham offering his son Isaac as a burnt offering (Genesis 22:1–10) and Jephthah sacrificing his daughter (Judges 11:29–40).

A story in which God, identified as a father, gives his son as a sacrificial "lamb without blemish" makes perfect sense within a cultural context in which fathers have the right to swap, sell, or sacrifice their children; where the consent of the father rather than the child is what matters; and where the father is the one who is perceived as taking the loss.

Of course, the Iron Age idea that one person can own another has changed over time, moderated by centuries of cultural and moral evolution. One can see this evolution even within the Bible itself when the texts are arranged chronologically. Today in the twenty-first century, in the post-Enlightenment West, people largely accept, at least in the abstract, that all men are created equal and endowed by their creator with an unalienable right to life, liberty, and the pursuit of happiness. But the concept of dominance over others has not disappeared.

On the frontiers of moral consciousness, where the arc bends toward justice, we are wrestling with questions about the equality and autonomy of people who are queer and gender queer. Fiction writers and ethicists boldly go where no man has gone before: exploring the moral standing or personhood of nonhuman species, aliens, and artificial intelligences.

And yet, as ongoing battles about racial equity and reproductive freedom show, we continue to struggle over who merits inclusion in the ideals of equality, liberty, and community that so many hold dear. "Love is love is love," say some, including some Christians. But others aren't so sure.

We struggle as a society, at least in part, because hundreds of millions of people believe that God put powerful men at the top and gave them the right to own others, literally or figuratively or both. If this seems like overstatement, let's let the Bible and the church fathers speak for themselves. I want to start at the root—to show how clearly the Bible says that some humans can own others, and then I will move on to show how the biblical view of women fits this frame.

Old Testament Endorses, Describes, and Regulates Slavery

The Bible's first explicit endorsement of slavery can be found in the book of Genesis, in the tale of Noah the ark builder. Everyone knows part of the story: God regrets making humans, who are universally lecherous and evil. So he drowns almost all of them in a global flood. But first he has Noah build a boat that holds two of each animal, along with Noah and his family, who will be the only survivors.

What many don't know is this: After the flood dissipates, presumably after the moose trundle off toward the Bering Strait and the kangaroos head for Australia across the soggy and decaying landscape, the biblical story of Noah resumes, with a tale that later will justify the African slave trade.

Noah's son Ham sees his father drunk and naked and, for reasons that have long been debated, is cursed. A recurring theme in Genesis is that guilt can be transferred from a guilty person to an innocent person (think of Adam and Eve's fruit consumption, which taints us all), and in this case, the curse gets put on Ham's son, Canaan.

When Noah awoke from his wine and knew what his youngest son had done to him, "he said, 'Cursed be Canaan; lowest of slaves shall he be to his brothers.' He also said, 'Blessed by the Lord my God be Shem; and let Canaan be his slave. May God make space for Japheth, and let him live in the tents of Shem; and let Canaan be his slave'" (Genesis 9:25–27).

Most likely, this story was intended originally to justify Israelite subjugation of Canaanite peoples, who, in other stories about the conquest of the Promised Land (the land of Canaan) get slaughtered or enslaved. Later, though, Christians and Muslims would use the story to explain why some people have dark skin, and Ham's curse became a justification for enslaving Native Americans and Africans. It was used explicitly to defend Black slavery in the American South as well as the vigorous slave trade in the Muslim world and around the Mediterranean.

Throughout the Hebrew Old Testament, God and his representatives show their approval of slavery with both actions and words. Patriarchs Abraham and Jacob both have sex with female slaves, and God blesses the unions with male offspring. After a battle with the Midianites, the Israelites tally captive Midianite virgins among the booties of war, and God provides explicit instructions for purifying the war captives before "knowing them." King Solomon, labeled the wisest man of all time, keeps hundreds of concubines, meaning female sex slaves, along with hundreds of wives.

The books of the Law provide explicit rules for the treatment of Hebrew and non-Hebrew slaves: "As for the male and female slaves whom you may have, it is from the nations around you that you may acquire male and female slaves. You may also acquire them from among the aliens residing with you, and from their families that are with you, who have been born in your land; and they may be your property. You may keep them as a possession for your children after you, for them to inherit as property. These you may treat as slaves, but as for your fellow Israelites, no one shall rule over the other with harshness" (Leviticus 25:44–46).

When punishing slaves, owners can cause any level of injury short of on-the-spot murder: "When a slaveowner strikes a male or female slave with a rod and the slave dies immediately, the owner shall be punished. But if the slave survives a day or two, there is no punishment; for the slave is the owner's property" (Exodus 21:20–21).

That said, the book of Deuteronomy explicitly forbids returning an escaped slave to his master, in a passage that was a favorite of abolitionists: "Slaves who have escaped to you from their owners shall not be given back to them. They shall reside with you, in your midst, in any place they choose in any one of your towns, wherever they please; you shall not oppress them" (Deuteronomy 23:15–16).

When confronted with distasteful scriptures, most Christians say that Mosaic Law is no longer binding, and that the life of Jesus ushered in a new period of grace and forgiveness, but that hasn't stopped Old Testament endorsements of slavery from shaping the course of Christian history. They are, after all, still in the Bible.

New Testament Encourages Kindness from Master, Obedience from Slave

Equally regrettable, from the standpoint of moral clarity, is the fact that New Testament writers fail to condemn slavery, either as practiced by their ancestors or as practiced by their peers. Slavery comes up regularly in New Testament texts, but rather than repudiating the practice, the writers simply encourage good behavior on the part of both slaves and masters.

In one parable Jesus compares God to a king who has slaves. When one slave refuses to forgive the debt of a peer, the righteous king treats him in kind, "and, as he could not pay, his lord ordered him to be sold, together with his wife and children and all his possessions, and payment to be made" (Matthew 18:25). On the surface, the moral of the story is *do unto others*…but the subtext is that a king has the right to own, punish, and sell slaves—and just below that is another layer of subtext: A man's wife and children are simply extensions of the man himself.

Messages about slavery in the New Testament are, to be sure, mixed. While in prison, the apostle Paul encounters an escaped slave, Onesimus, and sends a letter to his Christian owner, Philemon, tacitly endorsing Philemon's authority in the matter (Philemon 1:1). Paul sends Onesimus back to Philemon "not as a slave but as a brother"—but he does send him back.

Several letters attributed to Paul express the sentiment that in Christ all people are one:

- "For in the one Spirit we were all baptized into one body—Jews or Greeks, slaves or free—and we were all made to drink of one Spirit" (1 Corinthians 12:13).

- "There is no longer Jew or Greek, there is no longer slave or free, there is no longer male and female; for all of you are one in Christ Jesus" (Galatians 3:28).

Then again, he tells slaves to submit to their masters, even as he exhorts masters to treat slaves well.

- "Slaves, obey your earthly masters with fear and trembling, in singleness of heart, as you obey Christ; not only while being watched, and in order to please them, but as slaves of Christ, doing the will of God from the heart. Render service with enthusiasm, as to the Lord and not to men and women, knowing that whatever good we do, we will receive the same again from the Lord, whether we are slaves or free. And, masters, do the same to them. Stop threatening them, for you know that both of you have the same Master in heaven, and with him there is no partiality" (Ephesians 6:5–9).

- "Let all who are under the yoke of slavery regard their masters as worthy of all honor, so that the name of God and the teaching may not be blasphemed. Those who have believing masters must not be disrespectful to them on the ground that they are members of the church; rather they must serve them all the more, since those who benefit by their service are believers and beloved" (1 Timothy 6:1–3).

Small wonder that slave owners through history found in scripture the justification they sought for maintaining the practice.

Ripples Through History

It is easy to look back on Black slavery from the vantage of our modern moral consensus—that treating people as property is wrong, regardless of whether slave owners are cruel or kind. But the Bible deserves no credit for that consensus. The mixed messages in the New Testament supported Christian arguments on both sides of the slavery question, enabling the pro-slavery side to dominate for 1,300 years until a combination of changing economic conditions and changing moral consciousness elevated teachings about compassion and justice over biblical support for slavery.

Today the transatlantic slave trade of history is gone, and one person cannot purchase title to another, except, in some cultures, in the form of a marriage license. But forced labor or exploitation of the weak by the strong takes many forms, and because the Bible contains such mixed messages, Bible belief offers very little defense against coerced labor.

Nor does it offer much protection against a second form of chattel culture—that which treats children as economic assets belonging to their fathers. This, again, may seem like a tangent in a book about women. But it is impossible to make sense of Christianity's aversion to reproductive rights or full female equality without peering beneath the surface of Christian teachings about children.

A Modern View of Childhood

Modern Western secularists think of children as persons with rights based on their capacity to suffer and feel pleasure, to love and be loved, to be aware and self-aware, to have preferences and intentions that are expressed via decisions and actions, and to have dreams and goals that place a value on their own future. These capacities, which make human life uniquely precious, emerge gradually during childhood, which is why children can't take care of themselves. Parents are thought of as custodians who have both rights and responsibilities that change over time based on the ways in which a child's own capacities are limited.

In this view, as children become more capable, their rights increase within developmentally appropriate limits, while parental rights and responsibilities decrease. If a five-year-old prefers vanilla ice cream over strawberry, most people believe that, all else being equal, he or she should be allowed to choose. A seven-year-old has little say in a custody agreement, but a fourteen-year-old who prefers to be with one or the other parent can get a hearing from a judge. Similarly, the capacity for sexual consent emerges gradually during adolescence. Young teens may be capable of consenting with each other, but their vulnerability to manipulation and exploitation means they are protected legally by the concept of statutory rape.

In 1923, Kahlil Gibran published a much-loved book, *The Prophet*, which contains his poem "On Children." Gibran's poem, while deeply spiritual, reflects a modern view of childhood:

> Your children are not your children.
> They are the sons and daughters of Life's longing for itself.
> They come through you but not from you,
> And though they are with you yet they belong not to you.
>
> You may give them your love but not your thoughts,
> For they have their own thoughts.
> You may house their bodies but not their souls,
> For their souls dwell in the house of tomorrow, which you cannot visit, not even in your dreams.
> You may strive to be like them,
> but seek not to make them like you.
> For life goes not backward nor tarries with yesterday.[1]

Gibran's twentieth-century view would have been completely alien to the men who wrote the Bible.

A Biblical View of Childhood

In the Iron Age mind-set of the Bible writers, children are not individual persons who have their own thoughts with corresponding rights. Rather, like livestock, women, and slaves, they are possessions of the male head of household; and the biblical framework governing treatment of children is property law, not individual rights law.

As I said earlier, the legal term *chattel* refers to moveable personal property—economic assets that are not real estate. In the Bible, male children grow up to become persons, while females remain chattel throughout their lives—first as assets of their fathers, then as assets of their husbands. Because property rights at the time were patrilineal, male heirs

---

1 Kahlil Gibran, *The Prophet* (New York: Knopf, 2007), 17.

were particularly prized, as they have been in most cultures until very recently.

The texts bound together in the Bible were written over the course of hundreds of years, and they reflect the evolution of social and ethical norms within Hebrew culture during that time span. Some express a more compassionate and dignifying perspective toward children than others. But taken as a whole, the biblical formula for parenthood is based on several core assumptions, including:

- **Children are property of their fathers.** This is why God can allow Satan to kill Job's children during a wager over Job's loyalty—and then simply replace them (Job 1:18–19, 42:12–13). It is why a man who injures a woman causing her to miscarry must pay her husband for the loss (Exodus 21:22).

- **Children are born bad.** This mentality derives from the idea of original sin, which posits that all humans are basically evil because Eve defied God and ate from the Tree of Knowledge. This means that parents have a right and a responsibility to purge a child's natural tendency toward evil.

- **Children must be beaten to keep them from going astray.** In the Gospel stories, Christ's only teaching on the subject of physical punishment was "anyone among you who is without sin, be the first to throw a stone at her" (John 8:7). Unfortunately, many Christians prefer King Solomon's "spare the rod, spoil the child" admonitions from the book of Proverbs (Proverbs 13:24, 23:13).

- **A father's right of ownership extends even to killing his child.** This is why it makes sense for Abraham to sacrifice Isaac, or for Jephthah to sacrifice his daughter, or even for God to give his "only begotten son" as a human sacrifice. In the Torah, a man can send his child into battle or sell his child into slavery (Exodus 21:7–11). The Torah advises that a rebellious son should be put to death (Deuteronomy 21:18–21).

Of course, there are plenty of Bible verses that talk about love and tenderness. "Let the little children come to me and do not stop them," says Jesus, and "Is there anyone among you who, if your child asks for bread, will give a stone?" (Matthew 19:14, 7:9). He compares God to a loving father in heaven, with the implication that his Hebrew audience understands fatherly love. In the New Testament parable of the prodigal son, the father weeps with joy when his son returns home, even though the son has been greedy and rejecting (Luke 15:11–32).

The problem with Christianity's view of childhood isn't that exhortations to kindness and mercy are missing; it is that children, like other forms of chattel, lack the *right* to be treated well, and they lack the right to leave or seek protection if they are not. When beaten, denied education, denied medical care, or otherwise harmed, a Christian child's job is to submit, and society's job is to stay out of the way.

As a child who was being physically abused in a Christian home, author M. Dolon Hickmon collected bits he'd heard in sermons and adult conversations, trying to understand his fear and hurt. Ultimately he decided the fault lay in himself:

> Here are the messages I gleaned from the church of my childhood: that beating children is acceptable—good for them, in fact; bruises and welts are of little consequence; that fear is desirable, as is pained screaming and broken sobbing. I'd heard that kids were to be whipped for the least act of disobedience, with belts and sticks and plastic racecar tracks; on bare skin, and as often as an adult thought was necessary.
>
> A child abuser, on the other hand, is someone who doesn't love you. A parent who never gives hugs because he is angry all the time. A child abuser is a drinker, a druggie, or at best some kind of wild animal. An abuser has no reasons or explanations. He just burns kids with cigarettes and gives them broken arms.
>
> My abuser loved me and hugged me, and he overflowed with explanations. I once got an hour-long lesson on disobedience for leaving a crayon on the floor. While the belt clapped with the measured rhythms of chopping firewood, I struggled to commit verses to memory and to answer quizzes on the metaphysical meanings of the word *honor* in scripture....
>
> I tolerated being degraded, because that was what I thought a Christian child was supposed to do.[2]

Father knows best.

2. M. Dolon Hickmon, "A Survivor's Conversation with Christianity," *No Longer Quivering* (blog), *Patheos*, September 12, 2013, http://www.patheos.com/blogs/nolongerquivering/2013/09/a-survivors-conversation-with-christianity/.

What the Biblical View of Children Means for Women

If children are economic assets of their fathers, with male heirs being particularly prized, then it only makes sense that the value of an adult female links closely with her ability to produce male offspring of known paternity. This attitude is not unique to the Abrahamic religions, meaning Judaism, Christianity, and Islam. Some Hindus offer young women a traditional blessing, *May you be the mother of a hundred sons.* But it is Christianity that imposes this concept of womanhood in the West.

When my two daughters, Brynn and Marley, were young, I bought them a book of Bible stories. We had read Greek mythology and folktales from China and India, and I figured they should know the ancient stories that are woven into the fabric of our own culture. We started at the beginning, reading the creation stories and moving on to tales of the patriarchs; but on the third or fourth evening, as I began a story, Brynn burst out in a tone of defiance: "Let me guess," she said. "This is going to be a story about a boy. This lady is going to have a baby, and he's going to be a boy, and he's going to go on to do great things! It's all boys, boys, boys!"

"Yeah!" said Marley.

I couldn't deny it. We flipped some pages. I can't recall whether the sanitized stories included Lot's daughters getting him drunk and then having sex with him to produce sons (Genesis 19:30–38). And I don't remember whether they included the story in which Rachel and Leah send their slave girls to get pregnant by their husbands to up the boy-baby count (Genesis 30). But the pattern was clear.

Brynn and Marley went and picked another book from the shelf.

Had I been reading aloud from the Bible itself, the girls might have been even more offended. The idea that women are lesser beings who derive their value and stature from the husbands they marry and the sons they bear has some ugly corollaries. For example, because the Bible was written at a time when our ancestors had no way to control paternity save by controlling sex, female virginity gets treated as a matter of divine obsession, and a woman who lacks a pristine vagina may be better off dead.

The Good Book spells this out in no uncertain terms:

* **A wife is a man's property:** "You shall not covet your neighbor's house; you shall not covet your neighbor's wife, or male or female slave, his ox or donkey, or anything that belongs to your neighbor" (Exodus 20:17).

- **Daughters can be bought and sold:** "If a man sells his daughter as a slave, she shall not go out as the male servants do" (Exodus 21:7).

- **A raped daughter can be sold to her rapist:** "If a man meets a virgin who is not engaged, and seizes her and lies with her, and they are caught in the act, the man who lay with her shall give fifty shekels of silver to the young woman's father, and she shall become his wife. Because he violated her he shall not be permitted to divorce her as long as he lives" (Deuteronomy 22:28–29).

- **Collecting wives and sex slaves is a sign of status:** "Among his [Solomon's] wives were seven hundred princesses and three hundred concubines" (1 Kings 11:3).

- **Used brides deserve death:** "If, however, this charge is true, that evidence of the young woman's virginity was not found, then they shall bring the young woman out to the entrance of her father's house and the men of her town shall stone her to death" (Deuteronomy 22:20–21).

- **Women, but only virgins, are to be taken as spoils of war:** "Now therefore, kill every male among the little ones, and kill every woman who has known a man by sleeping with him. But all the young girls who have not known a man by sleeping with him, keep alive for yourselves" (Numbers 31:17–18).

- **Menstruating women are spiritually unclean:** "When a woman has a discharge of blood that is her regular discharge from her body, she shall be in her impurity for seven days, and whoever touches her shall be unclean until the evening. Everything upon which she lies during her impurity shall be unclean; everything also upon which she sits shall be unclean. Whoever touches her bed shall wash his clothes, and bathe in water, and be unclean until the evening. Whoever touches anything upon which she sits shall wash his clothes, and bathe in water, and be unclean until the evening" (Leviticus 15:19–21).

- **A woman is twice as unclean after giving birth to a girl as to a boy:** "On the eighth day the flesh of his foreskin shall be circumcised. Her time of blood purification shall be thirty-three days; she shall not touch any holy thing, or come into the sanctuary, until the days of her purification are completed. If she bears a female child, she shall be unclean two weeks, as in her menstruation; her time of blood purification shall be sixty-six days" (Leviticus 12:1–5).

- **A woman's promise is binding only if her father or husband agrees:** "But if, at the time that her husband hears of it [the vow], he expresses disapproval to her, then he shall nullify the vow by which she was obligated, or the thoughtless utterance of her lips, by which she bound herself; and the Lord will forgive her" (Numbers 30:2–13).

- **Women should be seen but not heard:** "Women should be silent in the churches. For they are not permitted to speak, but should be subordinate, as the law also says" (1 Corinthians 14:34).

- **Wives should submit to their husband's instructions and desires:** "Wives, be subject to your husbands, as is fitting in the Lord" (Colossians 3:18).

- **In case you missed that submission thing, take another look:** "Wives, be subject to your husbands as you are to the Lord. For the husband is the head of the wife just as Christ is the head of the church, the body of which he is the Savior. Just as the church is subject to Christ, so also wives ought to be, in everything, to their husbands" (Ephesians 5:22–24).

- **Childbearing is a form of atonement:** "Let a woman learn in silence with full submission. I permit no woman to teach or to have authority over a man; she is to keep silent. For Adam was formed first, then Eve; and Adam was not deceived, but the woman was deceived and became a transgressor. Yet she will be saved through childbearing, provided they continue in faith and love and holiness, with modesty" (1 Timothy 2:11–15).

- **Women were created for men:** "For if a woman will not veil herself, then she should cut off her hair; but if it is disgraceful for a woman to have her hair cut off or to be shaved, she should wear a veil. For a man ought not to have his head veiled, since he is the image and reflection of God; but woman is the reflection of man. Indeed, man was not made from woman, but woman from man. Neither was man created for the sake of woman, but woman for the sake of man" (1 Corinthians 11:6–9).

- **Sex with women is spiritually dirty:** "No one could learn that song [perfect song of praise for God] except the one hundred forty-four thousand who have been redeemed from the earth. It is these who have not defiled themselves with women, for they are virgins; these follow the Lamb wherever he goes. They have been redeemed from humankind as first fruits for God and the Lamb" (Revelation 14:3–4).

Some Christian leaders teach that women and men were created equal by God but for different roles. This view, called complementarianism, is a gender equivalent of "separate but equal." But that is not what these verses communicate. Taken together, they convey in no uncertain terms that women are lesser. Our worth lies in our reproductive capacity. Paradoxically, childbearing is also a curse, and our reproductive systems are nasty. The female body's ability to grow a new life, which makes us uniquely female, also makes us physically and spiritually unclean.

Church Leaders Take Up the Torches

The visceral disgust toward women that oozes out of so many Bible texts has echoed down through history in the attitudes and words of Christian leaders—from Catholic Fathers, to Protestant Reformers, to modern leaders of sects like Mormonism and Evangelicalism. In reality, women ended up as economic assets belonging to men simply because we are physically weaker and less aggressive. But for the church to justify subjugation of women— to make chattel culture righteous—women had to be defined as inferior: morally weak, spiritually debased, physically defective, promiscuous, and stupid. It is no accident that this caricature closely resembles the one that righteous slave masters spun up about Africans during the slave trade.

Again, the most powerful way to make this point is to let church leaders speak for themselves. I offer the following lists of quotes as ample evidence— though they are just a sampling and are in no way comprehensive—of Christianity's subjugation of women:

Early Doctors and Fathers of the Catholic Church

- "Woman is a temple built over a sewer."[3] —Tertullian, considered the father of Latin Christianity (ca. 160–225)

---

3. Tertullian, quoted in *Man, Woman & Priesthood* (Leominster, UK: Gracewing Publishing, 1989).

- "[Women's] consciousness of their own nature must evoke feelings of shame."[4] —Saint Clement of Alexandria, Christian theologian (ca. 150–215)

- "Nor are the women to smear their faces with the ensnaring devices of wily cunning.... The Instructor [Christ] orders them to go forth 'in becoming apparel, and adorn themselves with shamefacedness and sobriety...subject to their own husbands.'"[5] —Saint Clement of Alexandria

- "In pains and in anxieties do you bear [children], woman; and toward your husband [is] your inclination, and he lords it over you. And do you not know that you are [each] an Eve? The sentence of God on this sex of yours lives in this age: the guilt must of necessity live too. You are the devil's gateway: you are the unsealer of that [forbidden] tree: you are the first deserter of the divine law: you are she who persuaded him whom the devil was not valiant enough to attack. You destroyed so easily God's image, man. On account of your desert—that is, death— even the Son of God had to die."[6] —Tertullian

- "For it is improper for a woman to speak in an assembly, no matter what she says, even if she says admirable things, or even saintly things, that is of little consequence, since they come from the mouth of a woman."[7] —Origen (d. 258)

- "Woman does not possess the image of God in herself, but only when taken together with the male who is her head, so that the whole substance is one image. But when she is assigned the role as helpmate, a function that pertains to her alone, then she is not the image of God. But as far as the man is concerned, he is by himself alone the image of God just as fully and completely as when he and the woman are

4. "Women in the Patristic Age," *Wikipedia*, last updated April 1, 2016, https://en.wikipedia.org/wiki/Women_in_the_patristic_age.

5. Alexander Roberts and James Donaldson, eds., *Ante-Nicene Christian Library: Translations of the Writings of the Fathers down to A.D. 325* (Edinburgh: T. and T. Clark, 1869), 320.

6. Tertullian, "On the Apparel of Women," as quoted in New Advent, http://www.newadvent.org/fathers/0402.htm.

7. Vincent Ryan Ruggiero, "The Denigration of Women in History," *Catholic Journal*, November 15, 2014, http://www.catholicjournal.us/2014/11/15/denigration-women-history/.

joined together into one." [8] —Saint Augustine, bishop of Hippo Regius (354–430)

- "What is the difference whether it is in a wife or a mother, it is still Eve the temptress that we must beware of in any woman. I fail to see what use woman can be to man, if one excludes the function of bearing children."[9] —Saint Augustine

- "Woman is a misbegotten man and has a faulty and defective nature in comparison to his. Therefore she is unsure in herself. What she cannot get, she seeks to obtain through lying and diabolical deceptions. And so, to put it briefly, one must be on one's guard with every woman, as if she were a poisonous snake and the horned devil…. Thus in evil and perverse doings woman is cleverer, that is, slyer, than man. Her feelings drive woman toward every evil, just as reason impels man toward all good."[10] —Saint Albertus Magnus, Dominican theologian (ca. 1200–1280)

- "As regards the individual nature, woman is defective and misbegotten, for the active force in the male seed tends to the production of a perfect likeness in the masculine sex; while the production of woman comes from a defect in the active force or from some material indisposition, or even from some external influence."[11] —Thomas Aquinas, doctor of the church (1225–1274)

Protestant Reformers

- "The word and works of God is quite clear, that women were made either to be wives or prostitutes."[12] —Martin Luther, Reformer (1483–1546)

---

8. Tertullian, "Ethical Treatises," in *The Ante-Nicene Fathers*, vol. 3, *Tertullian, Parts I-III*.

9. Augustine, Epistle 243.10, in Peter Brown, *Augustine of Hippo, A Biography*, rev. ed. (Berkeley and Los Angeles: University of California Press, 2000), 52.

10. *Quaestiones super de animalibus* XV, cited in Vivian Phelips, *The Churches and Modern Thought: An Inquiry into the Grounds of Unbelief and an Appeal for Candour* (London: Watts, 1911), 203.

11. "Thomas Aquinas," *Wikipedia*, last updated August 29, 2017, https://en.wikiquote.org/wiki/Thomas_Aquinas.

12. Martin Luther, *Works*, vol. 12 (St. Louis, MO: Concordia Publishing House, 1956).

- "No gown worse becomes a woman than the desire to be wise."[13]
  —Martin Luther

- "Men have broad and large chests, and small narrow hips, and more understanding than women, who have but small and narrow breasts, and broad hips, to the end they should remain at home, sit still, keep house, and bear and bring up children."[14] —Martin Luther

- "Thus the woman, who had perversely exceeded her proper bounds, is forced back to her own position. She had, indeed, previously been subject to her husband, but that was a liberal and gentle subjection; now, however, she is cast into servitude."[15] —John Calvin, Reformer (1509–1564)

- "…Of what importance is your character to mankind, if you were buried just now, or if you had never lived, what loss would it be to the cause of God…Do not any longer contend for mastery, for power, money, or praise. Be content to be a private, insignificant person, known and loved by God and me."[16] —John Wesley, Reformer (1703–1791)

American Patriarchs (Puritan, Mormon, Baptist, Evangelical)

- "Even as the church must fear Christ Jesus, so must the wives also fear their husbands. And this inward fear must be shewed by an outward meekness and lowliness in her speeches and carriage to her husband.… For if there be not fear and reverence in the inferior, there can be no sound nor constant honor yielded to the superior."[17] —John Dod, Puritan leader (ca. 1549–1645)

---

13. Martin Luther, *Table Talk* (New York: HarperCollins, 1995).

14. Luther, *Table Talk*.

15. John Calvin, *A Commentary on Genesis* (London: Banner of Truth Trust, 1965), p. 172.

16. John Wesley: letter to his wife, July 15, 1774, quoted from *The Letters of John Wesley*, Wesley Center Online, http://wesley.nnu.edu/john-wesley/the-letters-of-john-wesley/wesleys-letters-1774/.

17. John Dod, *A Plaine and Familiar Exposition of the Ten Commandements* (1603), quoted from http://www.azquotes.com/quote/580394.

- "The second duty of the wife is constant obedience and subjection."[18] —John Dod

- "The root of masculine is stronger, and of feminine weaker. The sun is a governing planet to certain planets, while the moon borrows her light from the sun, and is less or weaker."[19] —Joseph Smith, founder of Church of Latter-Day Saints (LDS) movement (1805–1844)

- "Women are made to be led, and counseled, and directed.... And if I am not a good man, I have no just right in this Church to a wife or wives, or the power to propagate my species. What then should be done with me? Make a eunuch of me, and stop my propagation."[20] — Heber C. Kimball, venerated early LDS apostle (1801–1868)

- "A wife is to submit graciously to the servant leadership of her husband, even as the church willingly submits to the headship of Christ."[21] — Official Faith and Message Statement of Southern Baptist Convention (15.7 million members), Summer 1998

- "The feminist agenda is not about equal rights for women. It is about a socialist, anti-family political movement that encourages women to leave their husbands, kill their children, practice witchcraft, destroy capitalism and become lesbians."[22] —Pat Robertson, Southern Baptist leader (1930–)

- "The Holiness of God is not evidenced in women when they are brash, brassy, boisterous, brazen, head-strong, strong-willed, loud-mouthed, overly-talkative, having to have the last word, challenging, controlling, manipulative, critical, conceited, arrogant, aggressive, assertive, strident, interruptive, undisciplined, insubordinate, disruptive, dominating, domineering, or clamoring for power. Rather, women accept God's

18. Ibid.

19. Joseph Smith, *History of the Church of Jesus Christ of Latter-day Saints*, vol. 5 (Salt Lake City: Deseret News, 1909), 21121

20. Heber C. Kimball, *Journal of Heber C. Kimball* (Nauvoo, IL: Robinson and Smith, 1840).

21. Pat Campbell, "Husbands, Wives, Headship, and Submission: The Biblical Data on Two Key Words," *SBC LIFE*, April 1999, http://www.sbclife.net/articles/1999/04/sla5.

22. "Robertson Letter Attacks Feminists," *New York Times*, August 26, 1992, http://www.nytimes.com/1992/08/26/us/robertson-letter-attacks-feminists.html.

holy order and character by being humbly and unobtrusively respectful and receptive in functional subordination to God, church leadership, and husbands."[23] —James Fowler, contemporary Evangelical leader

- "Women will be saved by going back to that role that God has chosen for them. Ladies, if the hair on the back of your neck stands up it is because you are fighting your role in the scripture."[24] —Mark Driscoll, founder of Mars Hill nondenominational megachurch franchise (1970–)

Driscoll, a popular evangelical speaker and author of the final quote in the list, likes to remind people that every book in the Bible was written by a man. He sees that as confirmation that God wants men in charge, communicating his will to the rest of us. And what is his will for women? The answer of scripture and Christian history seems pretty darn clear: Women are lesser beings, mentally and morally feeble but nonetheless useful for breeding—if men can only keep us in our place. And one of the most effective ways to do *that* is to convince women ourselves that this is true.

The Power of the Almighty Penis

In this worldview, what does it mean for a girl to become a woman? Since females exist for males and our primary service to them is sexual and reproductive, Christianity for centuries has convinced girls that they must pick between three scripts, each of which defines a young woman in terms of her sexual contact with males and what her male owners get out of her. A young woman can be a Virgin, a Madonna, or a Whore. These three scripts have roots in the Iron Age assumption that women are chattel. But like the quotes we have read from the Bible writers and church leaders, they frame Iron Age economic scripts as spiritual absolutes. As should be obvious at this point, one way that religion enforces practical cultural edicts is by giving them spiritual significance and divine sanction.

---

23. James Fowler, *Women in the Church*, 1999, quoted from http://www.christinyou.net/pages/womeninchurch.html.

24. Eric Grandy, "Everclear to Play Mars Hill Church," *Stranger*, April 4, 2008, http://lineout.thestranger.com/2008/04/everclear_to_play_mars_hill_church.

The Virgin

Every girl starts out a pre-sexual *Virgin*, but this status is always at risk; any touch of a penis and it's gone. A young woman, still in her father's house, keeps her economic value and (consequently) her spiritual standing by keeping her vagina untouched. She safeguards herself as a family asset that her father can then give in marriage to another man. A used girl, by contrast, is an economic liability and a spiritual failure. She brings shame on her family. As a Christian, she may not have to fear honor killing by male relatives, as she might in a fundamentalist Muslim family or in the Bible itself, but the nature of her very being changes permanently once she has been touched by a male penis.

Female virginity is prized, spiritually, by all the major religions that emerged during the Iron Age. But in Catholic Christianity, virginity took on unparalleled spiritual significance. According to some teachings, the Virgin Mary remained a virgin for life, even after giving birth to Jesus. Following suit, young women who didn't want to marry pledged their untouched vaginas to Jesus himself and became brides of Christ, even wearing white gowns for the wedding ceremony. Magical tales sprang up about beautiful martyrs who died tragic and violent deaths rather than cede their precious purity to evil infidels.

The practical reasons that drove our ancestors to become obsessed with female virginity are gone. Today, with a modern, long-acting contraceptive like an IUD or implant in place, the typical woman's risk of unwanted pregnancy drops below 1 in 500 (Yes, 1 in 500!) For young men who don't want to get saddled with another man's offspring, paternity tests are nearly perfect. Even so, Evangelical churches hold purity balls and promote promise rings, pressuring young women to make vows of abstinence until marriage. The echoes of chattel culture couldn't be clearer: These girls explicitly pledge their reproductive tracts to their fathers who will then give them to a mutually-agreeable young man.

The Madonna

Once that hand-off happens, once a young woman's womb is given in marriage, then her value lies in her ability to please her husband—to serenely service his sexual wishes, produce babies as he and God desire, and keep the hearth fire burning. Since the husband is the head of the house, her role is to trust and obey, to pray and submit, even if she or her children are being hit or hurt.

At an extreme, the Madonna is obligated to welcome every pregnancy as a blessing, no matter how dire her health or the family's economic resources. Biblical tradition values quantity of children over quality, so a mother's prudence and wisdom, her sense of her own limits, her desire to bring every good thing to one child before having another, run counter to handed-down notions of what motherhood should mean.

Again, the practicalities aren't what they used to be. A high birth rate once made sense. Our Iron Age ancestors lost most of their infants to disease. Children died of injury or malnutrition. Conflict killed many more young adults than it does today. For tribal herdsmen, children were indeed economic assets—in contrast to our current conditions, where resource depletion and urban life have reversed that equation. Also, our ancestors had little ability to control their fertility even when they might have wanted to. So counting each pregnancy as a blessing, however difficult the circumstances, may have helped ensure that children were welcomed and loved.

I should note that still today the Catholic Church and some Protestant sects like the Quiverfull movement explicitly promote competitive breeding to build adherence. A high birth rate helps them take over territory and turf out other sects. In other words, their promotion of traditional gender roles has a utilitarian ulterior motive at the institutional level, as it has for many centuries. But for ordinary believers, these institutional growth strategies are lost beneath layers of pious language and a sweet sense of self-surrender.

"Let go and let God," women are told, and for some having a powerful authority figure in charge of complicated decisions feels really good.

The Whore

If a woman's spiritual weakness makes virginity and motherhood unappealing—or if her sinful nature should lead her into temptation, then only one option remains, because a woman who is neither Virgin nor Madonna is a Whore. She is still defined by her relationship to men, still defined by the male penis specifically, but now her identity and economic value are tied to sex itself rather than procreation. In the Bible, sexual slaves have a clear—if lowly—place in society, but a woman whose body isn't owned by a man is the lowest of low, a prostitute.

In this trinity—Virgin, Madonna, Whore—female sexual pleasure has no legitimate place, even in the person of the Whore—whose job is to satisfy male desires. A woman who seeks pleasure for her own sake is a temptress, a Jezebel, a Lilith, or a literal demon.

Now picture that after centuries of these scripts being handed from generation to generation, 1960 arrives, and a whole generation of women embrace their own sexuality. Picture further that new contraceptive technologies allow them to choose sex without risk of pregnancy. The rules have been ruptured! God is not in the heavens with all well on earth. In fact, all hell might break loose, literally, because God is maniacal about sexual sin, and there are no limits to the wrath of the Almighty. Think Sodom and Gomorrah and Babylon, then fast-forward a few thousand years. Think Phuket, Thailand, or New Orleans. Each of these towns suffered mass destruction because of promiscuity—or so we are told.

How the Bible Believer's Obsession with Outlawing Abortion Makes Sense

Now it becomes possible to understand the bizarre, fanatical, and seemingly contradictory priorities of Bible believers when it comes to women, our bodies, and the children we do or do not bear. How is it, for example, that so many Christians are indifferent to death and suffering caused by war or by gun violence, more broadly, and yet oppose abortion on the grounds that they are "pro-life?" How can so many single-issue anti-abortion voters be completely disinterested in the best methods we have to make abortion obsolete (contraceptive implants and IUDs)? How can they actively oppose birth control access knowing that this drives up abortion, poverty, birth defects, and a host of other ills? How can conservative Christians defend embryonic life while simultaneously defending the right of parents to abuse children or deny them medical care?

It all comes together in the ancient idea that women and children are chattel.

A man has a right to offspring. Woman was made to bear them. (As both Bible writers and church leaders have reminded us over and over, that is her purpose and her salvation, the way she makes up for Eve's act of defiance, even if it kills her.) A child is not a person with intrinsic rights but a man's possession, to bring up according to his own values and beliefs; and paternal rights have few limits. Within the hierarchy of the family, a woman has authority over the children only by proxy: she acts as an administrator of God's will and that of her husband.

For a modern reader, the concept of female chattel may be easiest to understand when applied to livestock: A rancher owns cows for the purpose of breeding them, and he guards their fertility carefully to obtain the kind of calves he wants. A young fertile cow is worth more than an older less fertile cow. A cow is worth more when she's pregnant, but only if bred by the right kind of bull. She has no right to avoid pregnancy, however unpleasant or risky, and no one but her owner can decide when she has given birth to enough calves. Someone who deliberately caused a cow to miscarry would be stealing from the owner. Once calves are born, they too belong to the owner, and he has the right to poke or prod or hit or kick (or castrate) them to get the kind of behavior he wants.

In chattel culture, female birth control violates male property rights.

To the extent that females are chattel, there is little room for reproductive agency on the part of a woman herself. With God in charge, every baby is an arrow for the man's quiver—one of his economic and spiritual assets, as the Quiverfull movement teaches "Let go and let God," women are told. If women can be sorted into virgins, mothers, and whores, then contraception, which allows women to engage in sex without pregnancy, turns the first two of these into the third.

Abortion—a woman's decision to end an ill-conceived pregnancy— violates the Iron Age worldview in yet another way. In the Bible, bearing and ending life are roles that clearly split along gender lines. Females may have the power to nurture life, but only males can end it.

In fact, the Bible gives men the right to kill for many reasons: to eat, to make religious sacrifices, to resolve territorial disputes, to secure power, or to punish over thirty different transgressions. However, it never endorses ending a life for reasons of compassion, mercy, or prudence—the reasons women often seek abortion. And it never gives this right to women for any reason at all. Man alone—he who is made in the image of God—holds the power of death, just as God holds the power of death over humans, his "sheep." Remember, the Bible says a man can beat his slave to the brink of death, and as long as the slave survives for a day or two afterwards, the owner is within his rights.

What about the religious right's fetal personhood advocacy, which seeks legal protections for embryonic humans? Doesn't this contradict the idea that a man can do what he will with his property?

Not really. Fetal personhood laws are legal sleight of hand intended to ensure that the rights of actual persons don't interfere with the hierarchy of God and man over woman and child. Consider, for example, an Alabama law that assigns personhood to a fetus—and then hands associated rights to an attorney, who could be, as in one well-publicized case, a male Christian.[25]

Abortion foes seek to redefine the term *personhood* in a way that undermines the empowerment of those traditionally thought of as chattel—women, children, and other species. Qualities normally associated with personhood like sentience, feelings, thoughts, preferences, intention and self-awareness—qualities that create the basis for autonomy and legal rights—are irrelevant in anti-abortion personhood.

By taking this approach, religious right leaders hope to co-opt centuries of human rights law and political philosophy while simultaneously undermining any concept of personhood that grants rights or autonomy based on the lived experience of another being.

Full Female Personhood—Beyond the Bible

To the Bible writers, a modern ethical framework—one that assigns autonomy and person rights to sentient beings based on what we are capable of thinking and feeling and preferring rather than who created or owns us—would have been as alien as the concept of democracy during the Iron Age. The idea that women might be fully persons—not mere helpmeets, not human incubators, not concubines, not virgins nor Madonnas nor whores—but rather individuals defined by our experiences, values, and capacities, each with life purpose of our own choosing…this idea would have been as ridiculous as saying that the earth is round or there is no land above the sky.

25. Molly Redden, "A New Alabama Law Lets Judges Appoint Lawyers for Fetuses. Here's What That Looks Like," *Mother Jones*, October 6, 2014, http://www.motherjones.com/politics/2014/10/alabama-abortion-law-attorney-fetus-lawyers.

Even Mary, the mother of Jesus and Christianity's most revered female, never breaks out of the chattel role in Matthew's much-loved nativity tale. In Matthew, Mary is simply the perfect archetypal embodiment of the Iron Age script, just like Jesus is the perfect sacrificial lamb. She is told (not asked) by a powerful being that the Holy Spirit will come upon her and she will become pregnant. Of course, she is thrilled—if a woman's role is to bear children, what greater honor than to bear the child of a god?! For the rest of her life, she will be uniquely exalted because she is both Virgin and Mother simultaneously. What more could she possibly want? What more might any woman want?

The story gives no indication that Mary faces a decision, that she actively consents rather than simply assents to the angel's pronouncement. Consent requires a choice; but for the author of Matthew to give Mary a choice, he would have needed a whole different frame of reference. Intentional, volitional decision making by females about childbearing is simply beyond the consciousness of the Bible writers.[26] Men (and gods and angels), don't ask women our preferences. They tell us what's coming.

It is not the fault of the Bible writers that they looked at the rigid, violent pecking order in which they lived and assumed that a warlord in the sky must want it that way. It is not their fault that women, children, animals, and members of less advanced societies ended up as possessions of the men with the best weapons or the most money, or that to them this seemed perfectly fine. It is not their fault that they mistook strength for virtue, and might for right, and the shape of the Iron Age for the shape of eternity.

But we have the advantage of history. We know better. Women have made much progress toward equality, which could only happen as Iron Age text-based religions like Judaism, Christianity, and Islam began to lose their grip on society. Women in the West have legal and social standing far beyond that of our ancestors and women in Middle Eastern theocracies, where Abrahamic religion maintains an iron grip. But even in the most egalitarian and forward-thinking communities, we still have a ways to go. For the sake of our sisters and daughters and generations yet to come, it is time to fully remove the shackles.

26. Valerie Tarico, "It's Not Rape If He's a God—Or Thinks He Is," ValerieTarico. com, December 16, 2014, https://valerietarico.com/2014/12/16/its-not-rape-if-hes-a-god/.

5

Women in Islam—Unveiled

Hibah Ch

The most important thing women have to do is to stir up the zeal of women themselves.

—John Stuart Mill[1]

According to a recent survey by Pew Research Center, 23 percent of the world's population identifies as Muslim, spanning across all continents with concentrations in North Africa, the Middle East, and South and Southeast Asia.[2] Close to half of this percentage are women from all ages. These women, even though many hail from completely different cultures, have Islam as a religion in common. Another thing that these women have in common is restrictions carved by their religious and cultural heritage, and they suffer varying degrees of oppression and subjugation due to

---

1. Hugh S. R. Elliot, *The Letters of John Stuart Mill* (London: Longmans, Green and Co., 1910), 209.

2. Michael Lipka, "Muslims and Islam: Key Findings in the U.S. and around the World," Pew Research Center, August 9, 2017, http://www.pewresearch.org/fact-tank/2017/08/09/muslims-and-islam-key-findings-in-the-u-s-and-around-the-world/.

their gender. While one cannot confirm that all women from Islamic backgrounds are suffering, one can confidently declare that the majority of women in Muslim-majority countries are not enjoying the liberties and freedoms like their sisters in Western liberal countries.

I argue in this essay that the Muslim world is better off with empowered and free Muslim women rather than with subjugated and submissive women, and I argue that one of the major means to their empowerment is to leave religion, in this case Islam, and live by the modern humanist understanding of rights. I will focus in my argument on the status of women in Arabia before the birth of Islam. Then I will move to the social role of Islam in undermining women's rights in the majority of Islam-dominated countries. Finally, I will portray examples from Muslim-majority countries where Islam has influenced jurisprudence to legally subjugate and humiliate women.

To delve further into the evidence for Islam's hostility against women, I need to introduce you to few technical terms that I will use in the coming sections:

- *Qur'an*: Islam's holiest book (equivalent of bible)

- *Surat*: chapter in the Qur'an

- *Hadith*: narratives collected by Islamic scholars describing the life of Muhammad, the founder of Islam

- *Hadith Sahih*: an undisputed narration about Muhammad

It is worth noting that this article is in no way an attack on Muslims (men or women) as a people, but a thorough and critical analysis of Islam's approach to women's role and rights in their society.

The Forgotten Queens of Arabia

Never will succeed such a nation as makes a woman their ruler.
—Sahih Bukhari 9:88:219[3]

---

3. Unless otherwise noted, all hadith references are taken from Hadith Collection, http://hadithcollection.com/.

Islam is an Abrahamic religion that was founded in the Arabian Peninsula around the sixth century CE. The story of the founder of the religion, Muhammad ibn ʿAbd Allāh, had a theme similar to all Abrahamic faiths—political rebellion against society. As the objective sources on Muhammad's life are very rare, I will adhere to the narrations in the mainstream sources of Islam according to the Sunni sect the majority of the Muslim world population adheres to.

From Islamic sources, Muhammad, a forty-year-old Meccan merchant, claimed to receive a message from the one God, in defiance of the dominantly polytheistic practices in his tribe at the time. Going back fifteen years from that historic moment, he had gotten a recommendation to work for a wealthy woman in Mecca. Her name was Khadija bint Khuwaylid and she was a follower of Nestorian Christianity present in Arabia at the time. She and her cousin Waraqah ibn Nawfal both influenced the message of Muhammad to the extent that the holy inspiration of Muhammad stopped for a period right after the death of Waraqah. Khadija, impressed by Muhammad's success, proposed to marry him, and he agreed. Their marriage was done following the Christian Nestorian tradition.

This marriage doesn't sound like the image that the Islamic scholars tell us about women in Arabia before Islam. We constantly hear that women before Islam were oppressed, they had no right of ownership and had no say over whom to marry. In fact, the Islamic tradition prides itself as the liberator of women in Arabia, but how accurate is this claim?

It is true that the Arabian Peninsula was a desert and was sparsely populated. However, archaeological evidence shows that many kingdoms and tribes that populated Arabia and the Levant since 700 BCE until the rise of Islam in 600 CE were ruled by queens. Examples include Zabibi the Assyrian queen of a kingdom in northeastern Arabia called Doumatoa; the Nabatean empress Julia Domna (170–217 CE); the queen of Palmyra Zenobia (240–270 CE); and the queens of the kingdom of Himyar in South Arabia, the kingdom of Kindah in central Arabia, the Ghassanids in Syria, and the Lakhmids of Hirah all between 300 CE and 500 CE.[4]

There were even women in Muhammad's local tribe, before the establishment of the Islamic state in Medina, like Khadija, a businesswoman;

---

4. Nabia Abbott, "Pre-Islamic Arab Queens," *The American Journal of Semitic Languages and Literatures* 58, no. 1 (January 1941): 1–22, http://www.journals. uchicago.edu/doi/abs/10.1086/370586.

Hind bint Outba, a leader who waged war against Muhammad; and Al-Shifaa bint Abdullah a physician wise woman even prior to Islam, all highly respected in their tribe.[5] Many examples found in the books outlining the history of Arabs before Islam portray women in powerful roles. Women had the power, the respect, and the freedom to participate in decision making. They also had the right to inheritance and the right to speak their mind among men in local tribal councils. They participated in the society and were even members of the local parliament in Quraish named Dar Alnadwa.

Indeed, each tribe had different traditions—some tribes had incidents of infanticide because of poverty and it was mainly female infanticide to prevent young girls running off with men from other tribes. But from the pre-Islamic tradition that survived the forgery of Islamic scholars, women had a strong status in the tribes in general and were viewed as partners who helped provide as well as the traditional role of mothers and daughters. Even from Muhammad's family tree, Salma bint Amr, the wife of Hashim ibn 'Abd Manaf, was a prominent trader in her tribe who ran her own business.[6]

In addition, the polytheistic society of Mecca worshipped a trinity of female deities—Al Lat, Al'uzza, and Manat—as the daughter deities of god. By contrast, Muhammad in many verses of the Qur'an mocks Quraish for choosing feminine attributes for god while favoring sons to carry their legacy—"So have you considered Lat and 'Uzza? And Manat, the third—the other one? Is the male for you and for Him the female? That, then, is an unjust division" (Qur'an 53:19–22).[7] In this verse Muhammad exclaimed at how Arab tribes favor having sons but give god daughters, as in the three deities mentioned earlier. This division according to Muhammad is not a fair division.

In multiple passages of the Qur'an, feminizing deities and angels is looked down upon, as femininity was viewed as a less favorable characteristic than masculinity. Needless to say, after Islam was founded,

---

5. Ahmad Ibn Hajar Al-Asqalani, *Al-Isaba fi Tamyiz al-Sahaba*, vol. 8 (Many of these references are not available in English and have been translated from Arabic by the author.)

6. "Salma bint Amr," *Wikipedia*, last updated July 2, 2017, https://en.wikipedia.org/wiki/Salma_bint_Amr.

7. All quotations from the Qur'an are taken from https://quran.com/.

all the temples of Al Lat in Taif (currently Saudi Arabia) and other sites in the Islamic world were destroyed, along with all the statues and shrines inside the Kaaba itself, the holiest site of Islam.

Another source for the status of women in pre-Islamic Arabia is the historical narratives about women and warrior leaders in Arabia and the kingdoms of the Levant not too long before Islam. For instance, Haleema bent Alhareth Alghassani[8] was a fierce woman leader who led the infamous battle against the Lakhmid kingdom in the sixth century CE. Another is Subai'a bent Abd Shams from the Kenana tribe, who was one of the architects of a peace deal to stop a war between the tribes of Kenana and Qais 'Aylan.[9] She gave a pledge to protect any member of the losing tribe Qais 'Aylan in her home, and her word was honored, thus helping to stop a bloody chapter in the wars known as Harb Alfojjar in Arabic.

Now we come to the important point of this discussion; after this generous display of feminine leadership in pre-Islamic Arabia, how did Muhammad's declaration of his message change women's status? The decline of women's status we still see in the modern Islamic world started with destroying any sign of a female deity in Arabia and beyond, accompanied by shaming any discussion that referred to god or the angels as feminine beings, and reinforced with the draconian set of laws identified as Sharia to regulate the society and govern the newborn Islamic state.

Muhammad introduced new laws to organize life; he introduced a new image of a moral society very close to, and inspired by, the classical Judeo-Christian patriarchal laws. For example, men were considered as the leaders of their households because they were considered the primary breadwinners for their families, despite the fact that this was not always true in pre-Islam Arabia. And women had to assume the role of the obedient partner whose sole purpose was to satisfy the physical needs of her husband. This assumption was displayed in Surat Alnesa':

> Men are guardians over women because Allah has made some of them (men) excel others (women), and because they (men) spend of their wealth. So virtuous women *are those who* are obedient, and guard the secrets *of their husbands* with Allah's protection. (Qur'an 4:34)

---

8. Khayr Al-din Al Zarkali, *Al-A'lam* (Beirut: Dar Al-ilm Li-al-malayin, 2002), 270.

9. Abo Faraj Al-Asfahani, *Kitab Al-Aghani* (Beirut: Dar Sader, 2008), 53.

Another issue regulated by Sharia was inheritance. Women's shares were cut down to half of that of their male counterpart, because they were considered the responsibility of their male guardian, be it a male relative or husband, as in Surat Alnesa': "Allah instructs you concerning your children: for the male, what is equal to the share of two females" (Qur'an 4:11).

In another attempt to weaken women's influence in society, Sharia introduced the idea of cleanliness, courtesy of the Judeo-Christian traditions. Men are supposed to reapply Woodoo', a mandatory special set of steps to wash the body before every prayer, in two cases: if a man farts or if a man touches a woman. This is described in Surat Alnesa':

> O you who have believed, do not approach prayer while you are intoxicated until you know what you are saying or in a state of janabah, except those passing through [a place of prayer], until you have washed [your whole body]. And if you are ill or on a journey or one of you comes from the place of relieving himself or you have contacted women and find no water, then seek clean earth and wipe over your faces and your hands [with it]. Indeed, Allah is ever Pardoning and Forgiving. (Qur'an 4:43)

Many Islamic scholars explain that the term "contacted women" strictly refers to having sex with women. However, there is no mention anywhere in the Qur'an for women to wash after having sex with their husbands, which shows that Islamic traditions consider women's bodies unclean, as in the Old Testament of the Bible.

After Muhammad began his series of wars and assaults on the surrounding tribes, he used the promise of female war slaves knows as *sabaya* to encourage his warriors by allowing them to enslave already-married women from the countering tribes. Such as in this verified Hadith in Sahih Muslim:

> Abu Sa'id al-Khudri (Allah be pleased with him) reported that at the Battle of Hanain Allah's Messenger sent an army to Autas and encountered the enemy and fought with them. Having overcome them and taken them captives, the Companions of Allah's Messenger (May peace be upon him) seemed to refrain from having intercourse with captive women because of their husbands being polytheists. Then Allah, Most High, sent down regarding that: "And women already married, except those whom your right hands possess (iv. 24)" (i.e.

they were lawful for them when their 'Idda period came to an end). (Sahih Muslim 8:3432)

A final example, which I consider the strongest blow to women's rights since the beginning of Islam, is the call for women to stay at home and not behave like women of the pre-Islamic era (Jaheleya). Muhammad realized that controlling the powerful women of the society would open the door for him to control the other half of the society. This verse details this idea clearly:

> And abide in your houses and do not display yourselves as [was] the display of the former times of ignorance. And establish prayer and give zakah and obey Allah and His Messenger. Allah intends only to remove from you the impurity [of sin], O people of the [Prophet's] household, and to purify you with [extensive] purification. (Qur'an 33:33)

It is important to explain that the term "times of ignorance" is the term used in Islamic scriptures to refer to life in Arabia before Muhammad's message. All these traditions continued and evolved after Muhammad's death to form the chains choking and marginalizing the majority of women in the Islamic world for centuries.

Of Women, Donkeys, and Black Dogs

The things which annul the prayers were mentioned before me.
They said, "Prayer is annulled by a dog, a donkey and a woman
(if they pass in front of the praying people)." I said,
"You have made us (i.e. women) dogs."

—Sahih Bukhari 1:9:490

Society tends to think of faith as a method to reach spirituality, serenity, and power to live. However, when women examine scripture, especially Islamic scripture, they can expect only severe signs of disturbance, disappointment, and a sense of low esteem. How can Muslim women possibly obtain this level of serenity and empowerment if they read that their mere existence around their male counterparts can make the prayer unacceptable in the eyes of god? To make matters worse, here is the infamous Hadith Sahih that will blow your mind:

Abu Dharr reported: The Messenger of 'Allah (Peace be upon him) said: When any one of you stands for prayer and there is a thing before him equal to the back of the saddle that covers him and in case there is not before him (a thing) equal to the back of the saddle, his prayer would be cut off by (passing of an) ass, woman, and black Dog. I said: O Abu Dharr, what feature is there in a black dog which distinguish it from the red dog and the yellow dog? He said: O, son of my brother, I asked the Messenger of Allah (may peace be upon him) as you are asking me, and he said: The black dog is a devil. (Sahih Muslim 4:1032)

Muhammad was explaining to his companion Abu Dharr Alghafari that if he doesn't put a barrier in front of him while praying, his prayer will be at risk of interruption if one of the following passes in front of him: a donkey, a woman, or a black dog.

What's more, how can Muslim women find empowerment when they are constantly sexualized in their holy book? In no context in the Qur'an and Hadith are a man and a woman together other than for the purpose of sexual relation, which defies the image we saw previously in pre-Islamic Arabia. In fact, women are considered among the material blessings of life with cattle and horses: "Beautified for people is the love of that which they desire—of women and sons, heaped-up sums of gold and silver, fine branded horses, and cattle and tilled land" (Qur'an 3:14).

In many verses of the Qur'an, women are referred to in terms like plowing land: "Your wives are a tilth for you; so go to your tilth when and how you will" (Qur'an 2:223) or dirty during menstruation:

And they ask you about menstruation. Say, "It is harm, so keep away from wives during menstruation. And do not approach them until they are pure. And when they have purified themselves, then come to them from where Allah has ordained for you. Indeed, Allah loves those who are constantly repentant and loves those who purify themselves." (Qur'an 2:222)

Women are referred to as devils in this infamous Hadith: "The woman advances and retires in the shape of a devil, so when one of you sees a woman, he should come to his wife, for that will repel what he feels in his heart" (Sahih Muslim 8:3240). They are also the most condemned to hellfire: "I stood upon the door of Fire and the majority amongst them who entered there was that of women" (Sahih Muslim 36:6596). As Abdullah Ibn Abbas, an infamous Islamic scholar, explains about the latter, most women complain about their husbands and deny receiving gifts from them, so they are deserving of hellfire:

> "O women! Give alms, as I have seen that the majority of the dwellers of Hell-Fire were you (women)." The women asked, "Why is it so, O Allah's Apostle? What is the reason for it?" He replied, "O women? You curse frequently and are ungrateful to your husbands. I have not seen anyone more deficient in intelligence and religion than you." (Sahih Bukhari 1:6:301)

Women are also called less intelligent and less pious. When asked about the reason, Muhammad explained that all this is due to menstruation. Muhammad forgot the legacy of his wife, Khadija—the strong woman who enabled him to be the leader he became while she managed her menstruation.

Women were used as a tool to seduce men to follow the orders, whether by describing the blond Roman women of Tabook (a city under Roman influence at the time) to encourage men to wage war there—"Do you not take of the Banu al asfar female captives and servants?" (Qur'an 53:19)—or by promising full-breasted women to pious Muslims—"Indeed, for the righteous is attainment, gardens and grapevines. And full-breasted [companions] of equal age" (Qur'an 38:45) In fact, Muhammad himself married Safiya bint Huyai, a woman from Bani Quraitha. Her tribe was viciously eradicated by Muhammad in a genocidal manner. He took her as a slave, and he had sex with her a few nights after her husband was murdered:

> "O Allah's Messenger! You gave Safiya bint Huyai to Dihya and she is the chief mistress of the tribes of Quraiza and An-Nadir and she befits none but you." So the Prophet said, "Bring him along with her." So Dihya came with her and when the Prophet saw her, he said to Dihya, "Take any slave girl other than her from the captives." (Sahih Bukhari 1:8:367)

A note to conclude these examples of humiliation of women in Islam: Muhammad was very focused on monotheism. However, he broke the rule when he asked women to worship their husbands. "The Prophet (peace be upon him) said: Had it been permissible that a person may prostrate himself before another, I would have ordered that a wife should prostrate herself before her husband" (Shama-il Tirmidhi 1:285). Muhammad forbade prostration to any being but god. However, in this hadith he presents the only case he may hypothetically permit prostrating to someone other than god. This case would be a woman prostrating to her husband."

Islamic Jurisprudence as a Source of Legislation

But no, by your Lord, they can have no Faith, until they make you,
O Muhammad, judge in all disputes between them, and find in
themselves no resistance against your decisions,
and accept (them) with full submission.

—Qur'an 4:65

When Muhammad established his state in Medina, and later expanded to Mecca, he enforced a set of laws of social contract to organize the society. The collection of these laws is called Sharia. I will display below some family law aspects and some criminal aspects of Sharia that are far from just for women.

Sharia's approach to family law is harshly patriarchal. Islam builds all its legislation in these matters of family on the concept of Qewama—men are superior to women. The modern Islamic argument is because men are commonly the breadwinners. However, in the environment when Muhammad started his message, women were known to participate as breadwinners as well. Hence, it is less likely that this argument is really the intent behind the concept of Qewama. Given this concept, if a woman disobeys her husband, the Qur'an details the steps that the husband must take to resolve this disobedience. First, try to talk to her. If the conversation doesn't deter her from disobeying, the man should ban her from sleeping in his bed. If it is still not working—brace yourself for this one—beat her up! Very clear wording, there is no way for any linguistic interpretation around the beating part: "But those [wives] from whom you fear arrogance—[first] advise them; [then if they persist], forsake them in bed; and [finally], strike them. But if they obey you [once more], seek no means against them. Indeed, Allah is ever Exalted and Grand" (Qur'an 4:34).

Ironically, the Qur'an has a completely different approach if a husband was difficult with his wife. The approach to resolve this difficulty is to have a council formed from both the husband's and the wife's families to discuss issues civilly: "And if you fear dissension between the two, send an arbitrator from his people and an arbitrator from her people. If they both desire reconciliation, Allah will cause it between them. Indeed, Allah is ever Knowing and Acquainted [with all things]" (Qur'an 4:35).

Next, we move to an example from inheritance law in Islam. Inheritance law is very complicated in Sharia. However, all the inheritance laws from Sharia, as was the case in family law, spring from the fact that women are never independent. They are always the responsibility of a male guardian in their family. For instance, if a husband dies and he has no children from his wife, she inherits a quarter of what he owns. The reason she inherits a quarter is because Sharia assumes that this woman must have a male guardian with money who will take care of her. However, if the wife dies and she has no kids, the husband inherits half. For children of a deceased father, the sons' share will be twice the share of the sisters' because the assumption is that the brother is the male guardian of the sisters: "But if there are two sisters [or more], they will have two-thirds of what he left. If there are both brothers and sisters, the male will have the share of two females. Allah makes clear to you [His law], lest you go astray. And Allah is Knowing of all things" (Qur'an 4:176).

Another instance of extreme patriarchy is the issue of child custody in the case of divorce. In Sharia, a woman automatically has the right and responsibility of custody for the kids (boys or girls) until the age of seven. Islam doesn't view the father as capable of taking care of children less than seven years old. It doesn't even call for shared custody below the age of seven. This traditional view of parenting doesn't account for women who are irresponsible toward their kids or for the man's right to be with his young children as much as the mother. The only way for the man to get custody of a child at age seven or younger is if the woman gets married to another man after the divorce. At any time in the life of the child, if the mother remarries, she loses the right of custody. However, if the man remarries, his right for custody isn't affected, as displayed in the following Hadith: "'O Messenger of Allah, this son of mine had my womb as a container, my breasts for drinking, my lap to contain him. His father has taken him from me.' The Prophet (PBUH) said, 'You have more right if you do not marry.'"[10] This sexist practice continues to this day, as do others.

One of the big battles liberal Muslim women face today is the fight against polygamy. This practice is legal by Sharia with the only restriction being that a man may have no more than four wives (though he may have an infinite number of female sex slaves). Liberal women enter the territory of apostasy when they deny men the right of polygamy—how dare they deny men a right granted by Allah? Consider this verse: "Marry those that please you of [other] women, two or three or four. But if you fear that you will not be just, then [marry only] one or those your right hand possesses. That is more suitable that you may not incline [to injustice]" (Qur'an 4:3).

It is worth noting that Muhammad himself married thirteen women. One of them was his cousin, whom he first made marry his adopted son but then made them divorce so he could have her. Another wife referred to in the previous section was Safiya bint Huyai, who was a sex slave. Muhammad later married her to ensure that any child she bore from him wouldn't be a slave.

We come now to the marriage contract details. First, a woman can't get married without the consent of her male guardian. If she doesn't have one from her immediate or extended family, a judge will be appointed as a guardian for her. Her approval is required as well, but in an almost ironic twist of fate, the silence of the virgin when the man makes the offer means consent regardless of whether she is silent from fear or shyness:

> "A matron should not be given in marriage except after consulting her; and a virgin should not be given in marriage except after her permission." The people asked, "O Allah's Messenger! How can we know her permission?" He said, "Her silence [indicates her permission]." (Sahih Bukhari 7:62:67)

Second, Islam requires two witnesses for marriage. These witnesses must be males. I will tackle the testimony of women on other types of contracts subsequently. But in the case of testimony for marriage contracts specifically, the requirement is strictly men: "No marriage can take place without the presence of a guardian and two reliable male witnesses and any marriage that was not done in this way is nil" (Hadith sahih in Tirmidhi).

---

10. As quoted in Yusuf al-Qaradawi, "The Woman as Mother," IslamCan.com, http://www.islamcan.com/women-in-islam/the-woman-as-mother.shtml.

Third, the dowry. It is defined as an amount of money paid from the man to the woman to complete the marriage contract. No marriage in Islam is valid without a dowry. The concept of a dowry is present in many cultures and religions in the world. In other Abrahamic traditions, dowry stems from the belief of Qewama just like Islam—the idea that women are not capable financially and are constantly in need of financial support by their male counterpart. In Islam, the dowry works as a down payment for pleasure service that will be provided by the wife, as detailed in this Qur'anic verse:

> And lawful to you are [all others] beyond these, [provided] that you seek them [in marriage] with [gifts from] your property, desiring chastity, not unlawful sexual intercourse. So for whatever you enjoy [of marriage] from them, give them their due compensation as an obligation. (Qur'an 4:24)

Another issue with marriage under Islam is a direct result of the concept of Qewama—Muslim women are banned from marrying non-Muslim men, while their male counterparts can marry any woman of their choice or just take women as sex slaves. The evidence for this comes from the following verse: "And do not marry polytheistic men [to your women] until they believe" (Qur'an 2:221). In his fight Muhammad ultimately banned Muslim women from marrying non-Muslim men overall, but this verse started with the polytheists as he conquered polytheistic tribes and took sex slaves from them. The goal was and still is to preserve the Muslim population. If a Muslim woman marries a non-Muslim, because she is viewed as the property of her husband, she automatically becomes non-Muslim. This would cost the Muslim society an expanding population. It was a risk that Muhammad couldn't afford at the time. Even now, women in Islamic countries fight hard to battle the legal ban on marrying men from other faiths or even the social ban and exile from family if the thought crosses a woman's mind.

In the case of divorce after having sex, the woman can keep all her dowry. But if she is still a virgin, she must return half of the dowry since she didn't provide the sexual services of a wife. She is still untouched merchandise: "And if you divorce them before you have touched them and you have already specified for them an obligation, then [give] half of what you specified for Dowry" (Qur'an Surat Albaqara 237).

For the last Sharia example, let's look at women's testimony in contracts. As mentioned, women can't be witnesses for a marriage contract. However, in financial contracts, women can testify, but a man's witness is equivalent to two women's testimonies, per the Qur'an: "And bring to witness two witnesses from among your men. And if there are not two men [available], then a man and two women from those whom you accept as witnesses—so that if one of the women errs, then the other can remind her" (Qur'an 2:228). Again, Sharia laws assume that women are not the primary breadwinners and are not well versed with business transactions. We already proved that this is a false claim. But what's more is the assumption that women have a bad memory compared to men!

We must also evaluate criminal law's influence in subjugating women in Islam. Muslims pride themselves on the equality of the punishment between men and women. I will discuss some aspects in Sharia practice that show just the opposite. In the case of murder, the punishment is death whether the culprit is a man or a woman. However, if it was an accidental killing, a sum of money, to be decided by the judge, has to be paid to the victim's family. This sum of money is called Diya. Very few countries still apply this concept of punishment for accidental killing, but in those that do, gender inequality is evident. In Saudi Arabia, the Diya for having killed a woman is half that for having killed a man. The evidence used to deduce this is called measuring. The value or worth of a woman is estimated as half of that of a man based on the concept of Qewama. A woman is not a fully independent person, thus her worth is half of that of a man.

Another case of discrimination in criminal law is apostasy. Apostasy is defined as the "abandonment or renunciation of a religious or political belief,"[11] and in Islamic culture, apostasy is punishable by death per Sharia. However, the Hanafi school of jurisprudence views that women apostates are not important enough to be killed because they are not strong enough to rebel against the society. This school of jurisprudence is dominant in the Levant, Turkey, Egypt, and Islamic central Asian countries.

One must admit that there is not a lot of discrimination in scripture between punishment for male and female culprits regardless of the nature of the crime. However, the conditions to prove the crime lead automatically

---

11. "Apostasy," *Wikipedia*, last updated August 29, 2017, https://en.wikipedia.org/wiki/Apostasy.

to gender discrimination. For instance, in Islam, adultery is punishable by lashing for virgins or by stoning to death for married culprits, and women are always considered the instigators of any sexual relation based on the previously mentioned Hadith, "The woman advances and retires in the shape of a devil." To prove a sexual interaction outside marriage, either the culprit confesses to the judge or the culprit must be caught in the act of penetration by four male witnesses. When there are not four male witnesses, there is often coercion to force the woman to admit committing adultery, many times in the form of the judge's manipulation or the public's smearing of the woman's reputation.

Also, women who become pregnant outside marriage along with women who mix with foreign men even if no sexual interaction has taken place tend to suffer consequences leading to punishment for adultery. After all, these societies have been subjugated to the concept of Qewama for centuries, and that view of women as lesser people facilitates manipulating their fate either for money, revenge, or power, as we will see in the next section on honor killings.

In the following section, I will display instances of practices common in the Muslim world even though there is no direct scripture to command them. I am going to argue that the reason these practices flourish among Muslim communities around the world is Islam and its Sharia principles.

What Do a Woman, a Slave, and a Camel Have in Common?

If one of you marries a woman or buys a slave, he should say: "O Allah, I ask Thee for the good in her, and in the disposition Thou hast given her; I take refuge in Thee from the evil in her, and in the disposition Thou hast given her." When he buys a camel, he should take hold of the top of its hump and say the same kind of thing.

—Abu Dawud 5:2155

The Muslim world is very diverse. Even though all Muslims believe in the Qur'an and the Hadith as the main sources on how to live, different cultures had various barbaric cultural practices preceding Islam. When Islam invaded these regions, it adopted these practices and made them part of the Muslim way of life.

Before proceeding to these examples, I would like to highlight more information about Sharia goals. We talked earlier about Qewama, which is a concept that outlines solving family law mediations and disagreements even for special cases that are not mentioned in the Qur'an or the Hadith. The goals of Sharia are the guidelines which Islamic jurists use to solve matters that were not common at the time of Muhammad. These goals are five—preserving the religion, preserving the self, preserving the mind, preserving the lineage, and preserving property. I argue that these goals led to the preservation and inflammation of many barbaric practices that existed before Islam, many of which still survive.

The most hideous case of female abuse in the Muslim world is female genital mutilation (FGM), also known as female circumcision. This practice includes a wide barbaric spectrum of cutting female genitals (clitoris and labia). Islam apologists claim that this practice is an African tradition that is only practiced in Africa. However, the latest UNICEF study shows that 200 million women in the world suffer from FGM in thirty countries across three continents.[12] Although twenty-seven of them are African countries, they have a majority Muslim population. The other countries are Iraq, Yemen, and Indonesia. The practice attempts to control women's sexuality and sex drive, and it is carried out by family women as an initiation of honor. To shut out any voice denying Islam's responsibility in the continuation of suffering for these women is this Hadith Sahih stating Muhammad's answer when asked about female circumcision: "Circumcision is a law for men and a preservation of honor for women."[13]

Next is the phenomenon of honor killing. This crime is common in the entire Muslim world including the Levant, Egypt, Turkey, South Asia, Albania, Iran, the Persian Gulf states, and even in Muslim immigrant and first-generation families in Western Europe and North America. This "honor" crime, one among other types of gender-based homicides, legitimizes killing a female member of the family if she is suspected or caught in suspiciously immoral acts. This is horrific, and yet the true problem is that the criminal system of many Islamic countries doesn't treat honor killers as regular murderers. In Syria, for instance, murder is

---

12 "Female Genital Mutilation/Cutting," Unicef, February 26, 2016, https://www.unicef.org/protection/57929_58002.html.

13 Ahmad Ibn Hanbal 5:75; Abu Dawud, Adab 167, as quoted in "FGM (Female Genital Mutilation) & Islam," TTEONB—Nonbelievers of Islam, June 30, 2015, https://tteonb.wordpress.com/2015/06/30/fgm-female-genital-mutilation-islam/.

punishable by execution. However, honor killers under the most updated Syrian criminal law get up to two years' imprisonment. A similar sentence reduction in other Islamic countries is also common. Muslim apologists ironically attribute these laws protecting honor killers to French and British mandate laws. However, these laws carry the fingerprint of the Abrahamic faiths' patriarchy all over them. Islam's obsession with virginity and marriage make any suspicion of adultery a direct threat to the goals of Sharia, specifically preserving lineage and self.

A practice that also serves the goals of Sharia is the virginity check. It involves using two fingers to check for the presence of the intact hymen in unmarried women as proof of no previous sexual intercourse for non-married women. Traditionally in many Islamic societies, in Egypt and the Levant specifically, a bride is expected to bleed after the first sexual intercourse. In the Egyptian country, a groom is expected to open the door after intercourse with his wife for the first time and present a handkerchief with blood on it to both his and her family as a proof of virginity. The largest Muslim country by population, Indonesia, mandates virginity checks for women enlisting in the police service. These women have to not only wear the hijab, but they also have to experience the humiliation of being tested to see if they are virgins—as if being a virgin affects their performance in any way. To take matters further, in Egypt during the revolution of 2011, women who opposed the Egyptian regime were subjugated to virginity tests as a way of humiliating them into submission. Even when the Islamist party won the elections of 2012, the case of these women who were subjugated to this humiliation was refuted, and no sentence was applied to the army officers involved in this shameful act. Again, there is no scriptural text that mandates virginity tests, but many verses in the Qur'an and Hadith emphasize the virtue of being a virgin and the increased worth of the woman who has not been touched or used.

Another issue that is mostly a problem in Arabic-speaking Islamic countries is the citizenship of the mother. In all these countries, with the exception of Tunisia, women don't have the power to pass their citizenship to their children. Only fathers give the citizenship to their children. It is true that the political conflicts in the region make this practice legally dominating. However, Islam with its concept of Qewama doesn't help women who are fighting to gain this simple right as a citizen of the state. It is utterly painful to see that a mother who gives birth to a child doesn't have the right to pass on this part of her identity because she is considered less of a person in the eye of the law. Currently, Lebanese women are taking this fight to the parliament in hopes of one day being treated as equal.

Finally, the fight for reproductive rights. Clearly, it is not only Muslim women who are fighting for their reproductive rights. It is a fight that springs from societies plagued with religion. Islamic countries may not necessarily have a problem with abortion for medical reasons, but abortion for any other reason, even rape, is illegal and punishable by law in many countries. Women in Islam are deemed worthy for marriage when they meet the standard set in the following Hadith: "Marry the one who is loving and fertile, for I will feel proud of your large numbers before the other Prophets on the Day of Resurrection" (Sahih Muslim). When the purpose for marrying is for women to have children in order to increase the population of Muslims, then abortion or abstinence become very sinful behavior in the eyes of Allah. Women can't under any circumstance favor a role different than wife and mother. Even though the numbers indicate that more women in the Islamic world are educated and working than ever before, if they have no control over their reproductive rights, their careers and aspirations will meet a quick end.

Muslim women must realize that their submission to these outdated principles is the main reason behind the deterioration of the living conditions and socioeconomic situation in their countries. Women won't be treated as fully independent individuals until they *believe* that they are fully independent individuals, capable of great things. Women can be mothers, astronauts, authors, teachers, engineers, mechanics—we can work at any trade or profession we desire. If my sisters in the Islamic world can't fight the pressure to be part of the submissive group, they will always remain second-class citizens, they won't be able to guarantee the prosperity of their children and their families, and they will remain prisoners to the subjugation and humiliation of Islamic Sharia.

6

Negotiations with God

Aruna Papp

My discussions with God began when I was about five years old. My father worked full-time for God. In fact, he worked for God twenty-four hours of the day, seven days a week. This also meant that he was away from home a lot. Father was an interpreter for the missionaries who came to India to save all the heathen people and make sure they were baptized so that they could have a mansion in heaven, which Christ was preparing for all the people who loved him. A few decades later, Father became a very famous pastor in India, often mentioned in the media as the "Indian Billy Graham."

When Father returned home from his travels, it was my job to update him on the neighborhood gossip. As the eldest of seven children, it was my job to take care of the chores such as fetching milk from the neighborhood dairy, going to the bazaar while Mother attended to the house and my younger siblings. It was also my chore to inform Father about all the chores that needed his attention.

While he was away, Mother would constantly remind me, "Don't forget to tell your father how many times the milkman refused to give us milk because he had not been paid for two months," or "Don't forget to tell him you had black tea for breakfast for weeks," or "If you forget to tell your father that we have no cooking oil, we will all starve." It never occurred to me that it should be our mother who should discuss our grocery bills with our father. It was many years later that I learned why Mother never discussed family maintenance issues with Father.

When I told Father about running out of food during his absence or the milkman demanding to be paid, Father would comfort me by saying that I should realize that he was busy doing very important work for God, saving "heathen souls for God's kingdom." There was nothing more important to us, and since we were God's chosen people, God would look after all our needs. Father assured me that because God loved us, he would provide us with just enough "worldly goods" that we required. I believed my father, and I began to trust God to take care of us. But the milkman or the vegetable seller did not seem to buy into my trust in God. And usually, I was the one left to deal with them.

The missionaries in India had managed to find a lot of heathens who needed to be saved. My father's job was to travel with the missionaries, and he reminded me constantly that this was the most important job in the world, which required that we all "sacrifice for Jesus." This would galvanize me into being a "young champion for Christ" and to stop complaining. I also withheld certain details from Father, such as when we had run out of food and I had stolen lentils or vegetables from the bazaar. I could never bring myself to tell him that I had visited the Hindu temple where worshippers had left piles of food and sweets before the "idol Hindu Gods" and I had helped myself to this booty. I was sure this would not be considered stealing and I was not breaking the Ten Commandments because we were Christians and the Third Commandment forbade us to worship before the idols. So stealing food from the temples might be our God's way of providing for us. But I felt that checking out these arrangements with Father was best left for another time.

In our home, a pastor's family, we prayed five times a day. Every morning our day started with morning worship, which was held before breakfast. If Father was not home, Mother presided, reading a chapter from the Bible and then having each of us say a prayer. Worship without Father was much shorter. Father's prayer was longer because he had to thank God for all the adventures and blessings he had experienced during his last missionary tour.

At each meal, we were required to pray and thank God for the food we were about to eat. Before going to bed, we had the sundown worship where we thanked God for keeping us safe that day, asked him to bring Father home safely, and begged him to make sure that we were all safe from any impending disasters that might occur during the night. During each prayer throughout the day, my three sisters and mother begged God to hear our prayers and bless us with a baby brother. It was understood that if all of us prayed and each one of us explained to God how important it was for us to have a baby brother, then he would probably listen.

From a very young age, I was aware that, in India, girls are less valued than boys, and my mother had given birth to four girls. Not only was she in danger, but so were my sisters and I. In the Indian culture, girls are considered a curse and a financial burden, especially in poor families because they are not able to bear the expense of dowries for their daughters. Boys, however, are counted upon to take care of their parents in their old age and carry the family name.

Songs about the blessing of being a mother of sons played on the radio day and night. Songs blessing a new bride "may you have a hundred sons" were sung at every wedding. The festival of Rakhi, which relates to the love and duty between brothers and sisters, is celebrated with great reverence and devotion. The duty of the sister is to obey her brother, live a moral life, and never bring shame to him or the family name, and the brother's duty is to protect his sister from all harm, physically and morally.

This gives the brother the right to select a spouse for his sister, and the sister's duty is to accept the brother's decision. If a sister rebels or insists on marrying a man of her own choosing, the brother has the community support to reprimand the sister, punish her physically, even kill her, because in rebelling, the sister has brought shame to the brother and the family. This is called honor killing. Honor killings can be carried out by parents and other relatives as well. It seems that I was aware of honor-based violence from a very young age, but I also worried that, since we did not have a brother, we did not have a protector.

I also have many happy childhood memories related to tent meetings that the missionaries conducted each year. Every year missionaries from America arrived in order to save as many heathens as possible. What was most exciting was that, for those two weeks, Father was at home. Father was responsible for hiring people who erected large tents and spread carpets for people to sit on. He hired local bands and invited choirs from various churches to sing before the sermon, which was to be delivered by the missionaries. The missionaries' sermons were always terrifying, especially for those who had not yet decided to be baptized. They told the people that they would burn in hellfire for eternity and that it would be too late to save their souls. But after the sermon, the missionaries gave out cans of milk powder and blankets to those who had agreed to join "the Lord's army" and be saved. During these sermons, I could not be more gratified and boastful because my father was working with the missionaries and we were sure to be first in line on our way to heaven. We had earned the privilege to sit at God's right hand; I fully intended to remind the milkman of this privilege when he yelled at me.

During the tent meetings, Father was always the master of ceremonies. He spoke four languages: Hindi, Urdu, Punjabi, and English. He had a booming voice and sang hymns with the band, warming up the crowd for the sermons from the missionaries. Father was also an excellent poet. He would read his poems about the wrenched life on earth and the love of God that would deliver the sinners. Sitting right in front of the stage with my mother, siblings, and families of other native workers, when I turned around to look at the crowd behind us, I could see many people with tears running down their faces. Their hearts were touched by the poetry Father had recited, and they were ready to receive God's word and be saved. I wanted to yell out, "That is my dad. That poet, that man on the stage, is my father."

To me, Father was like the greatest film star. He was handsome and charming with a thundering voice. I was so proud of him. My father was God's messenger. There were some who thought that the thousands of people who attended these tent meetings only came because they received blankets and powdered milk. I believed they came to hear my father sing and read his poems, and that they believed that he had direct contact with God who could make the mountains move.

No daughter could have been more proud of her father. I believed with all my heart that God would listen to Father and answer his prayers. I also believed that, because my father preached about the love of God and about saving the lives of all the sinners, Father would never let any harm come to me, my mother, or my younger sisters.

The person who threatened us harm was my father's mother—we called her Dadi ji. My grandmother hated our mother. Dadi ji was beautiful. She was fair skinned with light-brown eyes and long flowing hair, a Punjabi woman who had given birth to six sons and three daughters. My mother was dark skinned and had not brought any dowry with her as a bride. But worst of all, she had given birth only to daughters.

I was eight when, eventually, our brother was born. Those first eight years of my life, I witnessed Dadi ji threatening to throw my younger sisters and me into the well. She never called us by our names. We were called "the curse." Dadi ji would pound her forehead with her palm and wail, "God has been unkind to my wonderful son. He has been cursed with daughters who will be the end of him. I must find a way to remove this curse on my household." Neighbors would stop by with suggestions about visiting holy gurus who could help or visiting shrines or making a pilgrimage. Our mother had warned us never to eat anything Dadi ji offered us.

Dadi ji would hold up her finger at me telling me that, since I was the firstborn, it was my fault. I was the first curse to have befallen her son. I was responsible for my sisters being the wrong gender. When I asked Father about my being the first curse, he assured me that, if we prayed hard, God would hear our prayers and would give us a baby brother and all would be fine.

I prayed very hard five times a day, "Please God, this time around can you give us a baby brother?" I would then start to negotiate with God. I would remind him that I was not asking for myself. I wanted to make God realize that if we had a baby brother, our mother would not be terrorized by Dadi ji and Mother would stop crying all the time. I told God that keeping Dadi ji happy was the most important thing and, since he, God, could move mountains, make the rain fall on the desert, and resurrect the dead, he could also give us a baby brother. I always reminded him that this was not a favor I was asking for myself but for my mother and for my sisters, and I was willing to negotiate with God, mend my sinful ways if only he would give us a baby brother.

Every morning Mother would tell me, "I am busy with household chores and can't look after the new baby sister. It is your job to sit by her and, if you see Dadi ji coming close to the baby cot, scream as loudly as you can." So I had my eye on Dadi ji all the time.

Dadi ji also prayed several times a day. She prayed loudly so that we could all hear her pouring out her heart to God. So I prayed louder and harder and asked God to keep Dadi ji away from the new baby. I suggested to God that, if he broke one of Dadi ji's legs, or if a scorpion was to bite her, she would find it difficult to move and we would all be safe. Again, I was willing to negotiate with God and do his bidding in any way he saw fit. This prayer did not go well for me. Dadi ji, in tears, reported me to my father, and he used his belt to beat my back as punishment.

The Bible class for the children was conducted by the wife of the missionary, Mrs. Jenson. Mrs. Jenson spoke in English, which we did not understand, so a native pastor in training would interpret for her. Week after week I listened to her stories about how God had helped people out of difficulties when they had prayed for God's help. Mrs. Jenson told us that she truly believed that God could perform miracles, especially on behalf of the people who loved God. The one day she asked the children if we had a question she might answer, I raised my hand and told her about my ongoing negotiations with God and asked her if she had any suggestions on how to make God hear my prayer.

I am not sure if my question had been correctly interpreted, but the class was told that Mrs. Jenson said, "It is not your place to challenge God or test his motives. You have to learn to trust God completely and he will take care of your needs." I was told to have faith in God, and he would decide what is best for me and my family.

My dilemma was not related to God's judgment about what was best for the people who loved him, or if he could perform miracles when he was busy building mansions in heaven for all the people he was going to invite to live with him. My predicament was my Dadi ji—I wanted God to do something to mend my Dadi ji so that she would stop cursing my mother.

In the Bible classes, I also learned about God's instructions for women. Wives, I learned, were "subject to their husbands," which meant they belonged to the husband. Father was the head of the family just as Christ was the head of the church, and a wife must sacrifice herself and her desires in respect and honor of her husband.

Until my late forties, I fully believed this. If God said that women, or girls, were second-class citizens and property of the husband, the church said the same thing, and my father also preached this, then I felt that it must be true. This fact was also emphasized on a daily basis by the Indian culture. In the South Asian culture, women who give birth to daughters only are seen as being responsible for not living up to the wifely duty.

Therefore, they are viewed as being in shame. I felt that unless we had a baby brother, our mother too could be punished and no one would object.

Then Mother was going to have another baby and everyone was talking about it, and Dadi ji was very unhappy, sure that the curse would make this baby a girl too. She "accidentally" dropped a hot pot of tea on my mother's foot. Then she had "accidentally" opened the door just when Mother was passing by and hit her protruding belly. All I wanted was to have someone stop my Dadi ji from bullying our mother and threatening to throw us in the well. So I would negotiate with God in my prayer, which everyone heard and Dadi ji would report back to my father. Father would then take his belt and beat me for dishonoring his mother.

As much as I feared Dadi ji, a large part of me believed that our father would never let any harm come to us. Dadi ji seldom made threats when Father was home. She would say, "My son, you are doing God's work. This time around, I am sure he is going to bless you. I pray all the time for a grandson." Father would smile at his mother. He could never believe that she was cruel and threatening. In front of him, she was a kind, loving mother, worried for her son. My mother never complained to my father about his mother.

Still, I believed that Father would protect us. I told him all the things Dadi ji said when he was not around. But for this, I was punished. When I was punished, Mother would also reprimand me, saying that I could not bother Father with my trivial complaints. In my little heart, I knew that Father was working for God and so he could discuss things with God. I had heard Father preach about how "God is love" or "God loves his people." Therefore, it made sense to me that our father loved us and would never allow anyone to harm his daughters.

On one occasion, I knew that Father was going to leave early in the morning and would be away for several weeks, so I was determined to wake up before he left so I could say goodbye to him. When I came to my parents' room, I saw my parents kneeling beside their bed. My father had placed his hand on my mother's head, and he was praying. I heard him say, "Dear God, I have dedicated my life to you and to saving heathen souls for your kingdom. I am away from my family for long weeks, I am sacrificing my all for you, but you have not heard my prayers. You have not answered my prayer; you have not given me a son, which I need desperately. This time around, please give me a son."

Both of my parents were weeping as they begged God for a son. I crept back into bed and pretended to be asleep. I knew that moment, if Dadi ji managed to throw one of us into the well, Dad, who was always away, would not be able to protect us and, by the time he did get home, it would be too late. I was also sure he would not punish his mother. We—my sisters and I—were a curse. We were a burden and, because we were born the wrong gender, we were responsible for the torture our mother was being subjected to on a daily basis.

So it was when I was eight years old, those many years ago, around five in the morning, that our savior was born. We had a brother. I woke up to my father shaking me and telling me that God had finally heard our prayers. Father was sobbing. He was so happy, he could not contain himself. I jumped out of my bed, not stopping to put on my shoes, and I ran out and knocked on the doors of all our neighbors, screaming as loud as I could, "Wake up, our savior is born! We now have a brother. Come over and see our brother." I did not stop to check that my foot had been cut, leaving a bloody trail behind me.

Finally, after Mother had given birth to a son, things seemed to change for her somewhat. Our Dadi ji could no longer blame her for burying her son under the weight of daughters. By giving birth to a son, Mother had fulfilled her duty, and now her daughters had a protector, their brother. Our parents felt strongly that God had heard all our prayers and had blessed them. What is more, they felt that now that the "chain" of giving birth to girls had been broken, if they would try to have another child, it might also be a boy. In fact they tried twice, but alas their prayers must have been blocked by one sin or another because we ended up with two more sisters.

Now we were six girls and one brother, the poor little fellow burdened with the weight of six sisters. Our Dadi ji now lamented, "Where is my little grandson going to find money to buy dowry for all his sisters? How will he manage to find good homes to marry off his sisters?" We six sisters were not only a burden to our father, but now we were also a burden for our brother. But this time around, Mother had a response for Dadi ji's lament. "Don't worry about my daughters; they have a father and a brother. By God's grace they will manage to find good bridegrooms for my daughters." The plan was to marry off the girls as quickly as possible, and then all the family resources could go into educating the son, who would then look after our parents in their old age and bring glory to God.

I was seventeen when my younger sister told me, "You are getting married next month." Over the next few weeks, church aunties and Father's coworkers started to stop by the house and congratulate my parents on the upcoming wedding, to which my parents always replied, "God has been good to us. He understands our challenges." No one ever asked me if I wanted to get married. In church one day, my sisters pointed out my future husband. I noted that after the church services, Mother would go up to this man and invite him for lunch. I remained in the kitchen while the rest of the family ate lunch with my intended groom.

During the family prayers, my parents would be gushing their thanks to God for taking care of their burden. They were especially grateful because my future husband also wanted to be a pastor. He was one of the selected few looking forward to going to heaven. Thus began eighteen years of a loveless and abusive marriage to a man who also was working for God and keen on "saving heathens for God's kingdom." I was terrified at what the future held for me, but before God's will and my parents' determination to get me married off, I did not dare question them.

As a teenager I had been skinny, tall, and very dark skinned. Every time Dadi ji looked at me, she had something nasty to say about "the black skeleton" in her family. She would be wailing at my mother; "No man is going to marry her for her looks. You make sure she learns to cook well—maybe that will be her salvation." I enjoyed cooking and became a good cook. But that was not to be my salvation because, by the time I was nineteen, I had given birth to two daughters. Each time I was pregnant, I prayed and begged God for a son. I now understood my mother's fear, and when I prayed, I reminded God again and again about my father and the work he was doing to save all the heathens. I also mentioned my husband and begged God to forgive him for belting me. I reminded God that it was not my husband's fault that he lost his temper with me and beat me. After all, the fault was mine. I had given birth to daughters. If anything, it was also God's fault because he was responsible for the gender of my children. Again, negotiations with God became the focus of my day.

In the 1970s, there was a great influx of immigrants to Canada from India. The Canadian government had recruited the best of the best, mostly young professionals, a phenomenon referred to by the media as a "brain drain." A large majority of these immigrants were Christians who settled in urban centers such as Toronto. These new Canadians missed their homeland and wanted to worship in their native language. At this time, my father had made quite a name for himself in India.

The church officials in Canada sponsored my parents to provide for the spiritual needs of new immigrants in their mother tongue. Father's church in Toronto was an instant success, and he became very popular. I was the last of my siblings to arrive, with my two little daughters and their father. As a successful pastor in Canada, my father was determined to help my husband find employment with the church as well. However, this seemed much more challenging in Canada than it had been in India.

Regimented prayer sessions were again started, but this time around, we were all begging God for an employment opportunity where my husband would be able to wear a tie and a suit so that he would not be an embarrassment to my father. My father felt that it was more acceptable for my husband to be unemployed, "seeking work," than be working in a menial job. I, on the other hand, was encouraged to find any form of employment and support the family.

I started working at York University in Toronto as a short-order cook. I soon learned that, as a full-time employee, I was allowed to attend classes as part of my employment benefit. However, before I could register for any of the university programs, my educational background had to be assessed. This time around, my prayer regimen was all about me. I began to negotiate with God and remind him that it was, after all, his will that I give birth to daughters. I had accepted that. I did not mind working as a short-order cook. In fact, I was grateful for the opportunity, but now God had to come through for me and help me pass the assessment.

I did not tell my family that I was planning to take classes nor that my education was being assessed. Not having been assessed before, I was not aware of what this entailed, but I knew that it could prevent me from attending classes. Finally, my educational level was determined to be grade three, much too low to take college classes. I was devastated. Once again, God had neglected my prayers. He had not accepted any of the deals I was trying to make with him.

Seeing my disappointment, my supervisor suggested that I had the option of taking "upgrading" classes and that, in a year or two, I could be assessed again. I had nothing to lose, so I started the upgrading classes. I wanted to make sure that my family did not find out about my classes, especially when I became interested in seminars and workshops related to the empowerment of women.

I was terrified of these women and what they were preaching. It seemed to me that they were saying things that were in direct opposition to what God wanted his people to learn, what the church was teaching, and what my father and his colleagues were preaching. But I was also intrigued.

These women were demanding that women in Canada be given equal rights to men. I was sure that the church would view this as blasphemy. The women were demanding support for child care, shelter for abused women, and equal pay for equal work—a phenomenon that was new to me.

I was learning new terms, such as *domestic violence, wife abuse,* and *the right of women to call police* and have their husbands arrested for belting them. As I listened to these women, I was sure these were the same women the church had identified as the "devil tools," the "home breakers." I was scared of being seen by a church member and reported to my father. He would forbid me to return to work. And yet, I could not stay away. I prayed and asked God to forgive me for attending these seminars. I would promise God that I would only attend one more and then stop.

What I was learning from feminist professors at York University, people more educated than I, created confusion and terror in me. Confusion because they were saying that I was a human being and I had the right to live a violence-free life and the laws in Canada would protect me. Terror because if I stood up to the teaching of the church, I could go to hell, and the law of the land could arrest the men in my family. During sleepless nights, I would find comfort in telling myself that all these laws and rights only applied to white women and not women like me. But there was another power that would not allow me to rest. I wanted my daughters to have these rights, and I wanted my daughters to be protected by the law of the land. I wanted my daughters to grow up feeling that they were important to me. This thought put me on the path for a head-on collision with God and the teachings of the church.

I believed that if my father found out that I was meeting with feminists at York University and listening to their "propaganda," he would have no choice but to punish me. There had never been a divorce in our extended family. My father was the patriarch of a very large extended family, and he now had a very large South Asian church. He was well respected, and my contemplating a divorce would shame the family and bring dishonor to my father and the extended family.

While family honor is an abstract concept involving the perceived quality of worthiness and respectability, it definitely affects an individual's or family's social standing and self-evaluation in our community. I had heard from birth, "If a man can't defend his honor, he is not a man. He has no right to live." In Canada, when church members visited my father to discuss issues with their teenagers or wives wanting to leave the marriage due to domestic violence, I had witnessed my father supporting honor-based violence. He felt strongly that the Bible was very clear about a wife's duty toward her husband—total submission, complete obedience—and the husband's responsibility was to reprimand his wife and control his children.

In my prayers, I also presented a logical excuse to God about my behavior, because I felt that these women's advocates were all white women. They were tools of the devil, they were selfish and unsatisfied with God's will for their lives, and this made them immoral. I was not one of them, but I should, I told God, take the time to listen to what they had to say so that I would not become like them and I would know how to protect myself and my family. After all, I was a mother of two daughters who were growing up in Canada, and they were my responsibility. It was my job to make sure I brought up my daughters to be good, God-fearing Indian girls.

Every Sunday, after service in the Indian church, we would have a potluck lunch followed by a women's group. As the pastor's daughter, I was expected to help with the lunch and attend the women's group. Everything I was learning at the university from the women's advocates was the opposite of what the church expected of us. As the pastor's daughter, I was expected to be the role model as an obedient and passive daughter and wife.

While the women at the university threatened everything I was taught and believed in, there was some logic in what they were saying, and it kept pulling me back into those seminars. I justified my attraction by telling myself that I wanted a better life for my daughters, a violence-free life. I wanted them to have the opportunity to make decisions for their lives.

This was a very challenging period for me. For the first time in my life, I was hearing things that were new to me. I was being forced to think for myself. I would then be forced to make decisions about my life, my marriage, the abuse in my marriage, and the future of my daughters. But I had long since accepted the fact that I was a curse on my father and that I had to bow to the will of God.

My life plan was in God's hand, and he had chosen my husband, and my husband was the head of my household, and if he was beating me, then it must be that there was something wrong with me. The church's teachings were clear; women had to work hard to please their husbands. But no matter how hard I tried to please him, somehow, I always seemed to fall short. When my husband reported my failings to my parents, my father agreed with him and reprimanded me. When my husband's application to the church for a pastoring position was rejected, my father and my husband made it clear that it was my fault. I had not been a good and supportive wife, and the stress had caused him to fail.

Growing up in India, in a culture of honor, the concept of shame is all around us. It is like the weather—no one can escape it. What this means is that, in shame-based honor cultures, public humiliation, scorn, and censures are used as control mechanisms. The concept of shame allows the community to label an individual as flawed, defective, worthy of punishment.

While I wanted to have a violence-free life for myself and my daughters, I could not bring myself to walk out of my marriage and seek a divorce. My father had arranged my marriage, and seeking a divorce would state that *he* had made a mistake. The shame and dishonor in the community was unimaginable for me. I would have preferred to commit suicide to get away from my abuser than to humiliate my father. I could not imagine disobeying God, breaking the rule of the church, and dishonoring my extended family.

In honor cultures, women are expected to be modest, pure, obedient, virginal at marriage, and virtuous after marriage, and they must subjugate their personal autonomy, desires, and freedom in order to uphold the honor of their family and community. Through the church teachings, I had learned very early in life that the first honor killing is recorded in Genesis 34 when Jacob's daughter Dinah, a teenager of thirteen or fourteen, was raped by Shechem, a prince of his tribe. Jacob's sons felt that their tribe had been shamed and dishonored. Therefore, they massacred the tribe of the rapist Shechem to reclaim their honor.

As a fourteen-year-old girl in India, I had witnessed a young neighbor girl set on fire by her brothers because she refused to marry the man they had selected for her. I knew that I would have to face the wrath of my father and extended family and rejection from the church members, who were my community, if I sought divorce and a life of nonviolence.

My daughters, now growing up in Canada, were also learning that they are equal to boys, they have the same rights as boys, and the Charter of Rights in Canada states that everyone has the right to live a violence-free life. They were learning that they have the right to choose their own spouses and careers. My marriage to their father confused them, but I could not yet bring myself to bring shame on my father and extended family. For eighteen years, I lived in fear and terror. I worried that if I divorced my husband, no respectful Indian man would marry my daughters. I started new negotiations with God: help me to protect my daughters, and help me to teach my daughters to be confident and have power over their own lives.

As they marched toward their teenage years, my daughters began to challenge me. My daughters saw my negotiations with God as a farce. They saw my life as a travesty and my father's preaching as mockery. My Canadianized daughters were vocal about the choices I was making, such as choosing to live under the control of my father, their father, and my younger brother. At first this was shocking to me. I felt like I had failed to raise proper Indian daughters. But over the years I began to see my life through my daughters' eyes and to fear that they would not respect me because I did not stand up to my abusers—God and the men in the family.

It seemed, almost without my realizing it, that the shackles ingrained within my mind since birth, those cultural behavioral norms passed down for generations and instilled throughout my childhood, had started to loosen their grip on my thought processes. At times this was terrifying. The stark challenges from my daughters had created a gap through which I made a mental leap and, with stern resolve and great trepidation, I did divorce their father. Although the fallout cost me dearly, I remarried years later to a wonderful man who has been by my side for over thirty years and it has been a great honeymoon. This was only possible because I stopped negotiating with God and seeking my father's blessing.

For the past thirty-five years, I have been working with South Asian immigrant women in Canada who are victims of honor-based violence. During this time, I have met hundreds of women like myself who were programmed from birth that we must live our lives according to God's plan and honor our fathers, husbands, and brothers. We are taught early in life that we must sacrifice ourselves and our lives in order to protect our family's good name. We are taught that women are valued less than men simply because they are born the wrong gender, and this is God's will.

As people of God, obedient and virtuous daughters and wives, we must live within our cultural boundaries and not bring shame to our families. Mothers don't often see the full effect of the chains that bind them until they give birth to daughters and are faced with the overwhelming need to protect them.

Currently, there is little information about honor-based violence and immigrant women. Because police, lawyers, social workers, and other professionals lack detailed understanding of honor-based violence, they often fail to detect, record, or respond to this phenomenon in a culturally appropriate manner, further endangering the lives of victims seeking assistance. Unable to recognize the nature of this culturally rooted crime and abuse, which is related to family honor, the police and other professionals fail to act appropriately. When the police receive a phone call about abuse, for example, those who are not trained to recognize honor-based violence view it as domestic violence. If a brother is beating a sister, they will arrest the brother and charge him, but they will leave the girl with the real perpetrators—who may be the parents, grandparents, or uncles demanding the honor violence. All too often, this can result in the girl's death. These events have played out over and over again.

To be clear, all violence against women is unacceptable and should not be tolerated. But violence against women is manifested in different ways. In intimate partner violence, often referred to as domestic violence, the violence is between two individuals who have a sexual relationship—they are spouses, a couple. Therefore, the perpetrator of the violence is one of the spouses. Law enforcement may feel they have done enough in arresting a spouse because there is only one source of the violence. However, in honor-based violence, there can be many perpetrators. In North America in the majority of honor killings in Indian communities, the killers are fathers and the victims are teenage daughters. But in some cases mothers, brothers, uncles, and grandparents have also participated in murdering young women. In cases of honor-based violence, there may be a large number of potential perpetrators and an even larger number of persons willing to plan the violent act or shelter the perpetrator because the culture teaches that this violence is right and necessary to avoid shame on the family and community. We have second- and third-generation girls who are not being protected from their perpetrators because law enforcement is not trained to recognize the true danger.

In my experience, in domestic violence or intimate partner violence, there can be many reasons for conflict between the couple, including family honor. However, in a large majority of honor-based violence cases, the violence is related to controlling the woman's sexuality. A United Nations report on honor-related crimes defines it as:

> "Honour"-related murders involve a girl or woman being killed by a male or female family member for an actual or assumed sexual or behavioural transgression, including adultery, sexual intercourse or pregnancy outside marriage—or even for being raped.[1]

Over the past ten years, I have focused primarily on facilitating workshops and training programs for police officers, family court lawyers, and judges on how honor-based violence differs from domestic violence. I teach about the twenty indicators that are particular to honor-based violence, but unless officials know to look for these specifically, their risk assessments are flawed, which leads to inappropriate safety plans and, potentially, loss of life due to honor killings. Globally, honor killings are on the rise. In the past two decades, honor killings have been on the rise in Western countries as well.[2] However, there is very little documentation on honor-based violence.

Violence against women is a global phenomenon. It crosses all social, religious, ethnic, and class barriers. However, the manifestation of violence against women is rooted in patriarchal cultural traditions and practices. In order to assist the victims, it is important to have a full understanding of these cultural practices. To make matters more complicated, honor-based violence does not look the same from one culture to the next. Claimed reasons for the violence as well as the particular punishments vary depending on the cultural norms of the people committing it. Comprehensive training is needed for anyone who works with potential victims.

Some people worry that labeling certain forms of violence against

---

1. Fatma Khafagy, "Honour Killing in Egypt" (paper presented at a meeting organized by the UN Division for the Advancement of Women in collaboration with the UN Office on Drugs and Crime, Vienna, Austria, May 17–20, 2005).

2. Mandy Clark, "Honor Killings on Rise Worldwide," *VOA*, November 1, 2009, https://www.voanews.com/a/a-13-2008-02-05-voa19/406431.html.

women as "rooted in cultural practices" will stereotype certain groups, set up divisive attitudes of "them against us," or instill a prejudice against immigrants who have theoretically brought honor-based violence with them to Western countries. However, honor-based violence existed in Western countries for decades before the large influx of immigrants from honor-based cultures. Research shows that between 1950 and 1970, over 350,000 young unwed mothers were institutionalized in Canada. There is similar data in United States, Ireland, Australia, and the United Kingdom. These young girls were sent away from home because they were pregnant and not married and were therefore a source of shame and humiliation to the family and the community. While the families of these young women tried desperately to keep the exile a secret, the community knew but was complicit in keeping the secret by pretending that the young girls had been sent away to look after a sick relative. Many of the mothers lost their babies, and others were punished. Some even died. This is one form of honor-based violence in Western culture.

Although I lived in an honor-based culture for many years, I am free now. My second husband, David, and I also have a daughter, and with them I have learned to stop negotiating with God and start making choices for myself. Undoing the mental programming of self-sacrificing has been very challenging. Bringing shame and dishonor to the family name and to my father by getting a divorce and remarrying brings with it guilt which, at times, is debilitating. But in the autumn of my life, it seems each day is much better than yesterday because I ultimately have made the right choices.

7

Black Women and Christianity in the United States:

A Historical Perspective, Part I
(Colonial Era to Jim Crow)

Valerie Wade

First, we must realize that no such institution as the Negro church could rear itself without definite historical foundations. These foundations we can find if we remember that the social history of the Negro did not start in America.

—W. E. B. Du Bois[1]

Legba. Yowa. Asase Ye Duru. Ankh. These markings symbolize divinities, both male and female, and ideas. Along with several others, they adorn one of the most fascinating historical monuments in New York City, the African

---

1. W. E. B. Du Bois, *The Souls of Black Folk: Essays and Sketches* (Chicago: A. C. McClurg, 1903), 195.

Burial Ground National Monument. Under the operation of the National Park Service, the monument on the southern end of Manhattan serves as a reminder of the long, forgotten history of Black Americans in the United States, particularly during the seventeenth and eighteenth centuries.

By all accounts, the African Burial Ground is a sacred space: From the 1640s until the 1790s, more than four hundred bodies were buried there. It was chosen as a burial ground because Africans generally were not permitted to be buried in European cemeteries in the city. In the 1600s, its location was in a rural area in an African community on the outskirts of what would become New York City. Many of those bodies were interred with beads, shells, and motifs that demonstrate "cultural continuity between the New World and Africa."[2] This cultural continuity is the key to understanding the role of religion throughout Black American history.

The African Burial Ground, one of the most important archaeological discoveries of the last few decades, is replete with spiritual symbolism. What do we make of this? Clearly, these individuals held their various faith systems in high regard, and despite the harsh realities of life in the American colonies, they managed to create a rich body of syncretic burial practices. They did not, as some scholars have argued, forget their African sociocultural traditions as a result of the Middle Passage, at least not during the time the African Burial Ground was in use. But through the physical and psychological torture of slavery, these traditions gave way to Christianity, which has by now been the most popular religion among Black Americans for generations. One of the most deleterious effects of this transition was the loss of the divine feminine and the solidification of religious misogyny in Black American communities.

This essay summarizes the transition from the faith systems of the ethnic groups touched by the Atlantic slave trade to the patriarchal Christianity common today. Focusing on the Colonial era to the early twentieth century, it explores the role of Black women in Christian communities and makes a case for the dissolution of sexist practices in Christian churches.

---

2. "African Burial Ground Memorial, New York, NY," US General Services Administration, https://www.gsa.gov/portal/ext/html/site/hb/category/25431/action Parameter/exploreByBuilding/buildingId/1084.

The Erasure of West African Goddesses— Setting the Foundation for Sexism

When considering gender and Black American religion, I mourn the devaluation of the divine feminine and the consequent discrimination against women in traditional Christian churches. I do not think that goddess worship (or any religion in particular) would have been a cure-all for the layered discrimination that Black women have faced in the United States. However, I do posit that the existence of goddesses in the group's consciousness would have been an effective buffer between Black women's psyches and Christianity's harmful sexist teachings.

Throughout Black American history, the church has served as a channel for information, events, and ideas. The church offers "incredible power and security" for many Black women, but these same women experience obstacles "when they attempt to claim or exercise authority within the traditional church."[3] What we know for sure is that Africans in the United States held on to as much of their customs as they could, but due to myriad factors, goddess worship fell to the wayside.[4]

Western African cosmologies made space for goddesses like Mawu (of the Dahomey kingdom in Benin), Yemoja (of the Yoruba ethnic group in Nigeria and Benin), and Ala (of the Igbo ethnic group in Nigeria). These female deities were just as respected as their male counterparts. They were not minor figures in these religious traditions, but were revered as crucial entities in West African mythologies. For instance, Ala, who rules the underworld and morality, is consort to Amadioha, the god of thunder and lightning. Ala may be generally imagined as Mother Earth. She is the goddess of the land, and she controls the fertility of the fields.[5] Mawu is the sister-wife of Lisa. Mawu-Lisa is often considered to be an androgynous deity with male and female aspects. As the creator goddess, Mawu has the

---

3. Donald McCrary, "Womanist Theology and Its Efficacy for the Writing Classroom," *College Composition and Communication* 52, no. 4 (2001): 521–552.

4. This is a generality, of course. There are relatively small portions of the population that follow voodoo, Santeria, and other traditions that celebrate feminine divinity. The topic here is simply mainstream Christianity, broadly considered.

5. Immigration and Refugee Board of Canada, "Nigeria: Agbara the God of the Oba Cult or Religion as Practised among the Igbo in Abia State," Refworld, http://www.refworld.org/docid/3f7d4de0e.html.

power of the breath of life.[6] Living creatures would not exist without her. In contrast, Christianity ignores any concept of goddess worship, save for the Virgin Mary in some denominations.[7] The male creator god of the Judeo-Christian Old Testament controls nature and possesses the breath of life. The Holy Trinity of the Father, Son, and Holy Spirit leaves no room for feminine divinity. Affirming an equally powerful Mother, Daughter, and Holy Spirit is blasphemous for mainstream Christians.

As a patriarchal faith, Christianity helped set the stage for sexism in all aspects of society wherever it spread. Pre-Christian societies were not all matriarchal or egalitarian, of course. But in the context of the slave trade and the subsequent mass conversion of enslaved Africans to Christianity, the abandonment of feminine divinity has had very real consequences for Black women's lives. Mawu, Yemoja, and Ala had little room to thrive in a society that believed the downfall of humankind stemmed from a woman's choice to eat a piece of forbidden fruit.

Over time, as the United States developed culturally and economically, Black women's roles in society were increasingly constricted by patriarchal Christianity. The restrictive, dogmatic Puritan foundations of this country directly contributed to the erasure of African faith traditions by cementing Western patriarchal ideals of submissive femininity into the nation's consciousness during slavery. These restrictions did not suddenly dissipate at the end of the Civil War, when the country seemed primed for widespread cultural change. Even after Emancipation, safe spaces for Black women to speak, become educated, or conduct business were tenuous in an American society that relied upon the subjugation of women in sacred and secular arenas.

Considering differences between concepts of gender in the United States and West Africa helps to demonstrate why slavery and power were key factors in the proliferation of patriarchal Christianity. Precolonial West African societies consisted of distinct ethnic groups with their own languages, social hierarchies, and gender norms. Thus, they each responded and adapted to European colonization in various manners. In colonial African communities where women were permitted to grow

---

6. "Mawu-Lisa," African Oracles, http://africanoracles.com/gods/mawu-lisa/.

7. "Femininity and the Trinity: The Feminine Divine in Christianity," *Religions: The Feminine Divine*, BBC, August 3, 2011, http://www.bbc.co.uk/religion/religions/christianity/women/femininedivine_1.shtml.

independently wealthy, gendered European social norms had to be modified or cast aside altogether for the sake of practicality. Patriarchal Christianity simply could not operate fully in places where women had space to develop spheres of influence. The tension between European and African gender norms were evident in communities that flourished amid the burgeoning trading economy in Africa. For instance, there was a point in the seventeenth century when Luso-African women became prominent players in business transactions in Western Africa.[8] Those who "acquired wealth and influence from their capabilities as translators and traders" were called *nharas*.[9] In *Eurafricans in Western Africa*, George Brooks describes how society influenced the role of nharas in commerce:

> There were significant differences in the experiences of Luso-African women living in stratified societies compared to those in acephalous societies. Europeans trading with stratified groups in Senegambia… described Luso-African women as…intermediaries facilitating commerce between Europeans and male traders and elites.… By contrast, Luso-African women living in the numerous acephalous groups south of the Gambia River engaged in commerce on their own account, as well as acting as partners in commerce with Portuguese and Luso-African men.[10]

Brooks points out that the ability of nharas to gain status in the world of business influenced their relationships with men in other areas of life. Marriages in these communities were a mix of Portuguese and African traditions. "In some instances, marriages were consecrated by Christian clergy, but African customs and practices regarding mutual obligations, responsibilities, and expectations always constituted the core of these relationships," Brooks explains.[11]

The absence of this type of mutual respect in business and marriage in the United States can be directly traced to gendered notions of power

---

8. Luso-Africans were descendants of mixed-race Portuguese and African communities established during the slave trade between the sixteenth and eighteenth centuries in Western Africa.

9. George E. Brooks, *Eurafricans in Western Africa: Commerce, Social Status, Gender, and Religious Observance from the Sixteenth to the Eighteenth Century*, (Athens: Ohio University Press, 2003), 124.

10. Ibid., 125–126.

11. Ibid., 126.

inherent in Christianity. The apostle Paul writes in 1 Corinthians 11:3, "But I want you to realize that the head of every man is Christ, and the head of the woman is man." Women in any sort of leadership position, whether in business, marriage, or the church, challenged this hierarchy. Thus, "good" Christian women were urged to remain in their proper place behind and beneath men. Compounded subjugation was the ultimate, long-term effect of this mindset for Black women during and after slavery. Already disadvantaged because of their race, they faced additional difficulties because of their sex.

Perhaps most damaging, though, was the persistent notion that sexism was endorsed by God, as communicated throughout the Old Testament and in the writings of Paul in the New Testament. Over time, the violent cultural hegemony of American slavery obscured access to knowledge about African goddesses. This knowledge may have at least provided Black American women the philosophical tools with which to better resist Christian sexism.

My point here is not to romanticize traditional African faiths as a solution for the ills of Christianity. Rather, I argue that the very idea of powerful feminine divinity is a threat to mainstream Christianity, and that is why, despite all the cultural knowledge that Africans in the United States managed to keep, the names of goddesses like Mawu, Yemoja, and Ala were lost to most Black Americans by the turn of the twentieth century. This was no accident. If a Black woman could be a creator goddess, then certainly she should be able to lead a congregation, conduct business, and operate in positions of leadership within her community. Through those arenas, Black women could challenge slavery and racism on a larger scale. Given the importance of spirituality in African-descended people in communities across the world, one of the most effective ways to subjugate Black women was to remove powerful representations of them in religious practices.

The system of slavery became entrenched in the culture and economy of the United States, and patriarchal Christianity likewise grew to become the standard of religious practice among Black Americans. In the nascent Black Christian church, the divine could only be masculine, and the holy hierarchy outlined in the Bible—Christ, man, woman—must be respected. Besides smaller communities like the Gullah and practitioners of voodoo, the knowledge of those old goddesses was passed down only by the most stubborn of enslaved Africans. As Christianity grew to be the dominant religion in Black communities in the United States, the relegation of women to second-class citizenship almost destroyed the cultural safety net that some women had accessed in Africa.

Religion in American Plantation Life

In a 1918 speech to the American Sociological Association, Robert E. Park said, "In fact, there is every reason to believe, it seems to me, that the Negro, when he landed in the United States, left behind him almost everything but his dark complexion and his tropical temperament. It is very difficult to find in the South today anything that can be traced directly back to Africa."[12] This sentiment was, unfortunately, quite popular in scholarly circles throughout the twentieth century. Historical sites such as New York's African Burial Ground and the existence of Gullah culture in the Southern United States prove Park wrong. Africans who landed in the United States did not lose all their culture upon exiting slave ships. In fact, religion was a primary vehicle for sustaining vestiges of African culture over centuries of slavery. Park should have listened to W. E. B. Du Bois, who argued in 1915 that the Black church was deeply connected to African traditions:

> The vast power of the priest in the African state is well known; his realm alone—the province of religion and medicine—remained largely unaffected by the plantation system.... From such beginnings arose and spread with marvelous rapidity the Negro church, the first distinctively Negro American social institution. It was not at first by any means a Christian church, but a mere adaptation of those rites of fetish which in America is termed obe worship, or "voodoo-ism"...After two centuries, the Church became Christian, with a simple Calvinistic creed, but with many of the old customs still clinging to the services.[13]

Du Bois is describing the strength of the Black church throughout United States history. On one hand, as a conduit for cultural preservation and a mechanism for civil rights and social welfare, the church is an admirable institution. However, on the other hand, it has been an incubator of misogyny, ignorance, and complacency in the Black American community.

---

12. Robert E. Park, "The Conflict and Fusion of Cultures with Special Reference to the Negro," *The Journal of Negro History* 4, no. 2 (1919): 116.

13. W. E. B. Du Bois, *The Negro* (New York: Oxford University Press, 1970), 113.

Religion in communities of enslaved people developed out of praise meetings in slave quarters and secluded areas on or near plantations. Black plantation preachers were known to have a mastery of storytelling and "special oratorical skills."[14] But their talents were compromised by their status as slaves. John W. Blassingame notes:

> Trained by the white clergy, continually under suspicion of plotting insurrection, and often under the surveillance of whites, black ministers frequently joined their masters in preaching obedience and submissiveness to the slaves…. Many Black ministers preached obedience to the slaves because when they did not they were flogged. Others did so because the whites rewarded them with money, relief from labor, or manumission.[15]

This pattern has persisted from slavery to now: many Black preachers espouse a conservatism that preserves a position of favor in white society while simultaneously working against the interests of their congregations. For instance, Bishop Wellington Boone of Virginia is a Black megachurch leader and author who speaks out against the Black Lives Matter movement.[16] Du Bois noted this phenomenon in his seminal 1903 work, *The Souls of Black Folk*:

> In spite, however, of such success as that of the fierce Maroons, the Danish blacks, and others, the spirit of revolt gradually died away under the untiring energy and superior strength of the slave masters…. Nothing suited his condition then better than the doctrines of passive submission embodied in the newly learned Christianity.[17]

The first official Black Christian denomination, the African Methodist Episcopal (AME) Church, was founded in 1816 by Richard Allen in Philadelphia. Removed from Southern plantations, the AME Church

---

14. John Blassingame, *The Slave Community: Plantation Life in the Antebellum South* (New York: Oxford University Press, 1979), 131. See also Du Bois's chapter, "Of the Faith of the Fathers," in *The Souls of Black Folk* for his outline of Black preachers and religion on plantations.

15. Ibid., 132.

16. "About Bishop Wellington Boone," Wellington Boone Ministries, http://wellingtonboone.com/about.

17. du Bois, *Souls of Black Folk*, 117.

was a highly organized, stratified institution that was closely connected to Black American mutual aid societies in Philadelphia and other cities. Women were essential in the development of the AME Church and mutual aid societies, but their roles as official leaders were limited. Black women were revered leaders in the areas of prayer, music, and testimony within the AME Church and other Protestant denominations. Nevertheless, "preaching, officially, was left to men…who believed their dignity as free men depended on maintaining traditional gender roles, even if the tradition those roles were derived from was white and European."[18]

Yet, some Black women became preachers and directly challenged Christian sexism. Jarena Lee (1783–unknown) was given permission to preach in the AME Church.[19] Zilpha Elaw (1790–ca. 1845) preached alongside Lee before settling in England. In 1894, Julia Foote (1823–1900) became the first female deacon in the African Methodist Episcopal Zion Church. The stories of the small number of women who joined the ranks of church leadership in the nineteenth century evidences sexism in the church, but they bravely and eloquently spoke against it. Jarena Lee justified her call to preach the Gospel in a cogent argument against Christian sexism:

> O how careful ought we to be, lest through our bylaws of church governance and discipline, we bring into disrepute even the word of life. For as unseemly as it may appear nowadays for a woman to preach, it should be remembered that nothing is impossible with God…. If the man may preach, because the Saviour died for him, why not the woman, seeing he died for her also?[20]

Lee and her female contemporaries directly confronted sexist discrimination in the early Black church. Indeed, although the church largely rejected Black women's leadership in the clergy, they still managed

---

18. Darlene Clark Hine and Kathleen Thompson, *A Shining Thread of Hope: The History of Black Women in America* (New York: Broadway Books, 1998), 40.

19. Lena Ampadu, "Maria Stewart and the Rhetoric of Black Preaching: Perspectives on Womanism and Black Nationalism," in *Black Women's Intellectual Traditions: Speaking their Minds*, eds. Kristin Waters and Carol B. Conaway (Burlington: University of Vermont Press, 2007), 39.

20. Jarena Lee, "A Female Preacher Among the African Methodists," in *African American Religious History: A Documentary Witness*, ed. Milton C. Sernett (Durham, NC: Duke University Press, 1999), 173.

to carve out their own spheres of influence within the institution. However, they were still fighting for equality within spaces that, too often, had questionable effects on the overall well-being of the Black American community. As Du Bois, Blassingame, and other scholars note, Black Christianity during the Antebellum period was circumscribed by a false sense of hope and duty to slave owners. What began as admirable perseverance in the face of the extreme trauma of the Middle Passage and slavery morphed into a culture of longsuffering and acceptance of current circumstances, to the point that "waiting on the Lord" became an excuse for complacency. After the Civil War, many Black women tried to be more proactive in political and economic issues inside and outside the church.

Women and Religion from the Civil War to Jim Crow

In the late nineteenth and early twentieth centuries, the church grew to be increasingly central to the Black American community. The majority of church leaders felt that the church pulpit was reserved exclusively for men. This meant that women who aspired to be leaders in their churches had to learn to navigate and subvert patriarchal Christian social norms. For instance, women were excluded from church business meetings and were sometimes discouraged from creating their own societies and groups within churches.[21] Nonetheless, following the examples set by Jarena Lee and her contemporaries, Black women after Emancipation were indeed teaching and leading others in their church communities.

Black women preachers used feminist ideology as a tool to combat the opposition they encountered. In the years leading up to the Nineteenth Amendment, the discourse on gender equality spread from the political arena to the church. In that heightened political climate, a woman—much less a Black woman, and even less likely a Black woman outside the circles of the Black elite (or the "Talented Tenth," as upper-class Black people were called in the late nineteenth century)—seeking church leadership would have been an explicit political move, whether she intended it to be or not.[22]

---

21. Evelyn Brooks Higginbotham, *Righteous Discontent: The Women's Movement in the Black Baptist Church, 1880–1920* (Cambridge, MA: Harvard University Press, 1993), 120.

22. For some basic statistical data on the Black elite, see David McBride and Monroe H. Little, "The Afro-American Elite, 1930–1940: A Historical and Statistical Profile," *Phylon (1960–)* 42, no. 2 (1981): 105–119.

Negative sentiments and verbal disagreements from male counterparts were not the only thing Black female preachers faced within this political and religious context. Amid the tension surrounding gender rights, these women risked being ostracized from their communities, and they contended with threats to their safety. The path to religious leadership was not an easy one for most women. In the 1890s, Virginia Broughton, a Baptist leader in Tennessee, noted the intense opposition she and other Black women faced from male church leaders. As churchwomen began to organize and prophesy, some ministers locked their doors, denying the women spaces to speak. They were even faced with violence. Broughton writes that, "Dear Sister Nancy C. said, had not Sister Susan S. come to her rescue, she would have been badly beaten for attempting to hold a woman's meeting in her own church."[23] Furthermore, she gives an account of a woman whose husband pulled a gun on her, threatening to pull the trigger if she tried to attend a female-led Bible study meeting.[24]

The individuals who opposed female church leadership often supported their beliefs by a particular Bible verse, 1 Corinthians 14:34, which states, "Women should be silent in the churches. For they are not permitted to speak, but should be subordinate." A number of women countered the 1 Corinthians verse with one from Joel/Acts: "I will pour out my spirit on all flesh; your sons and your daughters shall prophesy" (Joel 2:28; Acts 2:17). The biblical debate doesn't end there. While Genesis 3:16 states that man shall rule over woman, chapters 4 and 5 of Judges recount the tale of Deborah, a successful prophetess and judge in ancient Israel.

If God stated in Joel that both sons *and* daughters would receive the Spirit and prophesy, then what do we make of the verse in Corinthians that mandates the silence of women, presumably whether they have received the Spirit or not? Mary Cook, who served as an officer in the American National Baptist Convention, asserted that 1 Corinthians 14:34 was addressed to certain women at the time who tainted the early church with glorification of pagan gods.[25] She considered the historical context of the verse, declaring that it was neither pertinent to the modern church nor

---

23. Virginia E. Walker Broughton, *Twenty Year's [sic] Experience of a Missionary* (Chicago: Pony Press, 1907), 84.

24. Ibid., 35.

25. Higginbotham, *Righteous Discontent*, 132.

applicable to all women.

Instead of dismantling the 1 Corinthians verse or the Bible as a whole, some women chose to focus on the aforementioned verse from Joel and Acts. Rosa A. Horn, a Pentecostal minister whose rise to fame began in the 1920s and 1930s, spoke about women's right to preach in her sermon entitled "Was a Woman Called to Preach? Yes!" on a New York City radio show. Horn used a wide range of Bible verses, including the Joel/Acts verse, to support her argument that God endorses female church leaders. "Time is almost out and millions and billions of souls are being lost," Horn urged. "Men, don't take time to fight the women. You need to use every moment of your life and all the breath that God gives you for the saving of precious souls."[26] This same sentiment is echoed in sermons of other Black American women preachers. I mention Black female preachers of this time period not to make a judgment on their theism or their steadfastness in fighting to gain leadership in an institution that did not value them, but to point out the ways that Black American women actively fought against discrimination on their own terms.

One way that women subverted sexism in the church was by developing social and professional networks of their own. In a more modern version of the mutual aid societies of the early nineteenth century, many urban Black women participated in service clubs, which were part of the National Association of Colored Women (NACW), founded in 1896. The NACW was a confederation of women's clubs whose aim was to lead and improve the race at a time when Jim Crow destroyed the country from within, and it was led by a group of dynamic women who devoted their lives to the belief that "a race could rise no higher than its women."[27] Much of the clubwomen's work included caring for orphans, building libraries, and volunteering in hospitals. The various groups of Black clubwomen were an important factor in the religious and political gender equality debates of the early twentieth century, and the NACW served to unite them in their battle against racism and sexism.[28]

---

26. Bettye Collier-Thomas, "Rosa A. Horn," *Daughters of Thunder: Black Women Preachers and Their Sermons, (1850–1979)* (San Francisco: Jossey-Bass, 1997), 173–183.

27. Deborah Gray White, *Too Heavy a Load: Black Women in Defense of Themselves, 1894–1994* (New York: W. W. Norton, 1999), 24.

28. Although the NACW devoted itself to community service, class divisions

Black clubwomen were highly critical of sexist church practices and were quite outspoken against the antics of Black male preachers. In *Too Heavy a Load*, Deborah Gray White explains that many clubwomen felt that most preachers "avoided hard work while living off the contributions of the more industrious." They were "corrupt," "ignorant," and "held the people back." One clubwoman said outright, "Preachers drank too much corn liquor, got girls pregnant, and often only came to the island [her home] to make money off the rural residents."[29] Black women were not monolithic in their relationship to Christianity. Some women sought to improve the lives of Black people from within the church, and others rejected the institution altogether in favor of more secular or intellectual organizations.

As Jim Crow laws strengthened their grip on the culture of the United States throughout the first half of the twentieth century, Black women's social activism employed themes such as faith and family to motivate their communities to work against lynching, voter discrimination, and other civil rights issues. Clubwomen and activists like Ida B. Wells, Mary McLeod Bethune, and their peers did not permit themselves to be silenced by sexist Christian norms.

Conclusion—Considering Black Women's Troubled Relationship to Christianity

According to the Pew Research Center's 2014 Religious Landscape Study, 53 percent of Black people in the United States identify as "Historically Black Protestant," a term that broadly defines traditional Protestant denominations in the Black American community, such as Baptist and AME.[30] With more than 50 percent falling into this one sect of Christianity, when we consider all other forms of Christianity as well, we can assume

---

plagued the relationship between Black clubwomen (who were often college educated and/or descendants of long-standing wealthy Black families) and the masses they tried to help. For information on Anna Julia Cooper, one of the leaders of the NACW, see Charles Lemert and Esme Bhan, eds., *The Voice of Anna Julia Cooper: Including a Voice from the South and Other Important Essays, Papers, and Letters* (New York: Rowman & Littlefield, 1998).

29. White, *Too Heavy a Load*, 73.

30. "Religious Landscape Study," Religion and Public Life, Pew Research Center, http://www.pewforum.org/religious-landscape-study/racial-and-ethnic-composition/black/.

that the percentage of Black American Christians is much higher. With the majority of Black Americans currently identifying as Christian as opposed to agnostic or atheist, it is obvious that faith remains important in the Black American community, but the demonstration of that faith has changed due to slavery. From the 1640s creation of the African Burial Ground to the early twentieth century, the formation of Black American religious life placed Black women in a difficult position. The church provided community, financial support, and tangible resources for education and civil rights advancements. But the violent sexism within religious spaces left much to be desired. Some women fought valiantly for equality in churches, while others dismissed church culture altogether. Playwright Lorraine Hansberry, actress Butterfly McQueen, and author Gwendolyn Brooks were Black women freethinkers who rejected traditional Christianity.

Hopefully, in the future, more scholars will conduct research on the ways that Black women rejected Christianity throughout United States history. Women have played a vital role in the growth of the Black Christian church; however, we could learn much about the ways that sexism functions in religious spaces through historical study of women on the margins of, and outside of, the institution. Did they leave the church to focus on deities with which they can identify? Or did they embrace atheism altogether? Perhaps, through new discoveries of archival materials and new analyses of historical records, we might learn that there has always been an undercurrent of rebellion against patriarchal Christianity in Black American culture. Perhaps this rebellion did not decline with the African Burial Ground or remain confined to isolated communities like the Gullah of the southeastern coast. In recent years, more Black American women are reconnecting to African religions, embracing ideas and practices like those preserved at the African Burial Ground.[31] I hope that, at the very least, this reconnection becomes strong enough that more people criticize and fight against patriarchy in Christian churches. All in all, the ideological complexities of Black American religion deserve considerations of gender and disbelief, particularly for the earlier half of United States history.

---

31. Yomi Adegoke, "'Jesus Hasn't Saved Us': The Young Black Women Returning to Ancestral Religions," Broadly, *Vice*, September 13, 2016, https://broadly.vice. com/en_us/article/bjgxx4/jesus-hasnt-saved-us-young-black-women-returning-ancestral-religions.

8

Black Women and Christianity in the United States:

A Historical Perspective, Part II
(Civil Rights Movement to the Present)

Deanna Adams

As my ancestors are free from slavery,
I am free from the slavery of religion.

—Butterfly McQueen[1]

As seen in the previous chapter, Black women in America have an intricate history involving their journey to Christianity. From predominantly West African societies to forced worship on plantations, perceived deliverance via the Civil War, and the disillusionment of the Jim Crow South and Redlined North, this journey has been filled with coercion and promises

---

1. https://ffrf.org/outreach/awards/freethought-heroine-award/item/11976-butterfly-mcqueen

that have yet to be truly filled. This essay will focus on the fight to gain true equality in the United States, and the failure of the Christian church to be the savior of Black women many thought it would become.

Civil Rights Era

The Civil Rights Movement presented another chance for Black people to advance post Civil War. Jim Crow laws were abolished in 1964. The Voting Rights Act of 1965 was also signed into law, giving African Americans a perceived avenue to equality. The Christian church undoubtedly assisted in some of these changes by offering meeting halls and training leaders with the necessary oratory skills to move audiences to action. However, due to current popular mythology and the romanticizing of the Civil Rights Movement, misconceptions about church involvement in the movement flourished. In *Through the Storm, Through the Night: A History of African American Christianity*, Paul Harvey writes:

> Black Christians empowered the post–World War II civil rights movement.... At the same time, movement activists held a conflicted relationship with churches. Whether because of indifference, fear, theological conservatism, or white coercion, many congregations and denominational institutions avoided involvement. Civil rights organizers gave them plenty of heat for their apparent apathy.[2]

Many churches wanted nothing to do with the burgeoning movement. Some felt their time would be better used focusing solely on the gospel. Some were actively afraid of retribution, manifested in church fires, bombings, and lynchings. Others believed their god would handle it, so they avoided the conflict all together.

When the church was instrumental in organizing, it could be a hindrance in regard to women's status as well as for people within the LGBTQ community, who often had to hide their sexuality or risk being relegated to the background. Women were often workhorses in the male-dominated movement, organizing without being able to hold leadership positions. Harvey goes on to say:

---

2. Paul Harvey, *Through the Storm, Through the Night: A History of African American Christianity* (Lanham, MD: Rowman and Littlefield, 2011), 109.

King and the male leaders of the Southern Christian Leadership Conference, the civil rights organization that emerged in 1957 after the Montgomery bus boycott as the primary instrument of King's civil rights leadership, garnered much of the media attention. However, behind their work lay the everyday efforts of generations of black churchwomen. Men led the civil rights movement in public, but women organized it behind the scenes.[3]

Black women were no more protected in the movement than Black men during this time. Six of the Little Rock Nine who integrated Little Rock Central High School in 1957 were girls. Claudette Colvin and Rosa Parks faced jail and violence for refusing to give up their seats on buses. Diane Nash, cofounder of the Student Nonviolent Coordinating Committee (SNCC), organized the highly effective but dangerous Freedom Rides throughout the South, which led to the integration of interstate bus travel. SNCC, with its focus on protest, marches, and voter registration, was initially organized by Ella Baker. Despite these contributions and more by Black women, not one was allowed to give a major speech at the 1963 March on Washington, though there was a brief tribute to "Negro Women Fighters for Freedom," led by Bayard Rustin with remarks by Daisy Bates. Surely much of the omission of women was due to the fact that many of the organizers were religious, and thus, accustomed to women playing support roles, as they did in most churches at that time.

The problems of women in the Civil Rights Movement were detailed and summarized in the "Student Nonviolent Coordinating Committee Position Paper: Women in the Movement," an anonymous paper written by a group of women in 1964 and submitted during a Waveland, Mississippi, SNCC meeting:

> The woman in SNCC is often in the same position as that token Negro hired in a corporation. The management thinks that it has done its bit. Yet, every day the Negro bears an atmosphere, attitudes and actions which are tinged with condescension and paternalism, the most telling of which are when he is not promoted as the equally or less skilled whites are.... This paper is presented anyway because it needs to be made know[n] that many women in the movement are not "happy and contented" with their status.

---

3. Ibid., 111–112.

It needs to be made known that much talent and experience are being wasted by this movement when women are not given jobs commensurate with their abilities. It needs to be known that just as Negroes were the crucial factor in the economy of the cotton South, so too in SNCC are women the crucial factor that keeps the movement running on a day-to-day basis. Yet they are not given equal say-so when it comes to day-to-day decisionmaking.[4]

Due to the prominence of self-professed Christian leaders like Rev. Martin Luther King Jr., we tend to believe the common myth that everyone found strength in their faith when there was nothing else to sustain them. But not all leaders of the Civil Rights Movement were Christian. Notable figures such as Ella Baker, Lorraine Hansberry, Bayard Rustin, and James Baldwin were openly nonreligious. In some cases, this lack of religious affiliation served to further relegate these figures to the background. James Baldwin, for example, was not permitted to speak at the March on Washington. Though not explicitly stated, some of the organizers believed him to be too radical or unpredictable. In *Baldwin's Harlem, a Biography of James Baldwin*, author Herb Boyd quotes Malcolm X: "They wouldn't let him talk because they couldn't make him go by the script...they wouldn't let Baldwin get up there because they know Baldwin is liable to say anything."[5]

Lorraine Hansberry, author of the acclaimed play *A Raisin in the Sun*, met with Robert Kennedy and others at Baldwin's request in 1963 to discuss racial issues of the time. During this meeting, she challenged Kennedy to listen to the voices of those who were on the front lines of the Civil Rights Movement, in particular one of the original Freedom Riders, who was in attendance. Hansberry famously left this meeting in frustration with Kennedy's lack of understanding. Previously, in a monologue widely accepted as autobiographical, the playwright spoke on her views of God through the character Beneatha:

---

4. "Student Nonviolent Coordinating Committee Position Paper: Women in the Movement" (paper submitted anonymously at a meeting of the SNCC in Waveland, MS, November 1964), Civil Rights Movement Veterans, http://www.crmvet.org/docs/snccfem.htm.

5. Herb Boyd, *Baldwin's Harlem: A Biography of James Baldwin* (New York: Atria, 2008), 70.

Mama, you don't understand. It's all a matter of ideas and God is just one idea I don't accept. It's not important. I am not going out and be immoral or commit crimes because I don't believe in God. I don't even think about it. It's just that I get tired of Him getting credit for all the things the human race achieves through its own stubborn effort. There simply is no blasted God—there is only Man—and it is *he* who makes miracles![6]

In an acknowledgement of the often-violent force of religion in Black households, this speech earns Beneatha a powerful slap across the face. This example of the repercussions of resisting religious conformity represented an ever-present threat that prevented more prominent Black activists from publicly asserting their lack of belief in the Christian God. With ministers and church officials serving as the face of the movement, it was highly unlikely that an openly atheist or even agnostic activist would be allowed to rise to prominence. Though many of the movement's leaders could be thought of as progressive, they weren't willing to risk the mistrust that would come from the masses they were trying to liberate. These masses were like Beneatha's mother, unwilling to even consider a world without a god to look to for strength.

For these everyday people, victory, in the form of the Civil Rights Act of 1964 and the Voting Rights Act of 1965, reinforced the idea that "God is with us." Though some would argue the victories celebrated were nothing more than small concessions leading to little systemic change, the hallmark legislation ushered in a period of transformation in the Black community. Black women, of course, were instrumental in and greatly affected by these changes.

1970s to Modern Day

The Black middle class, defined here as the percentage of African American families who have an annual household income from roughly $45,000 to $125,000 per year, grew substantially after the Civil Rights Movement. Many opportunities that had previously been closed to Blacks opened during this time period. Immediately after the civil rights laws were passed, overt racism in housing was outlawed, allowing many to purchase homes; educational opportunities opened, allowing many more to finish high

---

6. Lorraine Hansberry, *A Raisin in the Sun* (London: Samuel French, 1958), 39.

school and obtain higher-level degrees; and there was a shift from lower working class to middle class. Growth has been slow and barriers continue to exist, however, which creates confusion for those looking to participate in this apparent upward mobility. Many Black families began seeking an explanation for why they seemed to be unable to benefit from these gains, and sought to find ways to be included in this prosperous growth. This led many to turn to the prosperity gospel movement and megachurches. As Harvey writes:

> The civil rights movement opened opportunities for the growing black middle class, many of whom responded to a version of the black "prosperity gospel." The best known minister of this movement, Thomas Dexter (T.D.) Jakes, gained tremendous popularity with his novel *Woman, Thou Art Loosed*…. He preached a message of empowerment to black women who historically had been the backbone of the church.[7]

The prosperity gospel, in general, postulates that the Christian God wants his followers to be healthy and successful. He wants them to have businesses, own homes and cars, and live well. In order to do this, however, the followers must be faithful in their giving. Tithing, or giving one tenth of one's income, is demanded as a baseline for this faithfulness, with various extra gifts of money encouraged for extra favor, or blessings, from God. Most megachurch pastors, who have some of the highest rates of income in the clergy, preach this predatory message. Parishioners are asked to give and continue to give in order to receive. The idea of planting a seed when a need arises attaches the probability of answered prayers to the amount of money that can be sown with the petition.

In *Are You Ready? Nothing but the Blood of Jesus*, Jakes writes, "When God blesses you, not only will He bless you personally, but He will bless your family, your field, your crops, and your land. According to Deuteronomy 28, God will take you who used to be the tail and make you the head."[8]

Jakes certainly practices what he preaches. As the head of the over 30,000-member Potter's House Church, whose membership is mostly marginalized populations, the published author and producer oversees a

---

7. Harvey, *Through the Storm*, 126.

8. T. D. Jakes, *Are You Ready? Nothing but the Blood of Jesus* (Shippensburg, PA: Destiny Image, 2013), 6.

multimillion dollar empire and lives in the lap of luxury, in stark contrast to most of his congregants. Perhaps in an ironic acknowledgement of the unequal presence of women in minority churches, the Potter's House website states in the About section, "Men comprise 45% of the total congregation, which is unusually high for a mostly minority church."[9]

Black women have historically been the pillars of strength that hold the Black church together, and statistics show that they still are. While the Pew Research Center reports 87 percent of African Americans identified as religious in 2009, 62 percent of historically Black Protestants are women.[10] Furthermore, the center reports:

> African-American women also stand out for their high level of religious commitment. More than eight-in-ten black women (84%) say religion is very important to them, and roughly six-in-ten (59%) say they attend religious services at least once a week. No group of men or women from any other racial or ethnic background exhibits comparably high levels of religious observance.[11]

Even with this majority in the pews, women are rarely seen in church leadership roles. In a research study looking at social activism and gender inclusivity in the Black church, Sandra L. Barnes states that:

> Findings suggest that involvement in social activism does not necessarily correlate positively with support for women as pastors. Although frequent sermonic focus on Black Liberation and Womanist theology, and clergy involvement in protest efforts, engender such support, sermonic focus on general issues of racial justice actually undermine support for women in the pastorate.[12]

---

9. "About," The Potter's House, accessed August 21, 2017, http://thepottershouse. org/explore/about/.

10. Neha Sahgal and Greg Smith, "A Religious Portrait of African-Americans," Religion & Public Life, Pew Research Center, January 30, 2009, http://www. pewforum.org/2009/01/30/a-religious-portrait-of-african-americans/.

11. Ibid.

12. Sandra L. Barnes, "Whosoever Will Let Her Come: Social Activism and Gender Inclusivity in the Black Church," *Journal for the Scientific Study of Religion* 45, no. 3 (2006): 371–387.

Though there are more women in ministry today than in the past, the biblical teaching found in 1 Timothy 2:12 "I do not permit a woman to teach or to assume authority over a man; she must be quiet" (NIV) still hinders many women from leading congregations. They are able to cook, clean, teach small classes, and perform administrative tasks, but ascending to the role of senior pastor is elusive.

This second-class status persists even as Black women eclipse Black men in the area of education. Data from the US Census Bureau current population survey's 2016 Annual Social and Economic Supplement shows Black women with college degrees outnumber Black men at all levels above high school.[13] When taking the rate of educational attainment per noninstitutionalized population into account, 15 percent of Black women vs. 14 percent of Black men have attained a bachelor's degree, and 7.61 percent of Black women vs. 5.79 percent of Black men have attained a master's degree.

Unfortunately, the gains in educational status have not correlated to gains in financial independence. "Between 2004 and 2014, Black women's real median annual earnings for full-time, year-round work declined by 5.0 percent—more than three times as much as women's earnings overall."[14] While the reasons for this pay disparity are many, such as racism, sexism, and wage theft, this information begs the question: what is all of this church work profiting Black women in the short or long run?

Current Issues

In addition to educational and financial considerations, Black women today face a myriad of challenges in everyday life. From relationship struggles to social justice apathy, the historically Black Protestant Church in the United States sets Black women up to fail in many ways.

Many male church leaders, especially megachurch prosperity pastors,

---

13. "PINC-01. Selected Characteristics of People 15 Years and Over, by Total Money Income, Work Experience, Race, Hispanic Origin, and Sex," U.S. Census Bureau, last updated August 26, 2016, https://www.census.gov/data/tables/time-series/demo/income-poverty/cps-pinc/pinc-01.html.

14. Asha DuMontheir, "Black Women Are Among Those Who Saw the Largest Declines in Wages over the Last Decade," Institute for Women's Policy Research, August 22, 2016, https://iwpr.org/publications/black-women-are-among-those-who-saw-the-largest-declines-in-wages-over-the-last-decade/.

suggest women live a strict and holy life devoted to the church while they wait for the mate that God has sent for them. This "waiting for Boaz" mentality takes its cues from the biblical story of Ruth, who after becoming a widow, follows her mother-in-law Naomi to her native land. Boaz, a wealthy landowner, notices Ruth while she is working in his fields for food. Her mother-in-law encourages her to make herself available to him, and he eventually acquires her along with her mother-in-law's land. After this acquisition, they are wed and she begets a son in the lineage of David.

Prosperity pastors use this scripture to show that a woman's life can be substantially improved with the addition of a well-to-do man. The woman must be worthy, however, by being a hard worker, diligent, and chaste. Boaz took notice of Ruth because of her hardworking nature, and he rewarded her with marriage. When she lay at his feet as instructed by Naomi, he showed respect by not sleeping with her immediately, but instructing her on the next steps and telling her to wait until he met with the town elders. In essence, women must go about their daily lives, working hard in service to God at the church, and in service to their families at jobs and at home, and a wonderful man will appear when they least expect it. This wonderful man will respect her dutifulness and care for her, showing his dedication by securing her future.

In his book *Promises from God for Single Women*, T. D. Jakes writes:

> As a Christian woman, you have more important things to do than obsess about finding a mate. Don't worry. Know that God has someone or something waiting for you. Your only job is to fulfill God's purpose for you. You need to walk the path that He has laid before you, serve Him and only Him, and prepare yourself for all He has in store for you. Becoming too caught up in the dating/mating/relating game distracts you from your Heavenly calling and keeps you from the Lord.[15]

Unfortunately, this mentality leads to unreasonable expectations of men by women in the church. Heterosexual marriage is still an important goal of Christianity. Women under this teaching believe that they can go about their work obliviously and a mate will magically find them. While it is true that you never know when and where you will meet your significant other,

---

15. T. D. Jakes, *Promises from God for Single Women* (New York: Penguin, 2005), 4–5.

the odds of finding him in church when church membership is nearly 60 percent women are unfavorable. Add the desired qualities of financial success, spiritual health, and moral uprightness and we begin to see why so many women in this faith tradition struggle to find a suitable mate when one is desired. These thought processes also manifest in the pastor of the church becoming a surrogate husband until a suitable mate materializes. Women will go to him for advice on life decisions, model any potential mates after him, and in some cases, engage in sexual acts with him. When the pastor is put in this position, it is much easier for him to manipulate women further.

Of course, this phenomenon is not solely to blame for the state of Black women's marriage rates. It can be said, however, that this belief system is not helping the situation in the least. Current research shows:

> Racial and ethnic differences in marriage are striking. The median age at first marriage is roughly four years higher for black than for white women: 30 versus 26 years, respectively, in 2010. At all ages, black Americans display lower marriage rates than do other racial and ethnic groups. Consequently, a far lower proportion of black women have married at least once by age 40.[16]

Black women who marry experience less marital stability than most other racial groups.[17] Again, there are many reasons for this experience, but when devout Black women find themselves having marital difficulties, the first advice often given to them is to pray for their husbands and give the problem to God. Robust, secular mental health care practices are still shunned in much of the Black community, so any counseling that dysfunctional couples may seek out is likely to come from church leaders, if at all. Some of these church leaders give incredibly harmful advice to these couples, such as telling women to pray for their abusive husbands and wait for God to intervene, which can result in worsening of relations and escalation of abuse.

An analysis of women murdered by men in 2011 by the Violence Policy

---

16. R. Kelly Raley, Megan M. Sweeney, and Danielle Wondra, "The Growing Racial and Ethnic Divide in U.S. Marriage Patterns," *The Future of Children* 25, no. 2 (2015): 89–109.

17. Ibid.

Center yields some very sobering results for Black women in particular:

> In 2011, black females were murdered at a rate more than two and a half times higher than white females: 2.61 per 100,000 versus 0.99 per 100,000.... Compared to a black male, a black female is far more likely to be killed by her spouse, an intimate acquaintance, or a family member than by a stranger. Where the relationship could be determined, 94 percent of black females killed by males in single victim/single offender incidents knew their killers (415 out of 443). Nearly 15 times as many black females were murdered by a male they knew (415 victims) than were killed by male strangers (28 victims) in single victim/single offender incidents in 2011. Of black victims who knew their offenders, 52 percent (216 out of 415) were wives, common-law wives, ex-wives, or girlfriends of the offenders.[18]

Consequently, psychologically sound support for victims of domestic violence in historically Black churches is difficult to find. Men are regarded as the head of the household, and women are taught to submit to their husbands. Many women blame themselves for not being submissive enough or not praying correctly in an effort to correct the problems they experience. When this invariably doesn't work, women who try to escape may face social ostracism and a complete removal of what little support they have. Finding strength outside of the church may be the only way to save most of these women's lives.

Compounding Black women's difficulties when leaving abusive situations is the financial insecurity created by adhering to restrictive religious practices. Marriage ministries all over the country teach that a part of submission for women is to trust their husbands with finances. Even in modern families where both partners work, women are encouraged to commingle all funds to prove openness and faith. They are expected to give ten percent of their earnings to the church as a properly tithing family. Purchases should be discussed and agreed upon beforehand, and the woman may be given a small stipend for her daily needs. This hyperfocus on transparency puts women in a precarious situation daily, but especially when they need to rebuild after a failed marriage. Even women who earn

---

18. "When Men Murder Women: An Analysis of 2011 Homicide Data," Violence Policy Center, September 2013, http://www.vpc.org/studies/wmmw2013.pdf.

more than their husbands may find it difficult to save for an eventual divorce because all of her funds are either in joint accounts or under his control.

Unmarried women are financially harmed by many of these practices as well. In the prosperity gospel tradition, all church members are expected to tithe one tenth of their income, gross income in most cases. This is money that could go to savings or investment accounts, or even to pay off debt. Although Black women's wages are falling, they still faithfully donate to churches on a regular basis. Since their disposable income is lower than most other racial groups, Black women give a proportionately higher amount to charity, mostly in the form of church tithing and offering. Continuing this practice is devastating financially, especially when factoring in the lack of tangible benefit to doing so.

While donating to charity is certainly admirable, those who give to megachurches usually don't see the bulk of their donations used in the community. Findings from a 2016 survey of large churches shows:

- 98 percent of a church's total budget comes from congregational giving.

- 49 percent of total church budget goes to staffing costs.

- 54 percent of churches gave financial bonuses to the senior pastor in the last twelve months.

- 81 percent of churches say that knowledge about specific salaries is mostly limited to the board, a subcommittee of the board, or senior staff.

- For each $1 of annual increase in church-wide giving per attendee, the typical executive-level annual salary increases by $15.49.[19]

These findings demonstrate that at best, megachurches need to improve their financial transparency, and at worst, these houses of worship are nothing more than elaborate get-rich-quick schemes providing income for their charismatic leaders.

In regard to another current issue faced by Black Christian women, the overarching principle of letting go and letting God (handle your problems)

19. Warren Bird, "12 Salary Trends Every Church Leader Should Know: Executive Summary of the 2016 Large Church Salary Study," *Leadership Network*, September 26,,2016, http://leadnet.org/salary/.

creates a personal and socially apathetic individual who hesitates to fight for her own freedom or the freedom of her community. To be sure, many Black women are socially conscious and believe in activism, but the Christian tradition teaches them to first pray for changes instead of immediately getting involved. Once involved, much of that work is still done in the church, which leaves out groups that the church has historically shunned, such as the LGBTQ community.

At times, Black Christian women also become stagnant out of fear. They have been taught to seek God's approval in everything, so if they don't get an answer to their cries for help, they remain in unhealthy situations. Admonishments such as "One who is slow to anger is better than the mighty, and one whose temper is controlled than one who captures a city" (Proverbs 16:32) teach women to patiently wait for change instead of fighting for it. When tragedy strikes, Black women aren't allowed righteous anger or profound grief before they are told to forgive their enemies and let God handle the delivery of justice. Unfortunately in the United States, justice is rarely served when victims are Black.

When nine parishioners were murdered in a historically Black church in Charleston, South Carolina, in 2015, family members expressed forgiveness for the killer, even as he admitted to targeting them because of his hatred of Black people. In their faith tradition, forgiveness is essential. It is a requirement to be more like God, to be able to move forward and find peace in life. This simply does not work for many people, however. Rushing forgiveness hinders the hard work of emotional healing. It is extremely unfair to those who are not ready to forgive, as they now feel the initial pain in addition to the shame associated with their anger.

Finally, the piety of Black Christian women does not correlate positively with their health outcomes. It is widely reported that Black women experience disproportionately higher instances of most major diseases. Obesity, heart disease, diabetes, and depression are some of the ailments that Black women face more often than other races despite the church's suggestion that praying and tithing will be enough to ward off ailments and challenges if the Christian is pious enough.[20] Clearly, focusing on a closer walk with God and putting faith in his healing is not enough to overcome

20. "Health Disparities among African American Women," Movement Is Life, 2015, http://startmovingstartliving.com/wp-content/uploads/2014/04/MIL_HealthDisp AAW.pdf.

these very real medical issues. While there are many factors involved in these disparities, helping women feel empowered to help themselves must become a part of any plan to improve Black women's health overall.

In order for the modern Black woman to begin to heal from generations of religious zealotry, it is essential to be honest about the unhealthy relationships, abuse, and financial difficulties that are exacerbated by adherence to Christianity. Apathy for our health and social justice issues, especially those most concerning to Black women, must be addressed honestly within any plan to truly prosper.

Summary

As you can see, Christianity in particular has played a large role in how Black women navigate their lives in the United States. While there have undoubtedly been positive effects to this phenomenon, this belief system has also been incredibly harmful to women who are Black in particular, relegating them to accepting status as second-class citizens even while fighting oppression.

In a nonreligious state, we would have the freedom to use reason and logic in our fight against systemic racism and sexism. We will be free to make choices based on best outcomes, not on what we think an imaginary spirit would have us do. We will no longer continue to be shackled by the belief system our forebears were forced into—rather, we will move forward with clarity of thought and action.

9

Call for the Rise
of Nonreligious Latinas

Marilyn Deleija

*If we can just convince other people to get involved, this could make
some major changes in our society.*

—Dolores Huerta[1]

Born in Guatemala, daughter of an immigrant mother who came to the
United States and brought me at the age of three, I quickly found out that
life as a Latina American was going to be difficult. It is still tough to this
day. I was raised by a young single mother with the help of my maternal
grandparents. We were poor and did not have a lavish lifestyle. I grew
up like many other Hispanic children, trying to adjust to living in a new
country but also enjoying our family customs. We ate together as a family,
told stories of memories from Guatemala, listened to music, and genuinely
enjoyed each other's company. We were a regular family as far as I knew.

---

1. https://www.sdfoundation.org/news-events/sdf-news/interview-dolores-huerta-
discusses-grassroots-activism-and-weaving-movements/

Then I started school. That is where I noticed my family was very different. After every weekend, the classroom children would come back and talk about how their weekend went. Most would talk about going to church or church gatherings—weddings at churches, Sunday school, first communions, quinceañeras, and the list went on and on. Although I listened to their stories, I quickly realized I was spending my weekends quite differently—playing outside, exploring the backyard, studying nature, playing make-believe games, pretending to be a cook, and playing with my cousins. My grandfather had us reading books, reading the newspaper, and learning about history, science, animals, and music. In my household, we were encouraged to learn whatever we wanted to learn about. If we had questions, we were encouraged to look up the answers, research our questions, and come to a conclusion.

One question I asked my family at a very early age was why our family didn't go to church and why mostly everyone else did. That is when I figured out that we, as a family, were secular, had no religion, and rejected the idea of a god. At first I was dumbfounded, and then I wondered about my family's reasons for being secular. After all, if mostly everyone had a religion, why not us? Were we wrong? The kids at school would ask if I was scared of the devil, scared of going to hell, or having my family go to hell. At first I struggled to understand, and how can you defend yourself as a child from other children if you yourself don't know how to explain?

For these kinds of answers, I decided to talk to my grandpa. Our family's secular beliefs seemed to be rooted in him and his ideals, so I decided it was best to go to him to get some answers. What he told me was that he had an uncle who was actually very religious and was a missionary. He would go around town and to neighboring towns and villages in Guatemala to try to recruit people into joining his faith and church. He was a great man with good intentions, and he really had faith in what he believed in. One day after a church service, he went to one of the back rooms to try to talk to one of the church leaders, and he walked in on a handful of them sitting at a table. He noticed the donation plate in the center of the table and the members counting the money and splitting it into equal shares. My grandpa's uncle was shocked to see that the members were pocketing all the hard-earned money from the town and village people. That is when he realized that religion was a scam. That is when he realized that you do not need religion to be a good person and help your community. He vowed to never again help something that could quickly turn so corrupt and take advantage of people. He left religion and never looked back.

That story was impact enough for my grandpa to open up his mind and decide to teach his kids and the generations after to be nonreligious and freethinkers. This was the beginning of my family's emphasis on learning, and I learned to find the truth rather than believe fantastical stories. While the other kids were being told fairy tales about the Easter bunny, the tooth fairy, Santa Claus, ghosts, witches, and goblins, I was ten steps ahead. I knew the truth—that none of those exist and none of that is needed to appreciate life. I took the stories for what they were, just stories and myths.

The differences in how I was raised in contrast to my peers became more and more noticeable as I grew older, and as I gained life experiences, I came to see that I had an advantage over my peers. I realized that growing up secular as a Latina was going to be hard but also very rewarding in the end—this would be the reason I would succeed in life and overcome many tough situations.

Girls who grow up as Hispanic/Latina females have to deal with all kinds of negativity, from racism to sexism to being negatively stereotyped on a day-to-day basis, and religion does not help in overcoming any of it. And if it does not help, why keep it? Although being secular made me a minority among a minority, and there were challenges inherent in that, I ultimately found this to be valuable.

Religion, I believe, has reinforced negative and unrealistic stereotypes for Latina women, and that has affected us in politics, the economy, social situations, and education. Religion has kept us from moving forward in society and from breaking the culture barrier. Transcending these limitations is needed to move in a positive direction for the whole human race but more specifically, for Latina women.

From my point of view, I see religion affecting other Latinas in a negative way. While they might not see it at the moment because they are so invested in that lifestyle, I, as an outsider, have noticed many instances in which being religious did not help empower Latinas in building a positive future across all areas of life—from how religion affects people's perceptions of the world, to the limited roles women are allowed to pursue, to the brainwashing of young girls to behave a certain way, to Catholic guilt, to the lack of Hispanic representation in US politics, to limited education for young Latina women, to misguided sex education for Latina women, to damaged family and friend relationships, to financial ruin. I see religion as a pervasive threat to the Latino community in America. According to the Census Bureau, there are 56.6 million Latinos in the United States as of 2015.[2] According to the Center for Applied Research in the Apostolate at Georgetown University, 57 percent of adult Hispanics self-identify as Catholic—about 17 percent of the total population and growing.[3] With these statistics, we quickly realize that this affects many people.

I believe that religion, specifically Catholicism, can belittle Latina women, does not take them seriously, and influences women to settle for a mediocre life, all while they are being judged and treated as second-class humans. We see this in the gender roles the church enforces, the high percentage of unhealthy marriages, the frequency of disowned family members based on sexuality, and the very real glass ceiling that Latina women face.

Gender Roles

In the Catholic religion, women's roles are based on Mary, who is seen as the mother of the son of god, Jesus—the woman who miraculously got pregnant as a virgin and gave birth to the messiah. In the Catholic religion, Mary is depicted as the ultimate mother figure, full of purity, holiness, passivity, humility, and chastity. In Luke 1:26–35, we see Angel Gabriel explaining the situation to Mary about her future miracle child. She obediently listens to Gabriel's prophecy and follows through with god's plan. Again, she is depicted as passive, obedient, and just accepting of what is to come. Because she bears the miracle child and becomes the mother of Jesus, she is depicted as saintly and in a favorable light. I believe that if she had gone against the prophecy, she probably would have been seen in a different light altogether. In this same passage, Gabriel says Mary is "blessed among women" and "highly favored" because she is the chosen one who will be pregnant with Jesus. I think this is where religion latches on to a woman becoming saintly, lucky, and favored once she becomes a mother. The term "miracle of birth" that many people use seems to originate from that same passage.

---

2. https://www.census.gov/newsroom/facts-for-features/2016/cb16-ff16.html

3. http://cara.georgetown.edu/staff/webpages/Hispanic%20Catholic%20Fact%20Sheet.pdf

The problem is that the ideal that Mary represents is nearly impossible to live up to, especially in light of how much society has changed in the past two thousand years. With advancements in technology, knowledge, communication, science, and alternative life choices, in the modern world a pious mother is just one of the many roles in which a woman can be happy and seen in a favorable light. Think about this for a moment: Is your mother anywhere near a reflection of Mary? If the answer is no, you still might love her and respect her, right? When the world is filled with all kinds of women—from the childless who want to skip motherhood altogether, to women who have had abortions for unplanned pregnancies, to women who openly admit they love sex as a normal human function, to lesbian women who cannot biologically have children with their partners, and to women who do not like behaving saintly or holy—seeing the Virgin Mary as the ultimate role model is unrealistic for women in modern times. There are millions of different types of women, and not all should be a copy of one another like some dystopian *Stepford Wives* situation. The Virgin Mary stereotypes women into roles that some women do not care to be in. Women are strong and powerful, and we have minds of our own. We do not want to be boxed into one role, our value defined solely by our ability to mother, as the idolization of the Virgin Mary suggests.

The other strong woman featured in the Bible is Eve. Eve and Mary are contrasted, with Mary being the obedient and faithful one and Eve as the temptress and sinner. Eve is portrayed as the root of human sin, the bringer of a curse on all women after her, simply because she gave into temptation and ate a forbidden fruit. If the Virgin Mary is the ideal, what are the women who do not resemble her characteristics? According to the Bible, it would seem that they are Eve. Is the message that these women are not worthy of a good life? That they do not meet certain expectations? I believe that both Eve and Mary are judged unfairly. We, as women, understand that we are all different. In modern times, being different is praised. Knowledge is a beautiful thing. Not everyone lives the same, and not everyone has the same life goals.

For Latina women, the idolization of the Virgin Mary and the shaming of Eve create the foundation of Catholicism's edicts that passivity, motherhood, child rearing, and staying at home are the only respectable life choices. It's not uncommon to see women in this culture become mothers as young as ten to fourteen years old. Pew Research's 2012 survey ranks Hispanic women as having the highest percentage of first pregnancies under twenty among all groups in the United States.[4] I say this stereotype has been holding us back for generations, and as Latina women, we can do better.

Some of the most influential women in history were trailblazers who stepped out of these prescribed roles and cleared a path for future generations. In modern times, when we need strong, bold women stepping up for women's rights, children's rights, and family rights, do you still think the Virgin Mary qualities are necessary? Or do you think someone like Eve plays a better function in society? Women are not meant to be ruled over or forced to be quiet or passive. Women who played a major role in history, who fought for women's rights, did not stay home and let men take care of the problem. They were out there being strong, learning, reading books, gaining knowledge, and speaking up. Women like Elizabeth Cady Stanton, who had a leading role in the suffrage movement and criticized religion. Women like Margaret Sanger, who was one of the founders of Planned Parenthood and fought to make birth control readily available to women. Another woman was Simone de Beauvoir, who wrote about women being held back in history by the ongoing perception that being female was a deviation from the male norm. These women actually changed history and were crusaders and innovators for us. These are women to look up to and admire. Imagine if those women had been like Mary, had passively stayed home and done what they were told—the world would be a different place. The idolization of the Virgin Mary is an insult to these women who have fought for the feminist movement. All the Virgin Mary really did was give birth. Millions of women give birth, and many others do not want to give birth at all.

There are also many influential Latina women, freethinkers, who have fought and continue to fight hard every day for our rights. For example, Guatemalan Rigoberta Menchú, who was an activist who dedicated her time to help the world recognize Guatemalan indigenous rights and ran for president of Guatemala in 2007 and 2011. Then there is Dolores Huerta, who cofounded the National Farmworkers Association and fought for farmworkers' rights, helping them form a union and earning her a Presidential Medal of Freedom. There is also Ellen Ochoa, who was the first Latina astronaut and is now the director of the Johnson Space Center. These are just a few of the many influential Latina women helping the

---

4. "Births by Age and Race of Mother," Infoplease, https://www.infoplease.com/us/births/births-age-and-race-mother.

world become a better place, but I say we need more! We need amazing freethinking Latina role models influencing young Latina girls to fight alongside the great women in history. I say throw the idolization of Mary out the window and learn from women in history who have paved a way for the future generations.

Women's Familial Roles

Another limiting role that the Catholic religion puts on Latina women is that they should have many children, and this has created a cultural stereotype as well. Catholicism not only idolizes Mary as a mother but also does not condone birth control because it changes god's plan. Catholicism continues to try to overpower a woman's will, health, and life choices with this strict edict. I believe, though, that Latina women are growing conscious of the effects of multiple pregnancies and children on their personal lives, family structures, and finances. When you look at some facts, you see that the growth in the US Hispanic population has actually slowed down. Between 2007 and 2014, the US Hispanic population grew annually on average by 2.8 percent (its pace of growth has been an even slower 2.4 percent between 2010 and 2014).[5] This was down from a 4.4 percent growth rate between 2000 and 2007 and down from 5.8 percent annually in the 1990s. As a result, the Hispanic population, once the nation's fastest growing, has now slipped behind Asians (whose population grew at an average annual rate of 3.4 percent from 2007 to 2014) in its growth rate.[6]

Another way Catholicism becomes intrusive in the household, and in a women's lives, is by dictating what they can do and be involved in, in regard to roles in the family dynamic. Women are depicted as homemakers, having less education, and functioning nearly like a slave to their household. They are pressured into taking up the role of a traditional female as defined by Catholicism's gender roles. According to *Catholic Answers*, gender roles within a marriage are as follows:

---

5. Renee Stepler and Mark Hugo Lopez, "U.S. Latino Population Growth and Dispersion Has Slowed since Onset of the Great Recession," Hispanic Trends, Pew Research Center, September 8, 2016, http://www.pewhispanic.org/2016/09/08/latino-population-growth-and-dispersion-has-slowed-since-the-onset-of-the-great-recession/.

6. http://www.latimes.com/local/lanow/la-me-latino-asians-20160908-snap-story.html

The Catholic view is that men and women are equal in the sight of god. In marriage, each is to sacrifice himself or herself for the other. In marriage, they are to build a family together through cooperation with each other and mutual respect. There are differences in roles they naturally play. Women are more natural caregivers for children, and men more naturally work outside of home.[7]

In modern times, however, family roles do not have to be like that. Especially in Central and South America, women are often either the family's sole breadwinners or they have jobs they attend to while still maintaining their housework. The trend continues in the United States among many Latina women, who despite being told they should be stay-at-home moms, often work outside the home. The Catholic gender roles also completely disregard that men can have a wonderful paternal instinct and can be stay-at-home dads. They disregard women who do not have a motherly instinct and prefer to be the breadwinners. They insist that all women want to be caregivers and stay at home. This stops many Catholic women from wanting more in life and limits their education, careers, and even hobbies.

One Bible verse that is often quoted to support this belief is 1 Timothy 2:11–12: "Let a woman learn in silence with full submission. I permit no woman to teach or to have authority over a man; she is to keep silent." If this doesn't make you want to run away from Catholicism or religion, you need to reevaluate yourself. But this teaching is not just in ancient texts. The article "Liturgical Errors" states that "Catholic women have become political leaders, religious leaders, heads of corporations, and other organizations, even soldiers and law enforcement officers. Such is the teaching of our culture. But it is not a teaching of Christ."[8]

So the Bible tells us we are equal in the eyes of god, yet once we start taking roles over men, Catholic articles tell us our equality is no longer valid? Do you see the contradiction? Once women can potentially jail men, kill them in war, and have political and religious influence, our equality is no longer right in the eyes of Christ? But it is okay for men to have all that power? Not equal, not fair.

---

7. "What is the Catholic View of Women?" Q&A, Catholic Answers, August 4, 2011, https://www.catholic.com/qa/what-is-the-catholic-view-of-women.

8.. Ronald L. Conte Jr., "Proper Dress and Behavior for Catholic Women," *Catholic Planet*, http://www.catholicplanet.com/articles/article65.htm

To this day, the Catholic Church does not allow women to be priests. This is based on the belief that all priests are successors of Jesus's apostles, and because he appointed only men, this role is not open to women. Pope John Paul II, if there was any doubt, made it very clear in his letter of 1994 entitled "Apostolic Letter on Reserving Priestly Ordination to Men Alone" when he stated: "I declare that the Church has no authority whatsoever to confer priestly ordination on women and that this judgment is to be definitively held by all the Church's faithful."[9]

Catholicism has many rules, but with just this one, it has alienated half of its followers and has disempowered women from having leadership roles within its own community. This all stems from the idolization of the Virgin Mary and does not empower Latin American women. Any women who want to remain in the religion sacrifice the opportunity to be role models or leaders, as their only acceptable role is the submissive saint.

The core of this teaching is that men think they know what is best for women and what kind of roles women should have. We cannot be business owners, leaders of our community, or role models who empower other women. This has a deeply negative impact on modern society. This way of thinking no longer benefits society but instead sets it back and gives women many hurdles to overcome.

Despite these teachings, in reality, Catholic women do own businesses, are greatly involved in the community, take up political roles, and serve society in many positive ways. They teach at the college level, hold government positions, and make both male and female lives better. But the church does not see these as accomplishments because they are outside the role of the submissive woman. When society has changed so much, why continue to have such antiquated beliefs? It doesn't benefit us or anybody else.

Marriage Paradigms

Catholicism supposedly focuses on family and family values, and people wonder how that could be bad or damaging. Although Catholicism has some good intentions, there are many questionable ideals that have no

---

9. Pope John Paul II, "Ordinatio Sacerdotalis: Apostolic Letter on Reserving Priestly Ordination to Men Alone," *Eternal Word Television Network*, May 22, 1994, https://www.ewtn.com/library/papaldoc/jp2ordin.htm.

benefit to the modern family structure.

First, Catholicism abides by the male- and female-specific gender norms, which again, force the family structure to be just male-led households with the female supporting in the home. This sadly leaves out the LGBTQ community. According to the American Community Survey published by the US Census Bureau, in 2010 there were 594,000 same-sex-couple households, 115,000 with children.[10] These numbers will grow as society becomes more open-minded and accepting of the LGBTQ community. Catholic doctrine regarding men going to work and being the breadwinner and women staying home to take care of the household duties leaves out progressive couples with stay-at-home dads and breadwinning moms as well as gay and lesbian couples taking up both roles. If abiding by gender norms does not fit in your lifestyle, why continue to be judged for living in a way that works well for you? Who is the Catholic Church to tell you what is best for you and your loved ones? These antiquated gender norms of Catholicism cannot keep up with the ever-changing society and family dynamics. It is difficult enough to provide for our loved ones without religion specifically telling us what we are doing is wrong.

The second way that Catholicism ruins relationships is that child rearing is pushed upon the couple almost immediately upon marriage. Remember, it is god's plan to be fruitful and multiply. This can affect Latina women, whose whole worth is dependent on being a mother in our culture. This is downright insulting to many Latina women and Latino couples. It seems that Catholicism doesn't see past women's potential as incubators. While having children is a wonderful part of many people's lives, unfortunately many couples fall into the pressure of having children before they're ready, when they still have other goals and ambitions they wish they could spend their time on.

Outside of Catholicism, child-free households are on the rise as couples are skipping parenthood altogether. You can see where couples begin to have problems when religion has engrained into them the thinking that they must produce offspring. Many couples have decided to do many other things than to bow to religious peer pressure. They have decided to start their businesses, to work on getting their education, to focus on their health and fitness goals, and so on.

---

10. Daphne Lofquist, "Same-Sex Couple Households," U.S. Census Bureau, September 2011, https://www.census.gov/prod/2011pubs/acsbr10-03.pdf.

Times have changed so much that people no longer need big families to help them survive. In early human civilization, the more offspring a couple had had meant higher chances of the family as a unit living longer. More offspring meant more family members being able to help with food gathering, farmwork, housework, home building, and even providing more security against potential threats. As the world has evolved and progressed, though, we no longer live in a time where we need to have six or seven kids to have a successful home. Latinas should not feel guilty for having few kids or none at all. Women do not need to have children, and a couple with no children *is* considered a full family. Again, none of that peer pressure is on our shoulders when we do not have religion breathing down our backs, making us feel guilty for not having children.

Another limiting belief imposed on families is that Catholics are expected to marry other Catholics. How absurd is it to think that out of billions of people on earth, the love of your life will be the same religion as you? Young boys and girls are raised going to classes every weekend, and some weeknights, to prepare them in the Catholic tradition so that later they can go through with their first communion, then their confirmation, and eventually a Catholic marriage. Instead of letting them be children, having them explore and play and learn, they are told that if they do not go through these classes, their marriage will not be recognized by the church or by god.

This brings forth various assumptions about young people, and it teaches them limiting beliefs. First, it assumes that children want to get married eventually. Second, it assumes that they want to get married in a Catholic setting. Third, it assumes they will marry the opposite sex, and fourth, it assumes they will also find Catholic partners. Finally, it is put in the children's brains that they can only date Catholics, leaving out so much of the future potential dating pool. If they decide they do want to marry someone who is not Catholic, the spouse will have to convert. That is basically saying, "If you want to marry me, leave what you are and what you represent to conform and believe in what I do." This teaches children to be closed-minded in a world full of diversity, and for their spouses, having to mold themselves just to get married is beyond degrading. Not only do they have to leave their prior beliefs and customs, but they also have to change their identity because they are not good enough for Catholics until they become part of the flock.

Divorce

Another aspect I find disturbing is the topic of divorce and the fact that Catholic women are judged harshly for supposedly not trying hard enough to make their marriages last. I speak of this because it is very important to talk about the negative connotation Catholics give divorce. When a woman has been married more than once, she is seen and judged very harshly, as if there is something wrong with her. Many women endure very abusive behavior to avoid the stigma of being a divorced woman. Catholicism pressures unity no matter what, even through abuse. Spanish Archbishop Braulio Rodriguez stated that "the majority of cases of domestic violence happen because the woman's partner does not accept them, or rejects them for not accepting their demands."[11] This way of thinking blames victims and can lead to long-lasting abusive relationships, and the abuse can occur on every level: mentally, emotionally, financially, and physically. Instead of building women up, the religion blames victims and guilts women into staying, making women feel they themselves are in the wrong because of what is expected in their religious customs.

Since Catholicism is a denomination of Christianity, there are many similarities between them. You can find many articles like the information stated above where both non-Catholic pastors and Catholic priests come to the same conclusion about divorce. While the statistics I'll list next are about non-Catholics, I am extrapolating meaning for Catholicism to give a full picture of how divorce is stigmatized.

One mid-1980s survey of 5,700 pastors found that 26 percent of pastors would tell a woman being abused that she should continue to submit and to trust—telling her that god would honor her action by either stopping the abuse or giving her the strength to endure it.[12] Furthermore, 71 percent of pastors would never advise a battered wife to leave her husband because of abuse. Those results are scary and downright horrible.

While I personally do think people should be taught to work out

---

11. Michael Stone, "Catholic Archbishop Blames Disobedient Wives for Domestic Violence," *Progressive Secular Humanist* (blog), *Patheos*, January 8, 2016, http://www.patheos.com/blogs/progressivesecularhumanist/2016/01/catholic-archbishop-blames-disobedient-wives-for-domestic-violence/.

12. "Christianity and Domestic Violence," *Wikipedia*, last updated July 29, 2017, https://en.wikipedia.org/wiki/Christianity_and_domestic_violence#cite_note-christianitytoday-15.

issues in a mature way and leave the option of divorce as absolutely the last option, there are limits, and a woman in an abusive relationship with a husband who will not change is beyond one of those limits. We as a community, particularly a Latino community, should stop that stigma of failed marriage when lives depend on leaving and getting a divorce. We should learn that it is okay to accept when something is not working out and to move on. Why endure years of abuse? Why continue to be battered mentally and physically because of an outdated religion and tradition?

Divorce rates among married Catholic and Christian families range anywhere from 21 percent to 29 percent, while atheist or secular divorce rates were much lower.[13] This means that not only are secular couples less likely to get divorced, but religion is not needed to have a beautiful, healthy relationship.

Familial Excommunication

Still along the lines of the familial unit, I find it disturbing that some Catholics have disowned their family members for not believing the same as they do. According to Wikipedia:

> Homosexuality is addressed in Catholic moral theology under two forms: homosexual orientation is considered an "objective disorder" because Catholicism views it as being "ordered toward an intrinsic moral evil," but not sinful unless acted upon. Homosexual sexual activity, by contrast, is viewed as a "moral disorder" and "homosexual acts" are viewed as "contrary to the natural law. They close the sexual act to the gift of life. They do not proceed from a genuine affective and sexual complementarity."[14]

It continues to state, "The Catholic Church teaches that marriage can be made only between a man and a woman, and opposes introduction of both civil and religious same-sex marriage. The church holds that same-sex unions are an unfavorable environment for children and that the legalization of such unions is harmful to society."

That judgment, to me, fails the family unit. For example, if your son

---

13. http://www.religioustolerance.org/chr_dira.htm

14. As quoted in "Homosexuality and the Catholic Church," *Wikipedia*, https://en.wikipedia.org/wiki/Homosexuality_and_the_Catholic_Church.

or daughter comes out as homosexual, many people say it is a sin and an abomination, and they use their religious beliefs to validate their hateful and dangerous thinking. A 2013 report by the UCLA Williams Institute found that 1.4 million, or 4.3 percent, of US Hispanic adults identify as LGBTQ.[15] When 48 percent of the US Hispanic community is Catholic and believes that homosexuality is a sin, the odds are high that many of these LGTBQ adults' families and communities are guilting or even punishing them for who they love.

When a son or daughter comes out to their family, that is when they need the most love and support, but most do not get that. Instead they are banished from their families and shamed, and often their resources are cut off as well. Where is the family love and unity in that? Instead of preaching for families to love and support their kids, Catholicism separates many families and destroys what could be healthy family ties.

Catholic Guilt

"Catholic guilt" is an expression used to identify the reported excess guilt felt by Catholics or lapsed Catholics. It ties in with Catholic childhood religious indoctrination, in which children are taught at a young age that they are worthy of god's love only through divine grace. Catholic guilt has many lifelong consequences. Catholic guilt can occur when a person who was raised Catholic engages in behavior that the church has declared to be wrong or sinful. It is often identified with sins related to sexuality, such as premarital sex, extramarital sex, masturbation, homosexuality, abortion, and the use of birth control. Other sins for Catholic guilt also include divorce, not going to church, and interfaith marriage. In modern society, most of these so-called sins are seen as normal and not even taboo anymore, but the church still imposes guilt for them.

Catholic guilt has many lifelong consequences. Catholic children can grow up to be self-loathing adults. Some symptoms of people with Catholic guilt, according to Megan Brackeen, a lapsed Catholic and writer for the *Odyssey*, include: "You grow up to be a chronic people pleaser," "The idea

---

15. Laura Rodriguez and Brenda Arredondo, "New Report: Estimated 1.4 Million Latino/a Adults in the U.S. Identify as LGBT," Williams Institute, UCLA School of Law, press release, October 2, 2013, https://williamsinstitute.law.ucla.edu/press/press-releases/new-report-estimated-1-4-million-latinoa-adults-in-the-u-s-identify-as-lgbt/.

of skipping church gives you a mental breakdown," "You apologize a lot," and "When something bad happens to you, you can't help but think you're being punished for not praying."[16] All these symptoms can really affect Latin American women. Add Virgin Mary idolization and forced gender roles to the Catholic guilt, and you have a recipe for young repressed Latin American women who never feel good enough about themselves, lack confidence and self-esteem, and lack the ability to stand up for themselves and say *no* to people interfering in their choices. This can cause years of mental and emotional instability, which is difficult to repair.

Lack of Political Power

Taking a look at Catholicism's influence on women outside the home now, Latina women growing up Catholic are less likely to pursue or achieve political power. Not only are there few women representatives in government in the United States, but there are drastically fewer Latin American women in government seats and even fewer Latin American Catholic women in government seats. Latinas Represent cites current statistics regarding Latina women in elected governmental positions: "Catherine Cortez Masto took the oath of office in 2017 as the first Latina senator," "Only 14 Latinas have ever served in the United States Congress," and "Of the 1,972 seats in the state senates throughout the U.S., only 23 are held by Latinas."[17] Some of these Latinas consider themselves Catholic. These are very disappointing figures in representation, but not surprising.

If Catholic Latina girls are taught to be submissive—which by extension means not to be involved in politics—are told that leadership is a man's job, and are instructed to focus on other roles that would supposedly be better fitting for their gender rather than trying to bring about change, do you think they will strive to be leaders in the community, let alone leaders in politics? This lack of governmental representation contributes to the cycle of Latina women being pushed into submissive roles, being paid less, and not being treated equally in church or society. With Donald Trump in the White House leading by example of misogyny and xenophobia, I predict these numbers of Latina politicians will stay stagnant or even drop.

---

16. Megan Brackeen, "11 Signs You Have Catholic Guilt," *Odyssey*, March 14, 2016, https://www.theodysseyonline.com/12-signs-you-have-catholic-guilt.

17. "Get Informed," LatinasRepresent, https://latinasrepresent.org/get-informed.

I have pondered this many times, and I still do not understand why women do not try to vie for these important seats. While there are currently twelve countries whose leaders are women, the United States still has not had a woman president, let alone a minority woman president, let alone a Latina woman president. While other countries around the world have had their first woman leader or president decades ago, the United States is far behind. The more secular the country is, the more women are represented in government and are leaders in their communities. Even some South American countries—nations that are often considered highly religious and conservative—have already had their first woman leader. The United states was left behind in the 1950s.

Not only do women need more representation in the United States government, but Latin American women specifically need more representation. Even as the Hispanic population grows more each day, Latin American issues are left on the back burner when it comes to government.

Does this go back to young ladies being brainwashed into thinking their only goal is to reproduce and take care of the household? Does this go back to young ladies being told politics is a man's world and it is too difficult for women, that they should do stick to home-related tasks that "naturally" come to them? Right now in politics, not only do women need to stand up for themselves and be represented, but especially Latin American women need to stand up and take community and government roles to help one another.

It is interesting that as our society adopts progressive ideals, more and more Latinos are getting on board, even while a majority of Latinos are still Catholic and the progressive ideals do not align with Catholic teachings. Pew Research Center found that, "among Hispanic Democrats, 39% described their political views as moderate, 35% as liberal and 24% as conservative" in 2016.[18] Issues like a woman's right to choose, health care, immigration, social justice issues, and social welfare issues are all concerns for Hispanic Americans. According to Pew Research Center and National Election Pool exit poll data, 66 percent of the Latino population voted in very high numbers for Hillary Clinton, and more specifically 68 percent of

---

18. Rob Suls and Jocelyn Kiley, "Democratic Voters Increasingly Embrace the 'Liberal' Label—Especially Whites, Millennials, and Postgrads," FacTank, Pew Research Center, February 9, 2016, http://www.pewresearch.org/fact-tank/2016/02/09/democratic-voters-increasingly-embrace-liberal-label/.

Latina women voted for Hillary. You start to see a contradiction between Hispanics' faith and what we actually support when it is time to vote in this country.

So why do Latina women continue to hold on to their outdated religious beliefs when they don't vote with the same antiquated beliefs in mind? Does it go back to Catholic guilt? Not being able to let go of that old-fashioned way of thinking and fully move forward with what society has become? All these issues are worth thinking about and should not be taken lightly. Politics affect many people, but mostly the minorities. When a religion holds us back from making progress, it is time to let that religion go, for the betterment of the community and the entire country.

Glass Ceiling

The oppression of Latina Catholic women goes beyond the lack of women in leadership roles and politics. Catholicism affects Latina women's earning potential. According to recent research, Latinas own about one in ten women-owned businesses.[19] Latina women make 54 cents to the dollar when compared to White, non-Hispanic males. In comparison, white women make 78 cents to the same dollar. Latina women earn $549 per week compared to median earnings of $718 for white women. According to the US Bureau of Labor, 32.2 percent of Latina women work in the service sector, compared to only 20.5 percent of white women. From 2007 to 2012, the amount of Latina women earning at or below minimum wage more than tripled. Poverty rates for Latina women are at 27.9 percent and are close to triple those of white women at 10.8 percent. Compare this to white male counterparts, and it quickly gets even more depressing.

Some people try to dismiss these statistics as simply racial inequality and not religion affecting us directly. However, in a Pew Research Center report concerning the demographics of Catholics and atheists, Catholics are more likely than other Americans to be Hispanic (34 percent), and atheists are more likely than other Americans to be white (78 percent). So as you can see, religion—more specifically Catholic affiliation—does play

---

19. Mareshah Jackson, "Fact Sheet: The State of Latinas in the United States," Center for American Progress, November 7, 2013, https://www.americanprogress. org/issues/race/reports/2013/11/07/79167/fact-sheet-the-state-of-latinas-in-the-united-states/. The same source was used for the rest of the income data for Latina women in this paragraph.

a major role in income inequality, and it negatively affects the Hispanic population.

Some people will also say that this discrepancy can be explained by different education levels, and they are partially right—the income level mirrors the education level. Unfortunately, according to a Pew Research Center article, growing up Catholic affects Latina women's education levels, so again, religion plays a major role, and that is downright scary. Only 16 percent of Catholics have completed college, as compared to 26 percent of atheists.[20] Latina women do not fare as well as white women in education. The Department of Education in a recent study concluded: "Latinas graduate from high school at lower rates than any major subgroup; more than one in five has not completed high school by age 29. Latinas are also the least likely of all women to complete a college degree."[21]

So when you see that only 16 percent of Catholics complete college as compared to higher rates among nonreligious people or even those from other religions, it should be seen as a red flag and raise much interest as to why this statistic is very low. Even more concern should be shown because it directly affects the Catholic women in the Latino community.

When Latinas do earn degrees, they are most often associated with the service industry, like nursing, business, and so forth. While there is nothing wrong with getting these types of degrees, there is a bigger need in the science and engineering arenas. Does this trend to serve go back to Latina women being told they are natural caregivers, or that science and technology are for men? I am here to tell young Latinas to join us in molding the future. Get into the science and technology fields. Let us not fall into the same stereotypes that we are trying so hard to break away from. We are well worth a $100,000 income and more. We must try to leave the antiquated way of thinking and jump into these fields where so much advancement can be made.

With that being said, there are plenty of Latina women who do

---

20. "Chapter 3: Demographic Profiles of Religious Groups," Religion & Public Life, Pew Research Center, May 12, 2015, http://www.pewforum.org/2015/05/12/chapter-3-demographic-profiles-of-religious-groups/.

21. Patricia Gándara, "Fulfilling America's Future: Latinas in the U.S., 2015," White House Initiative on Educational Excellence for Hispanics, https://sites.ed.gov/hispanic-initiative/files/2015/09/Fulfilling-Americas-Future-Latinas-in-the-U.S.-2015-Final-Report.pdf.

overcome this educational barrier and do achieve degrees and build careers in science and technology. They do become high-earning professionals who are respected in the community for being very skilled in their field. These Latinas still experience another form of setback, not only for being women but also because of religious people giving their credit to a god that had nothing to do with their success. As an all-too-common example, let's say a young Latina gets her medical degree and starts a job saving lives or helping people live longer. She's treating a patient who makes an incredible recovery. In a highly religious community, that patient is likely to thank *god* for the recovery. Do you realize how many years of education, struggle, statistics, stereotypes, and obstacles this young Latina had to face just to be dismissed by this patient who says, "God played a great role." Do you realize how degrading that could be? How with one sentence the patient blows all her struggle and hard work away with thanks to an invisible, made-up deity? It's disrespectful to say the least, and it sadly seems that Latinas cannot win in a society like that.

The Cycle

All these concerns about income, professional level, role within the home, number of children, and lack of leadership in society are interconnected in a vicious cycle, and the undercurrent is lack of education, as evidenced in the topic of sex education. It is all tied together and affects people's livelihood. In its 2009 study "Family, Fertility, Sexual Behaviors and Attitudes," Pew Research Center determined that by nineteen years of age, 26 percent of Latina young women have had their first child already.[22] Furthermore:

> In the United States, not only do Latinos have children at younger ages than non-Latinos, they also marry at younger ages. Some 15% of Latinos ages 16 to 25 are married, compared with 9% of non-Latinos in that age group. What was also concluded was that nearly seven-in-ten Latino youths (69%) say that teen parenthood hinders the ability to achieve one's life goals.

---

22. "Between Two Worlds: How Young Latinos Come of Age in America; VIII. Family, Fertility, Sexual Behaviors and Attitudes," Hispanic Trends, Pew Research Center, December 11, 2009, http://www.pewhispanic.org/2009/12/11/viii-family-fertility-sexual-behaviors-and-attitudes/.

Included in this study, researchers found that despite sharp declines in overall pregnancy rates in America in recent decades, pregnancy rates remain relatively high among Hispanic teens. In 2005, almost 129 of every 1,000 Hispanic females ages fifteen to nineteen experienced a pregnancy. In comparison, the number of similarly aged females in the general population experiencing pregnancies was almost half that. Given these statistics, we can see why it would be hard to obtain a degree and make more money as a Latina. If you are busy taking care of a household and raising your kids, it can be difficult—but still possible—to advance in that aspect. However, over decades, these percentages have been declining as younger generations change and stray from the antiquated beliefs and customs of the older generations. Latina women are becoming more informed and are taking charge of their situations—hopefully this will continue to counteract the percentage of young pregnancies and the related rates of limited education and low career advancement.

This goes back to learning about birth control, how to prevent unwanted pregnancies, and having sex education available. In Catholic schools, most of these basic choices are not taught. So imagine a young Catholic girl not being taught pregnancy prevention. Her sex education is limited to abstinence and guilt about sexuality. Imagine how much harm is done to her by withholding true sex education and how much society is also affected. This is something that Catholicism has wrong and has had wrong for a very long time. The religion is for life and preserving life, but it does not teach anything in preventing unwanted pregnancies. Many of these girls are forced to go through with unwanted pregnancies that they are not ready for mentally, financially, or emotionally. How is any of this healthy for the mind of a young Latina woman? From the beginning, she is set back because of her exposure to limiting beliefs in Catholicism.

Now imagine a young, Catholic, Latina mother with no higher education trying to join the work force. She would have to compete with other people who have higher education and experience—but how can she rival that? She would have to fall back on low-paying jobs that do not require much skill in order to just be part of the workforce so she can provide for a family that her religion guilted her into having. Again, it all ties together. Keep all of this in mind.

Taking it a step further, in Latin American culture, many people get married and have kids at a young age. Those who do not do this by twenty-seven at the latest are seen as old maids, for lack of a better term. In reality, at twenty-seven years of age, most people are barely getting situated in adulthood. How are you supposed to graduate, go to college, get your degree, get a good job, find the love of your life, have children, and so on by such a young age? The truth is, the highest cultural priority among these women is starting a family—lowest is college and degrees. Despite the goals many young Latinos may set for themselves, the majority, especially young women, cave to social and religious pressure and do not accomplish their education and career goals. Latinas, especially Catholic Latinas, have to overcome obstacle after obstacle just to have a chance at a well-rounded and fulfilling life.

But it doesn't have to be this way. The solution to these types of problems already exists: let go of outdated religious and cultural beliefs.

Hope in a New Generation

This leads me to my final thoughts on what we as a society can look forward to. Many studies and surveys have been done among the Latino community in regard to religion and religious preferences. The studies show that most of the younger generation is abandoning old-fashioned beliefs and customs, and moving toward becoming secular, atheist, or agnostic. Most of them are running in droves from Catholicism as they realize that it does not fit in with what the world has become. We are starting to see whole countries with irreligion being the lead affiliation. A Wikipedia article on irreligion, in forms of secular humanism (human beings are capable of being ethical and moral without religion or god), freethought (positions regarding truth should be formed on the basis of logic, reason, and empiricism, rather than tradition, revelation, or other dogma), spiritual but nonreligious (takes issue with organized religion as the sole or most valuable means of furthering spiritual growth), theological noncognitivism (argument that religious language, specifically words such as "God" are not cognitively meaningful), and antireligion (opposition to religion of any kind) names a few countries with a high percentage of the population identifying as irreligious.[23] Countries like Estonia are at 70.4 percent, Netherlands at 68 percent, and Czech Republic at 67.8 percent. Alison Lesley, writing for *World Religion News*, states that Catholics are on the decline in Latin

---

23. https://en.m.wikipedia.org/wiki/irreligion

America as the population turns to atheism.[24] The Pew Research poll she reports on states that in the 1970s, 92 percent of Latin American countries identified as Catholic, which has now dropped to 69 percent. Studies have shown a wide awakening among younger generations, and people living wonderful, fulfilling lives without the influence of religion or a god.

Today, we find healthy, loving communities forming and growing. We are starting to see online communities like the Secular Latino Alliance Facebook page gaining momentum with about two thousand people. In this forum, members post about daily struggles that the secular, nonreligious Latino community has to endure. Most of the time they are there to support each other through living without religion in a religion-based culture. We also see Facebook pages like the Friendly Atheist, the Thinking Atheist, and Atheist Republic, where everyone and anyone is encouraged to join and express themselves without being judged. Outside of social media, we have started seeing secular, atheist, and freethinking organizations on the rise. Organizations like the American Atheists, the Richard Dawkins Foundation for Reason and Science, the Freedom from Religion Foundation, and the Secular Student Alliance, among many others. And the changes can even be seen on a global scale. In Latin American countries, we have the Brazilian Association of Atheists and Agnostics (ATEA), Atheist Alliance International, and International Humanist and Ethical Union.

I believe that over time, this way of thinking will outgrow any religion and Latina women will thrive, but change of this magnitude takes time and knowledge. While it is helpful that younger generations are embracing progress, we also need older generations to awaken to the needs of the movement and teach knowledge, truth, and reason to break the cycle of Latina oppression. It takes strength to understand that religion is not only a sickness and a delusion but also that it is no longer beneficial to Latina women of the modern world. And it takes courage to step up and fight the cruel cycle so Latina women—and society overall—can flourish.

---

24. http://www.worldreligionnews.com/religion-news/christianity/catholics-are-on-the-decline-in-latin-america-as-the-population-turns-to-atheism/amp.

10

Why Hispanic Women Should Abandon Religion

Hypatia Alexandria

*All formal dogmatic religions are fallacious and must never be
accepted by self-respecting persons as final.*

—Hypatia of Alexandria (born c. 350–370, died 415 CE)[1]

Author's Note: The terms *Latino* and *Hispanic* are used interchangeably in
this essay, and most of us, Hispanics, use them equally. The short explanation
that one is typically used on the West Coast and the other in the East Coast
is not widely confirmed or supported by most Latinos. Neither is the notion
that these terms are based on geography or language. I am Latina; thus, I
am qualified to retain the definition that I determine is more applicable to
us in the United States. I am not going to endorse a definition that non-
Latinos want to impose on us because they feel they have the authority

1. Hypatia Quotes, BrainyQuote.com, Xplore Inc, 2017, https://www.brainyquote.com/quotes/quotes/h/hypatia414122.html.

and knowledge to define us while dismissing a very important fact—the complexity of such a diverse community that has as many characteristics that unite it as those that fracture it. There are constant efforts by some non-Hispanics to come up with their own definitions of what and who we are and impose it on our community. If defining us were that easy, we would be a minority with a more solid and visible political and financial capital. Thus, I will use both nouns equally throughout this essay, and those of us who have a preference should embrace it and continue focusing on the main subject rather than on the definition of two words.

Many Hispanic women's lives are negatively affected by the culture's influences from the Spanish conquistadors and the Catholicism they brought with them, even to this day. Could these women benefit from leaving religion? The answer is a complex one rooted in a deep history of colonialism, racism, and misogyny, and the effects reach every aspect of Hispanic women's lives today, from gender roles in the family to lack of political representation and everything between.

Allow me to start with the arrival of the Spanish conquistadors to the Americas in 1519. They came looking for gold and used their affinity for fighting to subdue the native populations. During the next twenty years, settlers and administrators from Spain quickly replaced them in their authority roles and instituted governments among the colonies. Meanwhile a tiered relationship between the Spaniards and what they called the "Indian slaves" started to develop. The conquistadors began to establish a new colonial order that guaranteed their supremacy and also maintained ties to their homeland in the areas of economy, religion, politics, society, and culture. These colonial societies were extremely hierarchical and rigid, particularly in relation to the social mobility of persons of mixed races, persons of African ancestry, and Amerindians—the ancestors of today's Latinos.

Social status, honor, and wealth were assigned at birth, with the most powerful Christian settlers at the top, non-European men lower, and non-European women at the bottom. Changing such a hierarchy threatened god's natural order, according to Spanish settlers. But people could help themselves be in god's favor if they were believers. To that end, church officials started a crusade to incorporate the Amerindian population into the social order by converting them to the "true faith," Catholicism.

By the seventeenth century, religion and societal ranks had become more entrenched in the colonized territories. Colonial elites maintained control over the masses by instilling the belief that all social classes and sexes were connected in a hierarchical configuration predestined by god. The widespread belief that inequality was the natural order allowed elites to dominate the masses, and men to control women. The Catholic Church legitimized this credence by linking it to the will of god. Local populations repeatedly adopted these values of European culture superiority and the subservience of women to men. This is how the mental reshaping of the Amerindian population started, and it has held a persistent grip on Hispanic culture over the generations and centuries since. It has caused profound oppression to this day in Hispanic communities around the world, particularly for those of us who are Latino women. This essay will take a look at many of those areas of oppression apparent in the United States and then discuss a call for change.

Submissive Mentality

Among the many ideals religion teaches is that one shows respect by being submissive and not by questioning or challenging authority, opinions, or ideas. Thus, many Hispanics confuse having an opinion or disagreeing with other peoples' ideas with being aggressive. Our conforming mentality is one of the reasons we do not yet find ourselves in a place of progressive thinking that other minorities in the United States have either already achieved or are approaching faster than our community.

Since the conquistadors arrived in the Americas, Hispanics have been told that our place in life is predetermined at birth and linked to god's divine order. This teaching definitively restricts questioning religion, social status, and culture, preventing many of us from thinking critically about our barriers and working to move forward in society. Thus, it is important for the Hispanic community to retrain our way of thinking and accept that people, opinions, and ideas are constantly evolving—and we can too. The lack of critical thinking and the fear to question culture, religion, birth rights, and social status is common in the typical Hispanic community.

Being an ethnic minority in the United States comes with a set of intrinsic disadvantages in comparison to the general population. That begs the question, why do Hispanics continue to carry such archaic beliefs when getting rid of them could allow us to embrace equality and opportunity?

Our ancestors did not discuss the colonial hierarchy early in the process of independence from Spain. Their religion taught them not to question what they were told, but perhaps if they had, we would have already gotten rid of the tiers and would now be enjoying equality. Sooner rather than later, we should deal with this unwillingness to talk, this religion-based fear of questioning opinions and ideas. We should discuss these issues and stop pretending they do not exist.

As humans, we do not want to hear the truth if it goes against what we believe; that is true of everyone, including me. We constantly struggle to take criticism and resent our critics. However, if we were more successful in extracting what is helpful from those critics instead of concentrating on our hurt feelings, the message could be used as an outline to grow as human beings and hopefully avoid repeating those actions that earned us such criticism. Choosing not to be submissive any longer and to verbalize what we perceive to be obstacles and handicaps in our culture, particularly the hierarchies and religion passed down from colonialism, and addressing them in an analytical manner could help us improve the profile of Hispanics in the United States.

Within the Hispanic community, most women still act out this deeply ingrained submission edict, and in doing so, occupy an inferior place in society, although they are quick to refute it. Needless to say, no human being likes being told that they occupy a secondary place in society. The fact that such a comment is unpleasant does not invalidate it. Some Latinas have been conditioned to remain in such a place because their families still hold the same beliefs as the colonial elite did in the seventeenth century. And those Latinas who have dared to go out to the general community and ask to be included in decision-making processes are seldom formally included in leadership roles, and when they are included, they are rarely supported by the same community they are trying to represent.

Thus, it is imperative that we, in the United States, embark on a journey to undo this colonialist mentality. Hispanic women should be strongly encouraged and supported because we have started our journey to change archaic beliefs, and those changes will benefit the country as a whole.

Misogyny

One of the most noticeable oppressions carried from the old colonial mentality into Hispanic culture today is the hierarchy of men above women. While the colonial elites may not have power over us anymore, misogyny is still entrenched in Hispanic culture. Many men view Latinas— and many Latinas view themselves—in the same way they were taught to do in colonial times: inferior.

Latinas, throughout generations, have been taught to consider men their protectors, to believe that men are possessive over women because they love them. If men are not possessive, it is because they do not want them. Religion is still strongly influencing the place Latinas have in the community. Although Hispanics are no longer under the rule of the conquistadors, many are still Catholic, and these lesser roles are now reinforced from behind the pulpit during Sunday Mass sermons. Priests and deacons remind congregants that men are the head of the household and women are to serve them. In return, men protect and provide for the women. This tells women not only that they owe servitude to the men in their lives but also that women are not capable of protecting or providing for themselves.

But these gender roles are not just for adults—Latino children learn them from a very young age. For example, Latino boys are often encouraged to be strong and macho. When they fall down, they are often discouraged from crying. As they become teenagers, they may be given more freedom than females. They may be allowed to attend parties without a chaperone and to stay out overnight. Their parents may avoid talking to them about sex at all, and even if they do, because the Catholic Church expressly forbids birth control in any form, boys in Latino culture are not likely to learn about protection or contraceptives. It's not uncommon for Hispanic boys to be encouraged to enjoy their lives with little responsibility. There may be little discussion about furthering their education, resulting in a shortage in the kind of critical thinking skills that could incentivize leaving a life based on faith and imposed religious beliefs for one based on rationality and evidence.

In contrast, daughters may be pushed to be nurturing, submissive, devoted to their father first and their husband later, and trained to put their father's wishes above the needs of all females in the household. When young girls receive presents, they are typically dolls, tied to their eventual role as mother and caretaker. As the girls grow older, they may not have the freedom to choose their boyfriends or to attend parties alone. Parents fixate on their daughters' virginity until they are married. Despite this obsession with virginity, perhaps because girls are also often taught to submit to boys and men, they may become pregnant at a young age. Some girls may become single parents, and if they do, education is no longer a goal. They are often encouraged to marry in their twenties, and if they haven't already begun to have children, procreating is likely the next step. Women may be trained to value themselves by the number of children they have. This can turn into a cycle that perpetuates poverty by not allowing Latino women to become better educated and get better paying jobs. With so much emphasis on marriage and predetermined gender roles, young women might never consider that not having children is even an option.

Therefore, we as Latinas must explore what it is to live without the hierarchy that oppresses us, without the religion that still enforces that oppression—this is one of the most important issues we need to address in our community. We, Hispanic women, must strive for a more secular community where we can flourish and be respected as equals in our personal and professional lives.

High Birth Rates

Catholicism and colonialism have ingrained into Hispanic women that our value is based on how many children we have, and for centuries, big families have been a norm in Hispanic culture.

Although Hispanic immigration has been steadily declining and currently is close to zero, the US Hispanic population continues to grow. After 1960, the US Latino population increased from 6.3 million to 55.3 million by 2014.[2] It is projected to increase to 119 million by 2060. This growth in the Hispanic population is coming from the birth of Hispanics in the United States, primarily those born to women of Mexican descent. Between 1990 and 2004, the percentage of births in the United States from Hispanic women rose from 15 percent to 23 percent, while the share of the birth rate from Mexican Americans almost doubled from 9 percent to 17

---

2. Renee Stepler and Anna Brown, "Statistical Portrait of Hispanics in the United States," Hispanic Trends, Pew Research Center, April 19, 2016, http://www.pewhispanic.org/2016/04/19/statistical-portrait-of-hispanics-in-the-united-states-key-charts/.

percent.[3] Thus the highest fertility rate of all Latino subgroups comes from Mexicans in the US. I know Hispanics do not intend to take over the world by unlimited reproduction.

Although I try not to address any issue affecting the Hispanic community by country of origin, it is important to name the group with the highest fertility rate so they can understand that this particular practice affects the entire Latino community. I would hope that Mexican American women can realize that embracing old beliefs without questioning them in current times contributes to the oppression of Latino women. Taking a hard look at their birth rate and considering self-correcting could drastically help the Hispanic American population overall and their subgroup especially.

This message does not apply to Mexican American women alone, though. It is time for Hispanic women to start an open dialogue about reproduction today. We, Hispanics, bear the blunt pressure of raising large families with lower incomes. High birth rates cause financial pressure on many families that are already living under poverty lines. And the more families that fit that mold, the more the poverty and high birth rate cycles perpetuate, and the less likely we will see change in society. When parents are struggling to make ends meet, how can they be mentally and socially ready to become active members of their local communities?

We live in a society that wants our birth rates to remain high. Marketing companies are pleased with Hispanics' high birth rates, which clearly increase their sales and allow them to expect higher profits. Economists see this as good news too—a growing economy shows increments in sales. Furthermore, we live in a country that encourages child rearing by providing tax deductions, which reinforces reproduction even to a group that is already not inclined to do family planning as a result of their religious beliefs. Some employers also incentivize reproduction by pricing health care insurance premiums equally whether the family has one child or many children.

It is a delicate balance to advocate for population control within any particular group of individuals living in a democratic country. Governments cannot dictate how many children people should have, and even if they could, targeting one cultural demographic would be seen as

3. Emilio A. Parrado and S. Philip Morgan, "Intergenerational Fertility Among Hispanic Women: New Evidence of Immigrant Assimilation," *Demography* 45, no. 3 (2008): 651–71, https://www.ncbi.nlm.nih.gov/pmc/articles/PMC2782440/.

federally mandated oppression. Yet, we in the Latino community should recognize and agree that overpopulation is a problem regardless of what religion dictates.

Children are not sent by god. Couples should decide together when they are financially, socially, and psychologically ready for children and how many they can afford after analyzing the advantages and disadvantages of becoming parents.

The good news is that the birth rate among the US Latino population has begun to drop.[4] This could be the result of US-born Latino children furthering their education. Education is critical for building the skills to question and challenge information—in this case, passages from the Bible that promote having many children and link a woman's value to her fertility. Women have started questioning those archaic ideas handed down from colonialism through generations, and we have seen some women resist predetermined gender roles, other people's decisions over their bodies, hierarchical order, blind faith, and the expectation to submit to whatever religion tells them to do. However, the bad news is that this process has already taken too long, has already held too many families under the poverty line for generations, and we need to expedite it. The more educated a population is, the more social equality they can achieve.

Low Marriage Rates

Hispanics have higher rates of never legally marrying than other American demographics. According to Census 2000 data, over one-third of Hispanic men (38 percent) and 30 percent of Hispanic women have never married.[5] What these numbers do not explain is that for many Latino immigrants, especially those from Central America, most relationships with children are considered marriages even though unions are never registered anywhere.

These percentages have a devastating effect on women in couples that separate. Because the parents never got married, the father has no legal tie to the children. Their livelihood becomes the mother's responsibility, and going to the court systems to obtain child support is very difficult. If the

---

4. Jens Manuel Krogstad, "U.S. Hispanic Population Growth Has Leveled Off," FacTank, Pew Research Center, August 3, 2017, http://www.pewresearch.org/fact-tank/2017/08/03/u-s-hispanic-population-growth-has-leveled-off/.

5. "Marital Status: 2000," U.S. Census Bureau, October 2003, https://www.census.gov/prod/2003pubs/c2kbr-30.pdf.

mother did not advance her education, as many women in these situations do not, then it will be difficult for her to earn a family-supporting wage. Mothers and children in these situations often live in poverty.

Lack of Education

According to Pew Research, in 2000, the high school dropout rate among Hispanics in America was 32 percent.[6] By 2011, that had dropped by more than half to 14 percent. It is commendable that the numbers are showing improvement. However, we are still lagging behind other ethnic groups, with Black Americans earning an 82 percent graduation rate, Asians 91 percent, and whites 89 percent. This trend continues beyond high school as well. Census data from 2016 shows that 22 percent of Hispanics earn associate's degrees and 15 percent bachelor's degrees, compared to the national rates of 42 percent and 32 percent, respectively.[7] These gaps are what we, Latinos, need to be looking at closing down.

Education not only equips Latino women with higher level skills to secure better paying jobs, but it also teaches how to think critically, to question what we hear and learn. Statistics show that as people become more educated, they start leaving religion. And religion is a reason mentioned on why Hispanics do not question culture, gender roles, or when and how to start a family. Directly and indirectly, part of the Hispanic culture teaches, promotes, and encourages the submissive and secondary role most Latinas continue to maintain in our communities today. Education is the best way to combat that.

Religion

It's obvious that in the United States today, religion and colonial influences still play a large role in influencing the Latino culture. It has been a long-standing misconception that nearly all Hispanics in the United States are

---

6. Richard Fry, "U.S. High School Dropout Rate Reaches Record Low, Driven by Improvements among Hispanics, Blacks," FacTank, Pew Research Center, October 2, 2014, http://www.pewresearch.org/fact-tank/2014/10/02/u-s-high-school-dropout-rate-reaches-record-low-driven-by-improvements-among-hispanics-blacks/.

7. Camille L. Ryan and Kurt Bauman, "Educational Attainment in the United States: 2015," U.S. Census Bureau, March 2016, https://www.census.gov/content/dam/Census/library/publications/2016/demo/p20-578.pdf.

Catholic, and that was an accurate statement more than thirty years ago. However, a 2010 Pew Research poll found that about 67 percent of Latino Americans are Catholic.[8] The long-term decline in the share of Catholics among Hispanics may partly reflect religious changes underway in America, but that is not enough to shake the oppression Latinas face. Although our culture's affiliation with the Catholic Church has been decreasing for a few decades, preoccupation with religion is still prevalent, and many traditions based on the religion persist even in non-Catholic families.

These days, we often see Hispanics hopping from religion to religion and never questioning why they even need a religion. It is possible to speculate that religion continues to be a unifying factor among Hispanics, creating what they see as community but also acting as a catalyst for keeping women in a place of inferiority by making them dress in a particular way, by dictating the number of children they have, by obsessing over female "purity," by keeping women at home, by hijacking their uteruses in a religious context, and by keeping reproduction and sex as taboo subjects.

Perhaps, what we need is to have all Latinas get together and brainstorm to come up with a new unifying issue that is not religion. We see that many Hispanics, instead of leaving religion, just change their affiliation. They often become more fanatical in their new places of worship than they were in their previous churches. One thing that stays constant is that women remain in their submissive and secondary roles.

Lack of Leadership

Because of the emphasis on women to remain second-class citizens, there are very few Latino women in corporate leadership positions. And in my experience, those few who are, often mention religion when they are asked to be the key speakers at conferences. Because there are so few CEO Latino women, there is little public data to sustain my statement. Thus, I can only offer what I have observed while attending many chambers of commerce conferences during the last fifteen years as well as events organized by Hispanic business organizations, and it seems common for these women to proselytize.

---

8. "The Shifting Religious Identity of Latinos in the United States," Religion & Public Life, Pew Research Center, May 7, 2014, http://www.pewforum.org/2014/05/07/the-shifting-religious-identity-of-latinos-in-the-united-states/.

Religious affiliation seems to help them attain their positions as executives and leaders to an extent. If two Latinas are standing next to each other with the same set of skills and qualifications, religious affiliation being the only difference, the one with no religious affiliation will very likely not be a finalist and will be discarded as a candidate. The fact that this scenario plays out again and again further influences women to hold on to religion even if they've already begun to realize how overall detrimental the church's teachings are for women.

There is also a dire lack of representation of Latino women in politics, especially at the national level. This is true across both parties. During the 2016 Election, among Hispanic women voters, 70 percent said they supported Clinton while 25 percent said they supported Trump.[9] This is quite interesting because when looking at both parties, the GOP has been the more proactive one in giving a particular Latino woman, Ana Navarro, a highly visible role representing Hispanics' opinions in the party. On the other hand, Democrats remain very coy about giving prominence to any Latino man or woman, except for some political appointees whose loyalties are clearly to the party, not to the public.

When Democrats are asked about the lack of Latino representation, they cite diversity as one of the party principles. However, I often say diversity without inclusion is a just a photo opportunity. Even when we're offered a seat at the table, we are seldom included in the decision-making process. This lack of political inclusion by the Democratic party only compounds the feeling of alienation that Latino women are already experiencing. We can continue waiting until changes occur on their own, or we can expedite the process by getting Latino women acclimated to the political system sooner rather than later.

And yet, I hear the same answer over and over again: "We tried to get a Hispanic to come and speak, but we could not find anyone." This is causing a growing disenchantment with the system, particularly among Hispanic women. I say try harder or be ready to lose your Latino supporters in the immediate future. Most Hispanics do not get involved frequently. If no change takes place in the near future, women will start crossing party lines straight to the arms of religious fundamentalists, which is bound to

---

9. Aamna Mohdin, "American Women Voted Overwhelmingly for Clinton, Except the White Ones," *Quartz*, November 9, 2016, https://qz.com/833003/election-2016-all-women-voted-overwhelmingly-for-clinton-except-the-white-ones/.

continue the cycle that keeps Latinas sequestered to an inferior state of being like when the conquistadors colonized the Americas.

Division, Alienation, Racism

Another major issue affecting Hispanics today is the extreme fragmentation in the community due to many people's fanatical obsession with their family's country of origin. Some Hispanics do not easily become members of the general mainstream community when they immigrate. This may be in part because they want to preserve traditions from their home countries, but it is exacerbated by the fact of the new normal racism in America— although racism has unfortunately always existed, with recent glorification from government leaders, race-based hatred and discrimination has become more open and in your face. This creates a sense of alienation and makes many Latinos feel unwelcome, which leads to a glorification of their country of origin. This then validates and perpetuates antiquated traditions such as a blind faith in religion, which as this essay has shown, is damaging to the Hispanic community, particularly women.

This fragmentation makes it difficult to reach out to large groups in the Hispanic community to work toward any sort of common goal, whether that's better political representation, improving education statistics, or increasing awareness about problems related to birth and marriage rates. And at the core of all those issues is religion. The ability to unite to teach critical thinking skills would help Latinos start questioning whether religion actually makes our lives better. The point of teaching critical thinking skills is that each individual can come to the conclusion on their own on what to believe and what to dismiss.

Furthermore, it pains me to say that we do not need enemies, as we are our worst enemies. For those people who want to keep Hispanics "marching in the same spot," it must be satisfying to conclude that there is no easier and more effective way to conquer than by division. Sadly, many insist that it is okay for Hispanics in the United States to maintain, promote, and reward these blind connections to countries of origin. I suggest that it keeps us distracted from the problems at hand and keeps us entertained with unimportant activities. Hence, non-Hispanics do not have to worry about us becoming a unified group with political and economic power that can voice inequalities and lack of representation in companies, boards, government, and politics. If we could transcend these divisions within our community, we could work together to improve life for the whole community.

We, Latinos, are like a gigantic family, and all families have their dysfunctional moments. This means that we may appear to be fighting and criticizing each other, but when an attack is launched against any of us, we all feel and take it as an attack on all of us. When the president of the United States calls Mexicans bad hombres, drug dealers, and criminals, he is insulting each one of us. It is time for all Hispanics to unite against him and others like him.

Where Are Latinas Now, and Where Do We Want to Go?

The biggest issue that Hispanics, and more specifically Latino women, continue to face is that we are not represented in boards, leaderships and executive positions, government nonprofits, and so on. We're told that our interests are represented, but this so-called representation comes from just about anyone but one of us, implying we are not equipped to perform in leadership positions. As I mentioned at the beginning of this essay, there are often non-Latinos attempting to define what is a Latino or Hispanic or both as if we were incapable of knowing that ourselves. But this is what a passive attitude encourages—it leaves room for everyone to feel they are experts about our well-being.

Most Latinas really want to have a seat at the table and be part of the conversation. We are not pieces on a game board that are to be moved only for elections to facilitate the agendas of political parties, organizations, or corporations. We have skills and knowledge, and we are able and willing to make valuable contributions when given the responsibility and opportunity to move our country forward in business, government, research, science, construction, and other industries. We are not asking for special treatment; we expect equal access to all opportunities. The level playing field many politicians and corporate leaders tout always sounds good, but it is seldom truly accessible for Latinas. We do not want to be invisible anymore.

It is imperative that we, secular Latinas, uncomfortable as it may be, start a dialogue with our friends and families about living without religion. We live in a time where political correctness is expected. When someone disagrees, the audience quickly labels those of dissenting opinions as aggressive, and if those dissenting are women, they are the target of all sorts of condescending and dismissive insults. In today's social media frenzy, this has become the most common way to manipulate and control the nonconforming opinions on any subjects.

The Latino community has many positive traits, and it does not mean we cannot or should not improve in areas where we can do better. And the logical first step in improving in all these areas is to shed religion and its antiquated systems that hold us, especially women, back.

Giving Up Religion

What would Latinas lose and gain if they gave up religion? I have walked this path myself and work with many other Latinas who choose to take it too. By abandoning religion, Latinas will lose the perceived protection assigned to them because of their lower level in the hierarchy as established by the church. They will also lose the ability to justify every event in their lives as either a test to their faith—illness, death, or accidents—or god's blessing—recovering from surgery, taking a vacation, or getting better from sickness.

I hear some Latinas say they fear they will lose their families if they openly doubt their religion, but I am skeptical about the validity of this fear. The explanation may be simpler than that. Latinas generally receive financial support from either a husband or another family member, and in order to avoid being cut off financially, they work at staying quiet and unnoticed by completing their tasks without questioning them. The lack of financial independence, in many cases, is the defining factor in Latinas' decisions to stay firmly in place and not to question the status quo.

In reality, most Latino families have an extremely solid foundation. Although most are not happy when a family member tells them that religion is no longer working for them, the familial foundation eventually reunites them after a fight or disagreement. I have never met any Latinos— men or women—who were excommunicated by their families as a result of coming out as atheist. If that happens in Latino families, it is an exception to the rule; eventually most families come around, because in the Hispanic culture, family comes first.

After most Latino women confess their doubts about religion, they are often able to fulfill their lives in a different manner than when they were brainwashed to believe in something for which there is no evidence. I have observed that when Latino women decide to take a break from religion and get involved in other personal or community activities, they gain a more relaxed outlook on life due to the fact that they no longer have to lie about their lack of religiosity. They seem to enjoy life more without the constant fear of going to hell if they do not please god when they deviate from "moral" behaviors dictated by religion. Also, they enjoy pursuing fun activities previously forbidden by religion. They start meeting likeminded people; they strive to achieve a balance in their personal as well as professional lives without scheduling prayers to an imaginary being. They learn to accept that they were not born in sin and that they are *good* people, not *god* people. And many of them become more self-assertive. I can personally relate to that—as I open up about my atheism, I become more comfortable in my own skin.

Solutions

To my extended and sometimes "dysfunctional" Latino family, we may not agree on everything all the time, but I know that we can work together in educating all of us about the equal—not inferior—role women should have in society. Once we are strong internally, we can convey our opinions and ideas proudly everywhere. We owe it to our daughters, sons, and the community; our children need to be guided towards a path of critical thinking skills so they can achieve success in their future without being pulled down by old ideas. Building our opinions and ideas with knowledge based on evidence allows us to make better decisions than if we base our actions on Bible stories, colonial-based teachings, and blind faith.

My goal is to make the Latino community a powerful contributor to our country so we can gain the respect we deserve, dismissing the insults and lies endorsed by the current person occupying the White House. I would love for children to have an open dialogue with their parents about women's equality. Honesty and truth can set us free, and I know that women have never been inferior to men—at the least, we have always been equal to them. It is time to discard our self-inflicted wounds and assert our contributions to the economy, society, and institutions in which we are involved. There are several areas where we can take practical steps toward this goal.

Raising Children

Latino women can put a stop to the cycle of machismo and misogyny by raising our children differently. Let's start with raising daughters and sons with the same rights and responsibilities to do chores, to enjoy parties, and to participate in social activities. Girls and boys both deserve to have positive outlooks and see opportunity while growing up.

We must stop raising boys who will grow up to be "macho" men who get their confidence from putting women down because that is what they were taught by their own mothers. We can also empower our daughters to speak their minds, not be submissive, and make education, careers, and community representation priorities in their lives. We can encourage high school girls to go into STEM—high-paying fields where women are rare—and become professionals in all fields. We can teach them critical thinking skills so they can do what's best for them and for the community as a whole, not feel compelled to give up their self-worth for fear of losing their families and friends.

As a paper from the Brookings Institution states, "It is well-established that the circumstances into which children are born have a lasting impact on their later life trajectories." [10] Every Latina mother has the ability to influence the circumstances her children are raised in, and as such, influence her children's life trajectories.

Family Planning

The same Brookings Institution paper says, "Increasing access to effective, easy-to-use contraception is an important step in improving economic and social opportunities for children." Family planning is a combined decision. It does not rest solely with men, despite what religion and colonizers taught our ancestors. A woman's worth is not determined by the number of children she can push out. A child is a responsibility for the next eighteen years; the financial support must continue for that period of time, and although both parents should contribute to that support, women must recognize that they may be primary providers in certain circumstances.

---

10. Isabel Sawhill and Joanna Venator, "Improving Children's Life Chances through Better Family Planning," Brookings Institution, January 2015, https://www.brookings.edu/wp-content/uploads/2016/06/Improving_Childrens_life_Chances_through_Better_Family_Planning_sawhill.pdf.

Latino women have to start recognizing that it is their decision when and how many children to have. Having no children may be the preferable option for some of us, and there is no shame if that is what you choose. We should not forget that it is "Our body, our uterus, our decision"—not our family's, not the extended family's, not the government's, ours! Having children is not in all women's plans, and families should allow us the freedom to make such a decision without constantly pressuring us to procreate. Procreation is not the only activity that makes women special and valuable.

There is more than one option to have a family: One child is okay. More than one child should be carefully planned. Zero children is absolutely another option, and it should be perfectly acceptable. Any Latino woman should have the freedom to decide without guilt how to form her own family.

To that end, family planning programs should be offered for Latinas. Contraceptives should be easily available regardless of religious beliefs. Teach women to make their own decision about their reproductive systems and health. Ultimately, this decision should rest with each woman alone. Her body, her choice!

Although large families are often seen as a cultural practice, Hispanics must accept that *culture* is not a sacred word and that, like all ideas, cultural practices should be questioned. If they are harming any segment of the population, they should be recognized as damaging and changed.

Education

With the numbers pointing to a decline in Mexican immigration since the Great Recession, Hispanic immigration is almost zero at this moment. Since we do not have the distraction of trying to stop illegal immigration, perhaps we can focus our attention and reroute some funding to further improving literacy rates, college graduation rates, and the number of graduates earning master's and doctoral degrees.

Education is about more than improving statistics, though. Studies show that "women's access to education, health care, family planning and employment all affect family size," which we know affects financial stability.[11] Thus, promoting education specifically for women is one of the

---

11. "Human Population: Women," Population Reference Bureau, accessed August

most important solutions. It is the best way to fight the indoctrination that started when the conquistadors came to the Americas. The tools that come with education are what prepare and train individuals to analyze all factors that affect our lives from a social, scientific, and practical point of view rather than by what has been passed on from generation to generation. It's important to note that when I say *education*, I am specifically discounting theology and Bible degrees.

Educational programs should also be tailored to educate parents as well as students. Often, recently immigrated parents act as barriers to their children's education due to their lack of understanding of the social and cultural differences between their countries of origin and this country where their children are attending school and being raised. More open discussions about educational opportunities for young Latinos and the far-reaching benefits of education will help our community overcome this barrier.

Employment Opportunities

Latinos are going to be a large number of the US population in the future. We are a valuable and untapped market of people that can be trained to replace the retiring baby boomer workforce without having to wait for the next generation to mature. We have the youngest major racial or ethnic group in the United States—these are the country's future professionals. It is to our advantage to educate our young people and prepare them to move our country forward. Creating job training programs would benefit the country as a whole and would especially assist Latinas in gaining financial independence and improving their lives.

It is not wise to pretend that religiosity does not hinder young professionals' performance in their personal and work environments. While the technology industry is pushing forward full speed and is a valuable area for Hispanics to work, the tendency for Hispanic women to focus on having children because that's what her inferior status requires is inconceivable. Latinos should have the tools to make a rational decision on whether to stay home, have kids, pursue college degrees, have their own business, or all of the above based on their own personal decisions, not what the church teachings are. Education and equal-opportunity employment programs are critical in this area.

Unity and Inclusion

We need to stop saying the word *diversity* as a solution to anything and everything that is not right with our surroundings. Diversity without inclusion is merely a photo op or marketing campaign—it may seem to represent people from different races, incomes, religions, and ages from all protected classes but it does not actually ask people from these classes to be part of a solution.

More Latino women need to be involved in politics to represent and legislate on behalf of the growing US Hispanic community. Government leaders need to bring Latinas to the table and include us in the decision-making process. We should have a place at the table, and our opinions should be heard. The phenomenon of having us at the table but ignoring our opinions and contributions and then having us pose for nice photo opportunities should stop immediately.

Latinas must get involved in our immediate and surrounding communities. We have to become activists, civic leaders and run for office. The best candidate to represent Hispanics is generally one who is knowledgeable, familiar, and invested in the community they are representing. Many Hispanic women can meet that criteria. For those of us who are not inclined to fulfill leadership roles, we can still assist in supporting those women who are working on our behalf.

Furthermore, we must shed the submissive mentality that inclines Latinos to shy away from discussing problems and being "yes" puppets. Avoiding discussion with the idea that problems will go away is an absolute mistake. If we don't advocate for ourselves, we cannot rely on anyone else to do so.

The Hispanic community has many good qualities: we are hardworking and loyal, and we want to provide a decent life for our families. Many members of our community need assistance with access to equal opportunities. This is not a call for special treatment. As a country, we must make sure that the inequality gap does not become so wide that everyone on one side is left hopeless and angry. As politicians, advocates, and voters, it is up to all of us to make sure that collectively all contributions are valued, for the benefit of our nation. In order for Hispanics to get ahead in society, socially and financially, we need to offer our community members the tools to accomplish that. Without the right tools, obstacles may appear insurmountable.

Advocating for change from within the Hispanic community is as important as the help that may come from outside the community itself. It will take all of us to improve the profile of the Hispanic community. Change will not be delivered at our front steps just because we know change is needed.

And in order to advocate for change, we have to work together. Latinos should not show up at political rallies to elect US candidates to public office chanting, "Argentina," "El Salvador," "Cuba," "Bolivia," or any other country of origin. That sends the wrong message and keeps us from being invited to meetings on local issues that have big repercussions on the lives of Hispanics in America. We deserve to be at those meetings and influencing policy that affects our community and our interests.

The truth is that often the contributions of Hispanics are overlooked or diminished: we need to remind ourselves that we are part of our communities; that our roles in those communities are important; that living in the United States, whether as a new immigrant or as a descendant, comes with certain rights and responsibilities; that it is okay to honor our heritage and our country at the same time. We do not have to pick one over the other, but we do need to be involved in making our country a better place for ourselves and other Hispanics.

Hispanics who have been able to get ahead in their fields should give back to our own community. And that same community should sponsor those companies or individuals as well; it is a two-way street. This partnership between a community and its members and businesses will create financial and political capital within the Hispanic community—something we have absolutely zero of at present.

Latinos should unite under other issues different than religion so we can be heard loud and clear. Religion should be left in churches since they all teach the opposite of critical thinking—to just have faith that things will change is not good enough, even for a believer. No matter their religious affiliations, when people are uniting for other issues in the community or in business, they should realize that it is better to leave their faith at home or church. Big and small Hispanic organizations need to stop highlighting religion at their corporate events that turn out to be "mini revivals." Or they should clearly describe that the intention of the events is to ambush attendees with religious content so if members do not want to listen to it, they can skip the event. At the higher level, we should keep absolute separation between religion and government. In the current state of affairs in our country, that separation is under serious and constant attack.

Finally, we should never forget to focus on *education, education, and education*—that's what fights indoctrination. It teaches *how* to think, not *what* to think.

To summarize, why would it be advantageous for Latinas to abandon religion? The motives are simple and the implications are significant: gender equality, financial independence, more and better education, delaying having children and having fewer children, better paying jobs, better representation in leadership positions, and overall better quality of life.

11

Shaking the Ground:

Transgender Atheism

Kayley Margarite Whalen

Eventually you can't help but figure out that, while gender is a construct, so is a traffic light, and if you ignore either of them, you get hit by cars. Which, also, are constructs.

—Imogen Binnie, Nevada[1]

Origins

Everyone needs an origin story. Everyone needs a narrative as a way to understand their identity, their place in the world, who they are, and why they understand the world the way they do. Narratives help us advocate for our communities. They help us build empathy by emphasizing common human struggles that people of other identities can relate to. They infuse our lives with meaning and self-worth, and give us the ability to build community by finding those whose stories we can relate to.

---

1. https://www.goodreads.com/work/quotes/21399644

Atheists often find themselves telling an origin story of how and why we left religion and how we formed our own sense of ethics without the need for theological and supernatural guidance. We often have to explain how we can "be good without a God" to incredulous audiences who equate atheism with a lack of morals. Other times we share our stories in order to share how specific religious beliefs have harmed us and by extension harm others.

This is my origin story.

I want to share it as a transgender atheist, a queer woman, and a feminist.

So what is transgender? GLAAD, an LGBTQ advocacy organization, defines it in its media reference guide as:

> An umbrella term for people whose gender identity and/or gender expression differs from what is typically associated with the sex they were assigned at birth.... Many transgender people are prescribed hormones by their doctors to bring their bodies into alignment with their gender identity. Some undergo surgery as well. But not all transgender people can or will take those steps, and a transgender identity is not dependent upon physical appearance or medical procedures.[2]

I'll also use the term *cisgender* throughout this chapter, defined simply as "people who are not transgender."

At birth, I was assigned male. Much of my life, I was uncomfortable with many of the "typical" behaviors and gender expression associated with being male. At age twenty, I began publicly describing myself as transgender, after years of wrestling with who I really was. At the time of this writing, I have been out for over eleven years.

To most of the world, I describe myself simply as a woman. Yet other times, especially when I am surrounded by other feminists and LGBTQ people, I have also described myself as genderqueer, which means "people who experience their gender identity and/or gender expression as falling outside the categories of man and woman."[3] I don't consider this a contradiction or intellectually dishonest; as I'll explore in this chapter,

---

2. "Glossary of Terms—Transgender," *GLAAD Media Reference Guide*, 10th ed., GLAAD, October 2016, http://www.glaad.org/reference/transgender.

3. Ibid.

gender is both constructed and completely dependent on context in order to exist.

In spaces where gender is segregated into a binary system—such as accessing restrooms, or a "women's" support group, I feel most comfortable identifying as a woman. I am treated by the world as a woman, and as such I experience sexism, harassment, and discrimination like other women— experiences I stress when I am conducting feminist and transgender advocacy. In order to access medical care, especially transition-related care such as hormones and surgeries, I have had to navigate a highly binary system. And in order to debunk those who believe that transgender is a mental illness, against nature, or against science, I have to explain the scientific research validating that transgender identity is real.

Yet in spaces where others grasp that gender can be fluid and isn't limited to male/female, masculine/feminine—a microcosm of the world I am working to help build—I identify as genderqueer to indicate how I have always felt limited by binary categories and how I understand my gender has shifted over time and will continue to shift.

This gender binary, which reinforces oppressive forces like sexism, heterosexism (the privileging of heterosexuality over homosexuality and bisexuality), and cissexism (the privileging of being cisgender over being transgender) has been maintained in our society through many systems, including religion. I want to challenge oppressive systems that limit our imaginations and our ability to live beyond a binary understanding of gender. To be clear, I don't want to build a world where gender disappears—I simply want a world where people can choose and celebrate many unique gender identities without shame, fear, or discrimination.

Shame

For those who are religious, origin stories are easy to come across. They instill in each of us a set of values to live our lives in line with our particular theology—and those origin stories are subsequently exploited by those who benefit from that theology. The first origin story I was taught was the one in Genesis. The story of the Garden of Eden taught me that it's sinful to know about our own bodies and that man and woman are binary, God-given categories. Women are inferior to men and the root of sin.

Growing up, I wanted to be a good person. As a Catholic, being good meant avoiding sin by following the church's teachings on gender—including staying in my male gender role. To break out of the role you're supposed to play, to shirk from your duties as a man and wish to take on the "inferior" role a woman, is of course something that I internalized as completely against the order of creation.

The Catholic Church is invested in the binary and has described transgender people as a greater threat to this order of creation than nuclear weapons.[4] American Cardinal Raymond Burke recently said, "With gender theory, it is impossible to live in society. Already today, in certain places in the United States, anyone at all can change identity and say, 'Today I am a man; tomorrow I will be a woman.' That is truly madness. Some men insist on going into the women's rest rooms. That is inhuman."[5]

I did not know that transgender people existed as a child, and I never heard a sermon mention them. The church did teach me that sex should only be between a married man and woman for the purposes of procreation. Most of my life, I have primarily been romantically attracted to women, although I have explored relationships with men. The church's heterosexism caused me immense shame and confusion both about my early explorations with men and about my desire to be a woman who has relationships with other women.

My church, school, and parents were all complicit in keeping information about my body away from me, through shame and lack of early sex education. My first awareness that humans had different genitalia was bathing with my sister. Her body was different than mine, but I had no idea what that meant. But for some reason, I would have dreams of my penis magically disappearing so I could look like her. I remember being in the shower and feeling intense shame as I looked at my genitals, feeling like maybe if I covered them up with something, they'd go away or transform into something like my sister's.

During puberty, as I was discovering my genitals were a source of

4. J. Lester Feder and Ellie Hall, "Pope Compares Transgender People to Nuclear Weapons," *Buzzfeed*, February 20, 2015, https://www.buzzfeed.com/lesterfeder/pope-compares-transgender-people-to-nuclear-weapons.

5. Claire Chretien, "Cardinal Burke: Gender Theory Is 'Madness,' Transgender Bathrooms 'Inhuman,'" News, Life Site, August 1, 2016, https://www.lifesitenews.com/news/cardinal-burke-gender-theory-is-madness-men-going-in-womens-bathrooms-is-in.

pleasure, I became even more confused and aggravated. I'd punch the wall of my room if I felt "sinful" desire. I'd imagine being with a woman, but in my fantasies, the woman would always dominate me, control me, take control over my body—perhaps absolving me of blame for my own sexual desire.

These were dreams I ran from, buried deep down, as I wanted to be a godly, good person. Often I thought about what it would be like to live the life of a priest and renounce sex and sexual desire altogether. I volunteered as an altar server from childhood through age eighteen, and every Sunday I would assist the priest with the ceremonial aspects of the Mass, creating something beautiful for others to enjoy and bring them closer to God.

Perhaps less in line with the church's teachings, though, was how jealous I was of how pretty the priest's robes looked, how they flowed as he walked down the aisle, the beautiful colors and the rich fabrics. I also loved having my own robes; while nowhere near as elaborate as the priest's, they were fun to wear. It was one of the first times in my life I actually got to wear clothes that I enjoyed. Whether that was a signifier of a repressed urge to wear a dress or simply a joy in flowing, beautiful things, I could not say. Otherwise, I was typically satisfied enough with cargo pants with plenty of pockets—a practical feature I often bemoan the lack of in clothes available to me as an adult woman.

I respected my priests, and I felt respected by them and wasn't mistreated. But there was one moment that made me really question just how godly this idea of renouncing sex and sexuality actually is. Once, as a thank-you, a priest took a group of altar servers to an amusement park. It had an area with women doing traditional dances that were somewhat risqué. When we arrived at the park and were planning our day, the priest pointed to that area on the map and said, "I come here to see the dancing girls!" in such a sexually suggestive way, it shocked me. I could not reconcile his comment with the fact that he regularly sermonized about renouncing earthly desires, and it opened a major crack in my belief.

The Cracked Looking-Glass

The church played a huge role in denying me the language and history to understand as a youth that there might be transgender people like me. Religion has helped to colonize much of the world. In the process of colonization, it has erased the history, language, and traditional practices of countless cultures—including many cultures that had gender systems that weren't binary.

History is replete with examples of "third-gender" identities that existed outside of a gender binary. From *kathoeys* in Thailand to *takatapui* in New Zealand to *hijras* in India to *joya*/two-spirit Native Americans, third-gender people have always existed worldwide. Each has their own cultural context, and it's erroneous to apply the modern definition of transgender to all these identities. Unlike modern definitions of transgender, many of these third-gender identities combined sexual orientation and gender identity together, blurring the lines between homosexuality and transgender identity. While some of these third-gender identities have witnessed a recent resurgence in visibility and a reclaiming of their culture, much of their history has been systematically erased. As someone who is both Irish and Latinx, I have often looked to the history of Spain and Latin America, and the history of Ireland, to understand how Christianity was used to erase third-gender people.

Leslie Feinberg, a gender nonbinary-identified transgender activist, researched how Celtic third-gender history was erased by feudal Christian colonizers:

> Male to female transgender and cross-dressing were stigmatized by the Church as witchcraft. Yet cross-gendered expression, whether male or female was part of virtually all peasant festivals—including Halloween, a holiday with roots in Celtic, matrilineal society.... The Celt Winter Solstice persisted under Christianity as the Feast of Fools. Transgender played a prominent role in both holidays.[6]

At birth, I was named after a Catholic saint. When I transitioned, I chose a name that harkened back to pre-Catholic Ireland. Kayley, derived from the Gaelic *cèilidh*, referring to a celebration or dance, I found to be particularly appropriate based on this history of gender fluidity tied to Celtic celebrations.

The Spanish conquistadors also systematically erased third-gender identities in the Americas. For example, Deborah Miranda explores

---

6. Leslie Feinberg, *Transgender Warriors: Making History from Joan of Arc to Dennis Rodman* (Boston: Beacon Press, 1997), 70.

how joyas, third-gender indigenous people who were esteemed in their communities, were both systematically disciplined and murdered by soldiers and priests.

> The Spanish priests…approached the *joya's* behaviors through the twin disciplinary actions of physical and spiritual punishment and regendering. Both of these terms are euphemisms for violence. The consequences of being a *joya*—whether dressing as a woman, doing women's work, partnering with a normative male, or actually being caught in a sexual liaison with a man—included flogging with a leather whip (braided leather typically as thick as a fist), time in the stocks, and *corma* (a kind of hobbling device that restricted movement but allowed the Indian to work). Enforced, extended rote repetition of unfamiliar prayers on knees, verbal harassment and berating, ridicule and shaming in front of the *joya's* community were other forms of discipline.[7]

Harsh punishments for tolerating joyas led to the indigenous tribes exiling or sacrificing them in order to survive. This led to a restructuring of indigenous society, where third-gender people were treated as deviants and outcasts. This has continued in many tribes to this day.

Understanding the process by which the Catholic Church has violently reshaped cultures has helped me to understand why I had no concept for transgender as a kid.

Irish writer James Joyce has been highly influential to my atheism and transgender identity. In his book *Ulysses*, Joyce uses the metaphor of the "cracked looking-glass of a servant" to describe the colonial oppression of Ireland by both the Catholic Church and England. When Stephen Dedalus, one of the main protagonists, sees this "cracked looking-glass," he describes it as a "symbol of Irish art," implying that Irish art and culture will also be subservient and inferior to the dominant art and culture. Looking in this mirror, one can only see imperfection, a broken image distorted by one's own subjugation. The oppressed can only see themselves through the eyes of the oppressor as an inferior *other*.

This cracked looking-glass is a metaphor that I reenact almost every day as a transgender woman; that moment when I unwittingly catch myself

7. Deborah A. Miranda, "Extermination of the *Joyas*: Gendercide in Spanish California," *GLQ: A Journal of Lesbian and Gay Studies* 16, no. 1–2 (2010): 263–264.

looking in the mirror and wishing I was as beautiful as a cisgender woman. Transgender people constantly struggle to see their own beauty unmarred by what our culture says is not beautiful, not real, not valid about them.

Internalized oppression is insidious—it makes you understand yourself as inferior to others often without you even realizing it. If one can set the rules of what is sinful, unnatural, and shameful, and then get people to enforce those rules upon their own communities, one can have even greater power than a conquistador.

Astronauts, Skepticism, and Biased Science

When and how children develop self-awareness of their gender identity is a complex question that has seen a surge in recent scientific research. It is also an incredibly nuanced question, as proving that transgender identity is a naturally occurring phenomenon is not the same thing as proving that transgender people are really just men or women in the wrong body. However, sexologists, psychologists, and doctors who've dominated this field since the 1950s have ignored this nuance, as they were invested in upholding traditional values such as binary gender roles because of religious, financial, or political motivations. They've treated transgender people as mistakes that need to be corrected by medicine to bring them into alignment with their true gender of either male or female. More recent research, though, has increasingly shown that while yes, there are many possible biological bases for gender identity, what we observe as gender indeed has many different facets beyond simple biology or even a spectrum of masculine/feminine.

Informed by the growing visibility of diverse gender expressions in society, researchers have even posited gender as existing on a multi-axis spectrum or have used the metaphor of constellations of gender characteristics. By thinking beyond a binary of gender, we can discard dehumanizing notions that transgender people are somehow mistakes that need to be corrected by medicine—especially as many transgender people do not desire medical intervention to lead fulfilling, happy lives. Research on biological origins of transgender identity must not be used to eradicate transgender people through eugenics—a very real threat in the face of a society obsessed with "curing" us.

There is strong evidence of gender identity being heavily influenced by prenatal hormone exposure. Other research has pointed to various genes and epigenetic causes in addition to environmental triggers. Several studies have shown that a child's gender identity is often formed by age two or three and may become solidified by age six. Yet there is also a growing amount of research around how puberty affects the formation of gender identity, as genes are essentially switched on and off as hormones kick in. Anecdotally, while I know many transgender people who say they knew they were transgender dating back to being a toddler, many others—including myself—really did not begin to understand their gender identity as transgender until puberty or beyond.

LGBTQ and disability advocate Andrew Solomon has summarized much of this research in his book *Far from the Tree: Parents, Children, and the Search for Identity* in order to demonstrate how complex gender really is:

> Gender is among the first elements of self-knowledge. This knowledge encompasses an internal sense of self, and often, a preference for external behaviors, such as dress and type of play. Gender identity's etiology, however—posited to lie in genetics, in uterine androgen levels, in early social influences—remains obscure. Heino Meyer-Bahlburg, a professor of psychology at Columbia University who specializes in gender variance, has described numerous possible biological mechanisms, and said that as many as four hundred rare genes and epigenetic phenomena may be involved, genes associated not with hormone regulation, but with personality formation.[8]

Norman Spack, a leading endocrinologist in the field at Harvard Medical School, has also described how gender is so complex that science is only beginning to get a glimpse of its origins from a view seemingly hundreds of thousands of miles away.[9]

As people continue to express and be affirmed in new gender identities that are beyond male and female, I strongly believe we will continue to see more research showing that biology has indeed not predestined us to simply two genders, but opened possibilities for a vast array. I also believe that research will continue to show that gender identity is more fluid than

---

8. Andrew Solomon, *Far from the Tree: Parents, Children, and the Search for Identity* (New York: Scribner, 2012), 607.

9. Ibid.

we once thought; people can and do identify in new ways as they grow and change and society changes around them.

That said, most mainstream narratives of transgender identity—the narratives that lead to major book deals and reality TV shows—tend to portray transgender people as knowing that they were either a girl or a boy from a very young age. These narratives have a powerful effect on people who might otherwise dismiss transgender identity as not real and are commonly employed by advocates working to stop anti-transgender discrimination. The Movement Advancement Project (MAP), an LGBTQ advocacy organization, has collected extensive data on the efficacy of numerous strategies that transgender advocates have used when talking to voters and doing public education on transgender equality. This data has demonstrated that the stories about transgender equality that elicit the most sympathy in audiences who have limited knowledge of transgender people are stories of transgender youth and stories of transgender people who appear like "normal" men and women. This research has also shown that by discussing gender fluidity and nonbinary identities, advocates can lose public sympathy. Even in the last few years, organizations wishing to portray transgender people in a more nuanced way have seen their funders force them instead to follow MAP-approved messaging.

Jazz Jennings was one of the first transgender youth in the public eye who demonstrated that children often can and do develop an understanding of themselves from a young age. When Jazz Jennings came out as a transgender girl on national TV in 2007 at age six, it launched her career, which now includes two books, a reality TV show, and even a doll modeled after her.[10] The book *I Am Jazz* explores her and her parents' journey, beginning when she was age two, of understanding that she was a transgender girl. Beautifully illustrated and compassionate, it portrays both the pain and joy she experienced as she found her "true self"—a feminine girl who loves to wear dresses, play with dolls, and obsess over mermaids.

Jazz's story of acceptance has warmed the hearts of many parents who may grapple with fears about the happiness of their own transgender children, and it has moved many families to greater acceptance of their transgender children.

---

10. Katie Reilly, "First Transgender Doll Modeled after Teen Advocate Jazz Jennings," *Fortune*, February 24, 2017, http://fortune.com/2017/02/24/transgender-doll-jazz-jennings/.

But Jazz's story is not mine.

Unlike Jazz, I did not play with dolls or obsess over *The Little Mermaid*. I loved playing roller hockey and went to skate camp during the summer. I built model rockets, model planes, and painted science-fiction miniatures—in other words, toy soldiers. I subscribed to *Air & Space* magazine and dreamed of being an engineer or a scientist studying the cosmos.

Am I less valid as a woman today because I still paint toy soldiers, love science, and dream about space travel? What about girls who go into STEM fields and women who are gamers and sci-fi writers? My years of skating experience later became the foundation upon which I built a five-year semiprofessional career on a women's roller derby league, where I skated under the name Lenore Gore.

I didn't think there was anything specifically male or masculine about liking science and space. In third grade I was placed into the Gifted and Talented program, which emphasized math and science, and my teacher, Mrs. Cordell, was an astronaut. Our culture has often held astronauts as role models for our children; they dress up as astronauts and dream of meeting one or being one—including me when I was younger.

I interacted with an astronaut every day, and she was a woman.

If you're looking for Mrs. Cordell in the history books, you might not find her name except as a footnote to the *Challenger* disaster. She had been on the backup crew, and after the accident, she never went up. But she regularly told us stories of training with NASA, even once bringing us a tile from the space shuttle. Every morning she'd assign us a new logic puzzle to help us learn to problem solve in new ways and think outside the box. She helped foster in me the ability to question assumptions and biases in how we think as human beings, including in science, gender, and religion.

The Transgender Narrative

I have never understood or described my experience of being transgender as being a woman trapped in a man's body. As previously discussed, I believe that gender is much more complex than a male/female binary, and my identity does not fit neatly into either of these two societally prescribed categories. Yet despite all the ways I don't feel I fit this "typical" transgender narrative, I nevertheless have sought out medical interventions to transform my body. I have undergone transition-related care including hormone replacement therapy, breast augmentation, and genital reconstruction surgery including vaginoplasty. Rather than understand my reasons for seeking out these procedures as indicative of an innate desire to be a "true" woman, I understand them simply as a desire to be able to express my gender to others, and to experience my own body, in ways that more closely match my gender identity. I can't begin to understand all the biological and cultural factors that led to my intense desire to be able to seek out transition-related care so that I could experience living in a body more like a cisgender female. What I do know is that each of these medical interventions has made me happier, made me more able to feel comfortable in society, and allowed me to more fully enjoy relationships and sex.

Yet why do so many transgender people assert the "typical" transgender narrative that they are really a woman or man trapped in the wrong body? The history of this narrative is deeply tied to the struggles of transgender people to access medical interventions like I underwent, and to the struggles to assert our human rights, including the right to access health care. Historians including Dean Spade, Susan Stryker, Patrick Califia, and Joanne Meyerowitz have traced the development of this transgender narrative as a societal construction produced through patients seeking out transition-related medical care, doctors they went to for help, media, and scientific publications.

The vast majority of scientific and academic literature about transgender people has been written by cisgender people—and this literature is replete with examples of cisgender people cherry-picking stories about transgender people's lives in order to illustrate their own theories, access research funding, sell a hit book, or gain academic credibility in the eyes of cisgender people. As a result, even when transgender people do share their own stories, their stories are nevertheless largely understood by the public through the distorted lens—the "cracked looking-glass"—of what cisgender people have already written. In response to the historical trend, in their essay "Mutilating Gender," Spade asserts an ethical code that anyone researching or writing about transgender people's lives should follow:

> Sexual and gender self-determination and the expression of variant gender identities without punishment (and with celebration) should be the goals of any medical, legal or political examination of or intervention into the gender expression of individuals and groups.[11]

---

11. Dean Spade, "Mutilating Gender," in The Transgender Studies Reader, ed.

In the essay, Spade, who was assigned female at birth, describes how the process of seeking out medical intervention to make certain aspects of their body appear more masculine—a double mastectomy—yet does not desire transforming other aspects of their body through taking hormones or genital reconstruction surgery. When they speak with medical professionals who can help them access surgery, they are met with resistance every time they try to explain that they do not desire for the world to view them solely as male and that they did not understand themselves as transgender from a young age. They consistently refuse their counselor's frame of being a man trapped in a woman's body, and because of that, are initially refused access to surgery. Spade then attends a support group where other transgender people share their stories of lying and stretching the truth so that medical professionals would hear what they wanted to hear to approve transition-related care. Spade uses this personal narrative to demonstrate why and how we must change the narrow, limiting ways in which transgender identities are understood so that everyone can access the medical care that is right for them, not what biased cisgender medical professionals think is right for them.

John Money, a cisgender doctor whose work at Johns Hopkins University pioneered transgender and intersex care in the United States in the 1960s, had an extremely strong influence on shaping how transgender people's identities are understood. Money was infamous for the ethical disregard for his patients. He was obsessed with proving that one could control people's gender identities through medicine and psychology. In an infamous experiment where he forced a pair of identical twins to live as different genders, both twins committed suicide by their thirties. Money was incredibly homophobic and believed that a gender binary was absolutely critical to society—and that a doctor's role is to enforce a strict female/male gender divide and heterosexuality in children, including intersex children. He coached parents on how, by enforcing binary gender roles from birth, they could stop their children from ever becoming transsexual—which he viewed as to be avoided at all costs. The irony that one of the first doctors to treat transsexuals believed transsexuality absolutely was a worst-case situation—to be corrected immediately—and that homosexuality is wrong, is a contradiction that echoes throughout the

Susan Stryker and Stephen Whittle (New York: Routledge, 2006), 317.

history of medicine, where the same people who developed methods to treat transgender people also developed methods to punish and eradicate "deviant" genders and sexualities through practices like reparative therapy.

In the 1970s, Catholic psychiatrist Paul McHugh replaced Money at Johns Hopkins' Gender Identity Clinic and actively worked to dismantle the program. He commissioned a highly biased study which penalized male-to-female transsexual patients for not being stereotypically feminine enough, including if they were married to a woman or if they had a job in a male-dominated field. In addition to refusing to provide transition-related care to transgender women who were not stereotypically feminine enough in his eyes, he would systematically ridicule and dehumanize his patients, referring to them as "caricatures of women."

Dr. Ray Blanchard, a Catholic sexologist in Canada who also treated transgender women, took Money's and McHugh's theories even further in order to impose his moral views on his patients. He theorized that the only true transsexuals were ones who were attracted exclusively to men: all others were simply exhibiting symptoms of an immoral sexual fetish. This "fetish" is referred to by Blanchard as autogynephilia—someone who is "sexually oriented toward the thought or image of themselves as a woman." Blanchard would regularly diagnose transgender patients as autogynophiles to deny them transition-related care. He saw it as his duty to prevent patients from medically transitioning except in only extreme circumstances.

Even doctors who displayed more compassion for their transgender patients, including the 1950s pioneer Harry Benjamin, developed a gatekeeping system to determine if patients were "truly" transgender. While Benjamin's work was informed by his beliefs that variation from "normal" gender roles was pathological, he was an advocate for his patients' rights and helped author the first international Standards of Care (SOC) for treating transgender people. Now in its seventh edition, the SOC maintains this biased gatekeeping system on who can access transition-related care, making it difficult or impossible for many transgender people to access care if they don't fit the approved mold of what transgender is supposed to look like.

In addition to the SOC, the American Psychological Association's *Diagnostic and Statistical Manual of Mental Disorders* (*DSM*) has remained to this day a central piece holding together this gatekeeping system.

The criteria for assessing whether someone would be diagnosed with "transsexualism"—later described as "gender identity disorder (GID)" in the *DSM-IV* and now in the *DSM-5* as "gender dysphoria"—have rather transparently reinforced distinct, dichotomous gender roles and compulsory heterosexuality through the *DSM*'s various editions. The *DSM-IV* describes boys with gender dysphoria as those who "enjoy playing house, drawing pictures of beautiful girls and princesses...avoid rough-and-tumble play and competitive sports and have little interest in cars and trucks."[12] It goes so far as to state in its diagnosis of gender dysphoria that playing with Barbie dolls—a toy that's been critiqued by hundreds of feminists as reinforcing dangerous stereotypes about women—is an indication that a child might properly be diagnosed as a transgender girl.

Blanchard, a contributor to the *DSM*, has seen his theory of autogynephilia included in several editions. While separated from the diagnosis gender dysphoria in the most recent edition, it found a new place in the *DSM-5* under the diagnosis of "transvestic fetishism." Blanchard also added a new theory of his to the *DSM-5*, "autoandrophilia," which describes transgender men attracted to men as having a psychological disorder. This transvestic fetishism diagnosis continues to be used to demonize, discriminate against, and deny treatment to transgender people who—like myself—do not identify as heterosexual.

To respond to the gatekeeping system developed by doctors, transgender patients developed networks as early as the 1950s to coach each other on what to say in order to get treatment. Patients knew they had to say they believed they were "true" men or women, who had unfortunately been "trapped in the wrong body." As previously explored, this narrative has become reinforced through the media and through advocacy efforts, where repeating the same easily digestible formula helps sell magazines, books, and TV shows and helps fund transgender organizing.

Even though I understand the history of how this narrative was created and reinforced, I nevertheless constantly feel a dangerous pull on my own gender identity, trying to convince me that perhaps I am not a "true" woman because my story is not like Jazz Jennings's. It's an incredibly scary feeling, all the more so because I like to think that my academic research inoculates me. I often search through my memories for a way to validate

---

12. http://www.genderpsychology.org/transsexual/dsm_iv.html

my story—did I ever want to play with a doll instead of a spaceship? Even in sharing this origin story, I've highlighted a few details that match with the *DSM-5*: I liked wearing flowing robes and had early memories of wanting female genitals. Ultimately though, it is oppressive that anyone should have to cherry-pick their memories to validate one very sexist definition of being real.

Monsters and Existentialism

Siouxsie Sioux, frontwoman for the punk/goth bands the Creatures and Siouxsie and the Banshees, has long been a role model for me. In her 2003 song "Godzilla!," she describes how she never felt drawn to typical girl's toys and instead loved her toy Godzilla, because he "trashes cars" and "shakes the ground."[13] She also describes her affinity for swinging a "riding crop," suggestive of the sexually explicit and blasphemous BDSM themes present in her fashion and lyrics throughout her career. In her improvised reimagined version of the Lord's Prayer, which, in 1976, was the first song she ever performed, she sings about how "there's never ever been a heaven" and "claim me guilty [of sin]."[14]

Siouxsie's music and fashion demonstrated to me that there's no wrong way to be a woman. Sometimes you really do have to shake the ground and create your own path, including defying religion. As a teenager, I would spend up to half an hour a day teasing my hair and coating it with hairspray to look like hers. When I was published in the 2010 book *Gender Outlaws: The Next Generation* about being a transgender woman on a women's roller derby league, I used the pen name Uzi Sioux because I did not want to be outed at the time.

In one of my LiveJournal entries around age nineteen, I described why goth—a subculture that Siouxsie Sioux helped pioneer and inspire—was so important to my gender identity. It was a place where the gender binary was regularly called into question, if not ignored altogether, and it gave me a sense that there were possibilities beyond identifying as male:

---

13. The Creatures, "Godzilla!," Metrolyrics, http://www.metrolyrics.com/godzilla-lyrics-creatures.html.

14. Siouxsie and the Banshees, "The Lord's Prayer: Lyrics," Metrolyrics, http://www.metrolyrics.com/the-lords-prayer-lyrics-siouxsie-and-the-banshees.html.

What I also discovered through goth, which still resonates with me today even more than the music I listened to then, was a world where I could actually express my emotions, where I could wear makeup, where I could act femmey, dress androgynous, and where I could be somewhat accepted by a community of amazing girls who broke all the rules of what being a girl was supposed to mean…goth was the first time, ironically enough, that I could look outward to meeting other people, rather than just hiding in my books. And I could go to a club (there were some I managed to get into even though I was under 18, and well under 21), or maybe a renaissance faire, where I could live in a different world, and I could make myself look pretty and other people would like me, and they would talk to me, and maybe they'd even accept me as one of their own, and I could feel I had some sense of family or community.

Taking part in theater in high school also had a huge influence on my gender identity and atheism. There was a lot of crossover between my goth friends and theater friends, and several of them identified as LGBTQ. Also, theater gave me a monster I could identify with—Caliban from Shakespeare's *The Tempest*. I took part in two separate productions of the play—first while on stage crew, and second as an actor playing Caliban at the Folger Shakespeare Library Student Festival.

I related to how he was treated like an outcast, a survivor of a matriarchal culture that had been erased by the colonizing Prospero and Miranda. In a line I have always carried with me, Caliban articulates how it feels to have their own language and history replaced:

> You taught me language, and my profit on't
> Is, I know how to curse. The red plague rid you
> For learning me your language![15]

It was also through theater in high school that I first was exposed to existentialism, in the form of Jean-Paul Sartre's *No Exit*. While on stage crew, I studied the dozens of rehearsals and shows. Immediately afterward I checked out a lecture series from the library by Professor Robert Solomon called "No Excuses: Existentialism and the Meaning of Life."[16] It wasn't

---

15. William Shakespeare, *The Tempest*, act 1, sc. 2, *The Complete Works of William Shakespeare*, http://shakespeare.mit.edu/tempest/tempest.1.2.html.

16. Robert C. Solomon, "No Excuses: Existentialism and the Meaning of Life,"

just the rejection of supernatural belief that inspired me. I was completely enthralled by the idea that it was up to us, as individual human beings, to make a conscious choice to create purpose and meaning for our own lives. As someone who intensely experienced the injustices I saw in the world, including my own struggles with gender, I felt impassioned by the Sisyphean existential hero who would work to change the world.

As I graduated high school and began college, I began grappling with severe depression. Counter to the negative stereotypes of existential despair, I found the philosophy gave me intense hope and helped me keep going. In a journal entry from that time, I quoted Sartre:

> Existentialism is nothing less than an attempt to draw all the consequences of a coherent atheistic position. It isn't trying to plunge man into despair at all. But if one calls every attitude of unbelief despair, like the Christians, then the word is not being used in its original sense.... In this sense, existentialism is optimistic, a doctrine of action, and it is plain dishonesty for Christians to make no distinction between their own despair and ours and then to call us despairing.[17]

The philosophy of existentialism continues to speak to me to this day. It inspires me to fight for social justice, no matter how impossible winning against the powers of oppression might seem. It inspires me to value my time on this earth, because it is all we have, and to use that time to better the conditions of others and to fight for future generations.

Mental Health and Finding Affirmation

Like many transgender people, I've struggled with mental health. I have bipolar disorder. It was not diagnosed until I was in college, when the depressive episodes became more noticeable and severe. It wasn't until after I began treatment for bipolar—medication and counseling—that I began to have the mental stability and clarity to focus on exploring my transgender identity and ultimately transitioning.

The Great Courses, http://www.thegreatcourses.com/courses/no-excuses-existentialism-and-the-meaning-of-life.html.

17. Jean-Paul Sartre, "Jean Paul [sic] Sartre Quotes," iPerceptive.com, http://iperceptive.com/authors/jean_paul_sartre_quotes.html.

My worst depressive episode came my freshman year of college. I had freshly shaken off religion in high school, replacing it with extensive self-guided reading in philosophy and literature. I had a large number of LGBTQ and atheist friends. I was beginning to understand my gender identity. But after I graduated high school, I became trapped in what felt like a very nonsupportive college environment at Rice University. I am lucky I survived, as I contemplated suicide more than once.

Suicidal ideation, depression, anxiety, and other poor mental health outcomes are very common for transgender people because of the social stigma and marginalization they experience. In a 2015 national survey of over 27,000 transgender people, 39 percent had recently experienced intense psychological distress, and 40 percent had attempted suicide in their lifetime.[18] The psychological establishment, including the *DSM-5*, has recognized in recent years that gender dysphoria is not in itself a mental illness. However, many transgender people nevertheless struggle, which is directly correlated with the social isolation and discrimination they face. Figuring out that you are transgender, which involves questioning deeply held societal beliefs about your place in the world, is an incredibly scary process. Coming out as transgender at a school or a workplace makes you an easy target for bullying and harassment. For many, this leads to dropping out of school or losing a job.

The good news is that there's strong evidence that societal acceptance leads directly to positive mental health outcomes for transgender people. Several peer-reviewed studies have shown that children who socially transition in supportive environments—including among families, teachers, counselors, and other children—do not have significantly higher levels of depression or suicide than the general population.

However, the religious right has used the high rates of depression and suicide in the transgender community to argue instead for reparative therapy through coercive behavior modification. Medical science has widely discredited any evidence that you can forcibly change a child's sexual orientation or gender identity, and furthermore, has proven that such efforts actually lead to increased instances of suicide and depression in children. While religious organizations have generally stopped pushing "ex-gay" reparative therapy to "cure homosexuals," these same organizations

---

18. http://www.ustranssurvey.org/report.

still are publicly pushing "ex-trans" reparative therapy.

Dr. Paul McHugh, the same doctor who mistreated his transgender patients, continues to use his status as a professor emeritus as Johns Hopkins University to advocate for reparative therapy. Dr. Kenneth Zucker, a protégé of transgender researcher Ray Blanchard, also continues to promote behavior modification therapy to "cure" transgender kids—even after he was publicly ousted from the Child, Youth, and Family Gender Identity Clinic in Toronto for poor practices. The American College of Pediatricians are an especially influential and dangerous religious right group who are working to push reparative therapy in schools throughout the country—including by passing laws to criminalize parents who do not subject their transgender children to it.

Thankfully, I was never subjected to reparative therapy. However, my experience at Rice University included being surrounded by evangelical Christians who believed in it, which caused me intense psychological distress. The irony was that at Rice, I was supposed to be in the perfect place to follow my dreams. I was studying engineering at a college esteemed for its alumni's contributions to NASA, at a location right next to Space Center Houston. My grades were perfect. I was physically healthy; in fact, I was getting stronger every day through weight lifting with my roommate, Jim. But despite everything, I felt socially isolated. I felt I had lost my purpose and direction in life.

I had almost no LGBT people around me, and most of my friends, including Jim, were evangelicals. I knew one gay man, whom I didn't relate to at all. My friend Brad and his girlfriend, Esther, were both bisexual, and we'd go to a goth club each week. A few times Brad cross-dressed when we went out. But Brad was not transgender, and this one night a week was a pale reflection of the vibrant communities I'd been surrounded by in high school.

Other than the club, the hour in the weight room each day with Jim was the only time I felt okay. I had been picked on as a kid for being small and scrawny, and within months I had put on nearly twenty pounds of muscle. Jim and I loved music, and we would play a game in the weight room of trying to be the first to name whatever song came on the radio. Rarely would the conversation be serious, and I liked that, because otherwise it would remind me how different we were. But one day I decided I had to try to tell Jim what I was experiencing:

"Jim, I wish I could understand myself. I wish I made sense. I wish that, when a hot guy and a hot girl walked into a room, I was more attracted to the hot guy."

His response was: "Why would you want that?"

What I was trying to express, and struggling to do so, was that I wanted to be able to understand why I didn't feel at all like a straight man. I'll always remember that moment as the first time I ever tried to "come out" to somebody. But Jim never got it.

I increasingly felt trapped in my engineering program. Science and math had always been fun and intellectually challenging subjects—but now I faced the realities of an engineering career. It included an environment where I was surrounded by straight cisgender men who made sexist jokes and disparaged people like me who also liked arts and humanities. A recent longitudinal study by MIT showed that a major reason women drop out of STEM careers is the "hegemonic masculine culture of engineering" where they were not "taken seriously," and that is exactly what I was experiencing.[19] And while I still loved space, I didn't feel like the central thing that had made me interested in engineering over any other career path—my passion for creativity—could flourish here.

Then there was Campus Crusade for Christ (Cru). They were our campus's biggest organization, and they were everywhere. They'd hold huge outdoor gatherings, constantly try to recruit people by advertising with flyers and Bible quotes everywhere. It was a radically different experience than I'd had in my high school, which was incredibly secular. In an act of rebellion, I started putting quotes from existentialist philosophers under their Bible quotes, but word caught on, and I became a target. It also didn't help my popularity that I wore black every day with hair in a Mohawk or looking like Siouxsie Sioux's; at one point someone came up to me and explained how he was an ex-goth who could help me find salvation.

My isolation and depression was keeping me up at night, and I started taking over-the-counter sleeping pills to try to help me deal with it. But what started as temporary insomnia led to weeks of feeling like a zombie, barely getting out of bed during the day, yet being completely unable to fall asleep at night until I took one, two, three, maybe four pills. I dropped

19. Susan S. Silbey, "Why Do So Many Women Who Study Engineering Leave the Field?" *Harvard Business Review,* August 23, 2016, https://hbr.org/2016/08/why-do-so-many-women-who-study-engineering-leave-the-field.

classes. I could barely write, barely function, and saw no release. I started to wonder what would happen if I swallowed the whole bottle of sleeping pills—would it be enough to take me out?

Literally the one person who saved my life though was my English professor, Dr. Thad Logan. Professor Logan taught English 201 and was friendly to me outside of class, including giving me rides to events at the local bookstore. One of our assigned readings was *The Tempest*. Reading it, I relived the moment of self-discovery I'd had playing Caliban. The rigorous academic analysis of literature I was taught in Logan's class was also like nothing I had experienced in my science-and-tech–oriented high school, where Shakespeare had been dismissed as a hobby. I found her class even more challenging than my differential equations or mechanical engineering classes. I had a revelation, which I recorded in my journal:

> Halfway through the semester, we were asked to read *The Tempest*. Excited by the opportunity to revisit the happiness that that play had brought me [in high school], I emailed my teacher photos from Shakespeare Troupe's production of the play and offered to discuss them with the class. My wish granted, for the next two classes I lectured about the play, spurring on class discussion that really got people thinking. I was changing the world through ideas that came not from a science experiment, but from my knowledge of Shakespeare. The magic I had felt on stage found me again, except this time it was in a classroom. It was then that I realized that I did not have to go against my heart by studying engineering for the next four years, because all of the passion that I felt for English could be transformed into something worthwhile in the real world.

I started sharing with Professor Logan how unhappy I felt at Rice studying engineering. She encouraged me to consider both switching my major and transferring schools. I started researching and visiting other colleges. But my depression was still so great, I couldn't even start writing a college application—every time I tried, I'd delete my writing, completely doubting myself, and that just deepened my despair.

So one day, in a moment I will forever be thankful for, Professor Logan sat me down in her office to write my application. She stood over me at the computer, literally holding my hand if I tried to delete a single word, all the while saying, "just keep writing."

Performing Identity

I finished that application. And then another. And then another. And suddenly I started feeling I had hope. I made sure each college had an LGBTQ-friendly culture and wasn't heavily religious. One college I read about was in the top four for "students who ignore God the most," even though it was a historically Quaker college. After visiting, I knew it was the right one—and my sophomore year I transferred to Swarthmore College.

Swarthmore was finally where I could thrive. I immediately joined the Swarthmore Queer Union (SQU), where for the first time I met another transgender person and was surrounded by queer women I related to. Swarthmore held on to secular Quaker values that informed their dedication to social justice and the idea that everyone had an "inner light," which meant that we were all encouraged to be individuals. I was in an environment where engineers, sociologists, historians, and poets sat at the same table for meals and were part of the science-fiction club together, and no one believed that a particular course of study meant that you were inherently smarter, more creative, or more dedicated to your career than others. I started wearing a skirt and enjoyed that others did not find it strange. Even before I changed my name, I asked members of SQU to use female pronouns to refer to me, which felt very validating. By my junior year, I came out as both genderqueer and a transgender woman, and I found the college community to be incredibly accepting. My senior year I began a medical transition, taking my first dose of hormones while at the women's resource center, where I was already regularly volunteering.

My studies revolved around my interest in theater, modernist and postmodernist thought, and the history of gender and sexuality. Queer theory helped me understand how modern culture created the concepts of sexual orientation and gender identity. The very notion of identity, often celebrated as something deeply personal and liberating, also has its roots in systems meant to oppress us. A culture that demands that we *know* who we are has reasons to make that demand of us—to determine what capitalist products to sell us, to calculate what our labor is worth, or to divide us as competing political constituencies.

At the same time that I was studying philosophy, I was learning how to perform a character on stage. Using stylized movements and often wearing a mask, I learned to portray the archetypal male and female characters from commedia dell'arte—characters whose identities are defined by how they interact with each other. Arlecchino is always trying to trick his master, sometimes for food or personal gain, while Arlecchino's love interest Columbina uses disguises and wits to trick him or aid her mistress. Their roles are entirely defined by relationships established in the sixteenth century; because of those roles, the audience can easily understand a plot that is improvised and involves pantomime. Like the commedia plot, gender has been performed so many times that we need very little context to understand it. The context is so embedded in our memories that a million different improvisations will still register as only one of two options: male or female, Arlecchino or Columbina.

As Judith Butler writes in her foundational queer theory text *Gender Trouble*:

> Gender is always a doing, though not a doing by a subject who might be said to pre-exist the deed.... [As Nietzsche said,] "There is no 'being' behind doing, effecting, becoming; the 'doer' is merely a fiction added to the deed—the deed is everything."... There is no gender identity behind the expressions of gender; that identity is performatively constituted by the very 'expressions' that are meant to be its results.[20]

Arlecchino and Columbina do not actually exist as beings; they are performed using stylized expressions understood by the audience because of the characters' relationships to each other and to the masters they serve. Male and female do not actually exist as identities; male and female are performed using stylized expressions defined by their relationships to each other, and to the systems of power that they serve. Just as Columbina is the subject of her mistress, in society, women are subjects to many forms of oppression: colonialism, racism, sexism, cissexism, classism, ableism, and more. These forms of oppression are maintained through systems of power including religion, medicine, science, media, capitalism, government, and even the nonprofit organizations we form to serve our communities.

My senior year, as a leader of SQU, I invited queer theorist Dean Spade to speak at our 2006 LGBTQ academic conference about their nonprofit advocacy work at the Sylvia Rivera Law Project (SRLP). I was at the time

---

20. Judith Butler, *Gender Trouble: Feminism and the Subversion of Identity* (New York: Routledge, 1999), 179.

interning at an organization in Philadelphia called the Trans-Health Information Project (TIP), which served a similar clientele to SRLP: primarily low-income Black and Latinx transgender women, many of whom engaged in sex work. These women's experiences with gender were vastly different from mine; while I had a campus that gave me free rein to wear what I wanted, the clients I worked with regularly risked physical and sexual assault if they did not pass as feminine women. Several of the women who ran TIP were former clients, including GiGi. I looked up to GiGi immensely. GiGi could command anybody with her wits and charm, took shit from nobody, and had a fierce and beautiful femininity. As a Black transgender woman, GiGi personally knew the struggles of the community she was serving, and I wanted to know why more people like her weren't running LGBTQ organizations.

I invited Dean Spade to Swarthmore to speak to my predominantly white and middle-class LGBTQ campus community on how those of us with privilege can support the leadership of people like GiGi. His lecture explored the history of how nonprofits advocating for the rights of gay, lesbian, and bisexual people have erased the contributions of transgender people of color to the LGBTQ movement, including Latinx transgender pioneer Sylvia Rivera. As a lawyer, he had founded SRLP to empower local transgender people of color to conduct legal advocacy on their own behalf, and he'd stepped away from leadership once SRLP was being led by them. After hearing Spade's lecture, I never expected that years later I'd find myself working at an LGBTQ nonprofit: but every day I carry with me a dedication to support leadership of those more marginalized than me—and step away from leadership if need be to make space.

Feminism and Trans-Misogyny

My experience interning at TIP also included attending a funeral for a client. Erika Keels, a young Black trans woman, was murdered in a hate crime in 2007. TIP was informed by a harm-reduction approach to sex work, meaning our goal was to keep clients as safe as possible, including providing condoms, observing the police, and monitoring areas they worked. Volunteers saw Erika exit a vehicle driven by a john; the john then backed up, ran her over, changed gears, and ran her over again. When other trans women and TIP volunteers asked the police to investigate, the police refused, saying, "It was nothing," "She was nothing," and then harassed the trans women, demanding they tell them their "real" names.

There was nothing in my studies that could have prepared me for the emotional impact of attending her funeral. People like Erika were dying every day from violence—violence ignored by police complicit in a culture that punished blackness as the *other* and punished femininity as being fake.

Feminism has been complicit in this system. White feminists have often reinforced racism and cissexism in their single-minded quest to defeat sexism. In the 1970s and 1980s, radical feminism, inspired by feminist theory that exposed femininity as a social construct, proposed that in order to be liberated as a woman, one must transcend femininity. This radical feminism celebrated an androgynous, gender-free aesthetic as a more enlightened form of femaleness. Radical feminists critiqued all power dynamics as oppressive including how one practiced sex: BDSM was bad; porn was bad; top/bottom or butch/femme dynamics were bad; penetration was bad; penises or even dildos were inherently bad. Radical feminists launched crusades against those engaged in the sex industry, conspiring with police and religious right organizations and police to lock up sex workers "for their own good," and in the process regularly targeted women of color and transgender women struggling to survive.

A subset of radical feminists began a cultural movement known as lesbian-separatism, in which they sought to completely free women from sexism by forming "women's only" spaces such as Michigan Womyn's Music Festival (MichFest). However, these "women's only" spaces were truly welcoming only to a small set of predominantly white women—and transgender women were often explicitly excluded by radical feminists. These trans-exclusionary radical feminists (TERFs) were emboldened by feminist theorists like Janice Raymond, who portrayed transgender women as dangerous examples of people "duped" by sexism into embracing an oppressive form of femininity. Raymond demonized transgender women who underwent medical transitions as "cyborgs" created by sexist doctors in order to "rape" women's spaces. TERFs have used these theories to justify all sorts of attacks against transgender women, often colluding with the religious right to pass anti-transgender laws. As someone who attended MichFest twice as a transgender activist trying to peacefully protest the exclusion of transgender women from the space, I know how dangerous TERFs can be. Friends of mine who attended were verbally assaulted, publicly slandered online, and even accused of being sex offenders, causing them to lose their jobs. I personally was traumatized by the constant hate speech and public displays of anti-transgender hate present at the event.

Although MichFest closed in 2015, Raymond's theories still remain quite popular, including the idea that transgender women always have male privilege. This argument of male privilege is used to invalidate transgender women's experiences of sexism, arguing that they don't really experience discrimination in the same way as "real" women. It's used to minimize their experiences of harassment and sexual assault, and even to exclude them from spaces like domestic violence centers. Ultimately, it's a tactic to silence transgender women in order to say that their issues are not women's issues, that their experiences dilute feminism, and that fighting cissexism takes resources and attention away from the "real" fight against sexism.

This is nothing new—it's the same tactic used by white feminists who claimed that women of color fighting racism were taking resources away from the "real" fight against sexism. As Black transgender woman Raquel Willis has pointed out, "When cisgender women do this, it reminds me of how white women in the United States were initially viewed as a more valid type of woman than black women."[21] It's completely self-defeating to claim that one group has a more authentic claim to womanhood than another, just as it is self-defeating to believe that we can somehow eradicate sexism while leaving racism or cissexism intact.

In fact, the particular way transgender women experience sexism gives us a unique insight into how to fight it, and a strong motivation to do so. Transgender women are taught from a young age—through shame, through violence, through religion, through medicine—that being female is wrong. Every expression of femininity we exhibit is an invitation for a priest to denounce us as a sinner, a bully to attack us, or a counselor to put us in reparative therapy. We are denied the language to describe ourselves. We are told by doctors that we aren't "real" enough to get hormones or surgery. We are told that we don't understand feminism, that we have no claim to womanhood. Yet even with all these acts of violence, our femininity persists, our identity persists, and we demand dignity and recognition. Why wouldn't we be on the front lines fighting for our liberation?

21. Raquel Willis, "Trans Women Are Women. This Isn't a Debate," *The Root*, March 13, 2017, http://www.theroot.com/trans-women-are-women-this-isn-t-a-debate-1793202635.

Feminist and transgender writer Julia Serano has coined the term *trans-misogyny* to describe the uniquely harsh ways in which trans women are "ridiculed or dismissed not merely for failing to live up to gender norms, but for their expressions of femaleness or femininity."[22] As long as femininity is understood to be inferior and artificial compared to other forms of gender expression—including by feminists themselves—transgender women will bear the brunt of sexism through trans-misogyny. But if feminism instead is truly trans-inclusive, then together we can expose the ways in which all gender identities are constructed by society, and how no gender is more real or superior than any other. I'm happy to call myself a feminist and be part of that fight.

Our Commitments as Atheists

As atheists, we have a unique perspective on how religion has been used to discriminate and disenfranchise people by those in power throughout history. As humanists, we know what it is like to be told that our ethics, our morals, are not as valid or as real as those held by theists. As a religious minority, we know what it is like to be marginalized by Christianity, and we know that the dominant form Christianity has taken in this country has been white supremacist, anti-woman, and anti-LGBTQ. We must demand that when we fight oppression, we do so in a way that addresses how all our struggles are tied together. As women, when we take on sexism, we must approach it knowing that we are at the same time working to dismantle cissexism, heterosexism, racism, classism, ableism, colonialism, and all systems of oppression.

Intersectionality cannot be just a buzzword; it must be embedded into the DNA of our political organizing. Our struggles are intersectional because our lives are intersectional. Atheists are also women, we are also Black, we are also transgender, we are also immigrants, and we are also disabled.

We are living at a time when theocracy is threatening us like never before. With Donald Trump and Mike Pence taking political office in 2017, we have two right-wing Christian white supremacists in office who

---

22. Julia Serano, *Whipping Girl: A Transsexual Woman on Sexism and the Scapegoating of Femininity* (Boston: Da Capo Press, 2016), ebook, "Trans Woman Manifesto."

have no issue with passing laws to target LGBTQ people and women. They have and will continue to manipulate "religious freedom" in order to do so. As atheists, we must take leadership in educating progressives and the political left in this country about the dangers of the increasing erosion of church/state separation. The Trump administration has put religious-right groups into the center of their policy agenda, groups like the Family Research Council who want to write Christianity into our laws, write laws to force LGBTQ people out of existence, and write laws that ban abortion and reproductive health access.

We have a moral imperative to stand in the way of faith being used to harm transgender people, including literally putting our bodies on the line. Violence against transgender people is already increasing at an alarming rate, as are transgender suicides. Police have never been the answer to anti-trans violence, as one of the greatest perpetrators of such violence. We must resist the Trump administration's efforts to expand policing and the criminal justice system. We must see that system for what it really is—a system built around slavery, one that functions to keep racism and anti-Blackness intact. It's a system where trans women are forced into men's prisons, where they are regularly attacked and sexually assaulted, and where their labor is exploited.

Atheists are highly visible online. Like transgender people, we're often isolated physically and often have to gather our communities at conferences or events that happen only a few times a year. We understand how to organize our communities digitally, whether it's through social media, email, or blogs. We know how to fundraise for each other. We must use our digital skills and online platforms to support other struggles, including transgender people and people of color who have far fewer resources than we often do.

Atheists must stand arm in arm with people of faith against discrimination. When Muslims are attacked, we stand up. When transgender people of faith are rejected by their religious families, we support them with food, housing, clothes, and jobs. We cannot allow our different beliefs to distract us from our common struggles. At the same time, we must continue to demand that we have the moral high ground as atheists and humanists; that we are indeed more moral than white supremacist Christians.

I'm proud to be an atheist, a humanist, a transgender person, a Latinx person, a queer person, a woman. My many identities give me tools and perspectives through which I can fight for justice. I hope that atheists will join me in working together for collective liberation for all people, so we can be our full selves, in all our identities.

12

Biology, Women, and Conservative Abrahamic Religions—A Bad Combination

Abby Hafer, PhD

Other societies and other religions have been just as patriarchal and disrespectful of women: it wasn't much fun being a woman in traditional Hindu, Buddhist, or Confucian societies either. But nowhere else was there the same male sexual panic, the profound, ingrained fear of free women that infests all the Middle Eastern monotheisms.

—Gwynne Dyer[1]

Religion and the Natural World: Sex and Gender

In the beginning, there was one sex and it was female. An individual

---

1. https://www.straight.com/news/gwynne-dyer-fear-free-women-middle-eastern-monotheisms

reproduced by growing a copy of *herself* and releasing that copy into the environment. This was certainly the case with the first self-copying molecule. Since life began with the first self-copying molecule, this means that females are the first, original sex. Let that sink in for a while. In the beginning, it wasn't Adam and Eve; it was Eve.

So Eve (that first self-copying organism) made copies of herself, and those copies made more copies, and more copies, and more copies. In biblical terms, Eve begat Eve and Eve and Eve and Eve.

Eventually, one of those Eves had a mutation—that is, a slight genetic change—and begat a line of slightly different organisms. Let's call them Evelyns. Some of these mutated further and begat lines of Ediths and Ednas. Meanwhile, the Eves were still busy begetting more Eves, but some of those mutated and became Esmes and Esmereldas. So females were really doing pretty well before males came along, thank you very much.

Please note: Any religion that doesn't put females front and center in its creation story is a religion that misrepresents reality. Men may have made up their creation myths long before people knew any better, but we know better now. So those myths should not be perpetuated. Now let's get back to evolution.

The problems began when some of Eve's daughters—let's call them Edith and Esmerelda—started competing with each other. This probably happened very soon after life began. Once there is competition, organisms with mutations that provide an advantage in that competition will breed more in relation to those without the advantageous mutation. This results in a population in which there are many more organisms with that beneficial mutation than there are ones without it. That's the way that evolution works.

For example, the mutation that allowed adult humans to digest milk was incredibly beneficial because it opened up a new food source to adults. Teens and adults with this mutation were less likely to die of starvation and were therefore much more likely to survive long enough to reproduce themselves, and survive long enough to reproduce for many years, and survive long enough to raise their children. This beneficial mutation spread rapidly throughout northern European populations, to the point where now, most humans of European descent can digest milk as adults.

When a new, beneficial mutation comes into existence, the individuals without that beneficial mutation may eventually be so unable to compete for resources that they die out completely. This type of evolutionary competition is sometimes referred to as an arms race. It's a good analogy.

Let's get back to the problem posed by competition between Edith and Esmerelda. The problem was made worse by the fact that Edith continued to mutate and therefore continued to get new advantages over Esmerelda. Meanwhile, poor Esmerelda's offspring didn't always mutate fast enough to keep up. Many lines of Esmereldas were wiped out because of this, and that was the end of their evolutionary line.

Then a mutation took place that allowed some Esmereldas to *swap genes* with other members of the population. Members who were not Esmereldas. And this gene swapping saved the day. That's because some of those newly acquired swapped-in genes allowed the New Esmereldas to compete successfully with that pesky Edith. The New Esmerelda was no longer a pure Esmerelda, but by golly, she was alive. So the New, Improved Esmereldas got ahead in the evolutionary arms race, and it was good. And that, folks, is how sex was born. And it was *good*.

According to evolutionary biologist W. D. Hamilton, one major benefit that sexual reproduction gives us is the ability to stay ahead of parasites. Parasites work by adapting precisely to a very specific host species. The only potential hosts that are likely to survive are those that have the ability to mix their genetics quickly through sexual reproduction, and spread those beneficial mutations through the population quickly, also by sexual reproduction. This allows them to stay ahead of the parasites. Other biologists have also suggested that the gene exchange done by sexual reproduction also means that siblings are not exact copies of one another and are therefore less likely to compete directly with one another for survival. But one way or another, that's what males are for. Males are genetic mixers. They speed up evolutionary change.

Please note: The evolved situation that I described above is very different from the relationship between men and women as it is described in the Bible: "Woman is the reflection of man. Indeed, man was not made from woman, but woman from man. Neither was man created for the sake of woman, but woman for the sake of man" (1 Corinthians 11:4–10).

So according to the Bible, women come from men. Even without our current knowledge of evolutionary biology, this is a bizarre stance, since it is observably true that women give birth to other human beings, both male and female, and that men do not. But it is particularly perverted to state or preach this given our current knowledge about the origins of sex. Suffice it to say that women were not created from men or for men, and that men have no natural authority over women. Now let's get back to evolution.

Evolution and the Problem of Being Male
Since a male's genes can only survive by contributing to somebody else's reproduction, males across the animal kingdom have evolved a wide variety of mechanisms for trying to persuade a female to mate with them. Here's a list containing a few of them:

1. Showing off: Everybody knows about peacocks using their tails to show off and try to attract mates, but did you know about glow-in-the-dark vomit? Crustaceans called ostracods vomit luminous mucous in order to attract mates. Isn't that sexy?

2. Showering females with gifts: Humans do this. Did you know that bowerbirds do too? A male bowerbird makes a really showy nest in order to attract a female.

3. Trapping females, or rape: Trapping females is known to zoologists as "forced copulations." Humans call it rape. Rape is immoral, but evolution should never be taken for a good moral code. People sometimes get confused about this, but the natural phenomenon of evolution doesn't have good morals or bad morals any more than the natural phenomenon of gravity has good morals or bad morals.

4. Penis length: There's growing longer penises than the competition. This is what barnacles do. Barnacles are stationary as adults, so getting sperm to the nearest female is a challenge for male barnacles. They also have to compete with each other over this. They are up to this challenge. Male barnacles can grow penises up to eight times the length of their own bodies. Barnacles have the longest penises in the world, compared to their body length, anyway. Remember this the next time somebody brags about the size of *theirs*.

So I've explained why sexual reproduction is useful, and I've explained the general challenge that males face in trying to reproduce. Let's move on to the whole question of what is natural. People will spend a whole lot of time telling you what kind of sex is "natural" and what kind of sex is "unnatural," but these opinions are generally based on religious and social expectations rather than on actual nature. However, you have just learned that sexual reproduction exists as a means of genetic mixing. That's all it is! This genetic mixing does not require a specific set of gender or sexual characteristics.

Unnatural Acts?

Unfortunately, over the many millennia of our existence, human beings have imagined many mistaken assumptions about sex, and then believed that those assumptions were the solemn and immutable truth. So, I'm going to state a bunch of mistaken assumptions that people have about sex and gender, and then I'll take a look at males and females throughout the animal kingdom. You will see how brilliantly creative evolution by natural selection can be and how diverse the results are in the animal kingdom! There's no one set of rules! Sexuality is a free-for-all! This is what's truly natural, as it's found in nature. You will also begin to notice how many of these mistaken assumptions are based on a particular human's wishful thinking, usually about what they would like to see in their own human society.

Mistaken assumption #1: "Evolution means that males will have no parental involvement and will leave care of the infants and children to females, right?" Wrong. Here's just one example: emus, those big flightless birds from Australia. Once the eggs are laid, the male emu is the one who takes care of the eggs and incubates them. Once the eggs hatch, the male raises the chicks.

Mistaken assumption #2: "Evolution means that males will always be bigger than females and will dominate them." Wrong. For instance, male anglerfish are tiny compared to females. To continue their existence past a certain age, a male anglerfish must attach himself to a female and fuse his tiny body with hers. A female anglerfish may have more than one attached male.

In the biological sciences, having different sexes of different sizes is called sexual dimorphism. You can tell that the people who invented this term were men, since the term *sexual dimorphism* is defined as "males being bigger than females." When the females of a species are larger than the males, this is called *reverse sexual dimorphism*. In other words, human male biologists just assumed that males being bigger than females was the natural state of being.

Mistaken assumption #3: "Males are always the ones with Y chromosomes, right?"[2] Wrong. Birds. All birds. All male birds have two X chromosomes. It's the females who have the Y chromosomes. This is true for some male insects like moths and butterflies as well, and some crustaceans and some reptiles, including the huge lizards called Komodo dragons. It's called the ZW system instead of the XY system, but that's just to make it easier for people to talk about it. So if anyone has any assumptions about "maleness" being ineffably and magically conferred by a Y chromosome, then I'm sorry—it's just not true.

Mistaken assumption #4: "Females and males have separate bodies, right?" Wrong. Many animals are hermaphrodites. That is, they have both male and female reproductive organs. Most snails are hermaphrodites. So are many worms and many jellyfish. In fact, if you exclude insects, about one-third of all animal species are hermaphrodites!

Mistaken assumption #5: "Male input is *always* required for reproduction, right?" No—bonnethead sharks, blacktip sharks, zebra sharks, small white-spotted bamboo sharks, many snakes including boa constrictors, and fifty species of lizards including Komodo dragons can *all* reproduce without males.

Mistaken assumption #6: "But we always see pictures from the Bible of animals being saved from Noah's flood by going onto the ark, two by two. One female and one male. That's what's natural, right?" Two by two, one female and one male? Right? Wrong. First, many species have some male homosexual individuals. For instance, rams. Yes, rams, that very symbol of raging male horniness. Rams are male sheep. About eight percent of all rams form exclusively male-to-male pair bonds, forsaking all contact with female sheep. Some animals routinely practice lesbianism. For instance, the

---

2. For those who need a refresher course, humans have forty-six chromosomes that come in twenty-three pairs. The last pair determines the sex of an individual human. If there are two large chromosomes (known as X chromosomes) in that pair, then the individual will be female. If there is one large X chromosome, and a much smaller chromosome (known as a Y chromosome) in that pair, then that individual will be male. This XY system is what determines sex in most (but not all) mammals. Bird chromosomes look similar to ours, and they too have a final, sex-determining pair of chromosomes. However, if an individual bird has two large chromosomes (the bird equivalent of X chromosomes) in that final pair, then that individual will be male. If a bird has one large chromosome and one small one (the latter being the bird equivalent of the Y chromosome) in that sex-determining pair, then that individual will be female.

species of albatross called Laysan albatrosses has many same-sex female pairs, who nest and raise chicks together. Some animals form trios. Some trios are for child rearing. For instance, skuas often nest as mixed-sex trios and raise chicks together. Some trios are for sex. For instance, a female North Atlantic right whale was photographed by a group of scientists having simultaneous sex with two males. Both penises were in her vagina at the same time. That, by the way, is an example of a multi-male breeding system, where each female may have many male partners.

For something more biblical, there are also multi-female breeding systems, that is, where one male may have many female partners. For instance, northern fur seals. A male northern fur seal will maintain exclusive mating rights with forty or more females. Just like the Old Testament.

But what about primates? Our near relatives in the animal kingdom? Well, it turns out that our fellow primates have all different kinds of breeding systems. Some species of our fellow primates have multi-male breeding systems, some have multi-female breeding systems, and some have monogamous breeding systems. In addition, homosexuality, lesbianism, and bisexuality are all found within nonhuman primates as well.

Mistaken assumption #7: "But at least males are males and females are females, right?" Wrong. Transsexual fish are common!

First: barramundi. These fish transition from male to female. Most of these fish grow up as males. Then, after a breeding season or two, they become female. For that reason, most of the larger individuals are female.

Second: blue gropers. These fish change from female to male. The females are green, and the males are blue. All blue gropers begin life as females. Usually, gropers live in small groups with one male, one or two females, and several juveniles. When the male dies, the largest female grows, changes color and sex, and becomes male. Blue gropers are a type of wrasse, and wrasses are famous for changing their sex, usually female to male.

Third: clownfish. These change from whatever to male or female. Yes, Nemo himself was a transsexual! Clownfish start life with no functioning gonads. They are neither sex. There is one breeding pair, with a large female, a smaller male, and a bunch of nonsexual, or sometimes male, smaller individuals. If the female dies, then the male becomes female. If the male dies, then the largest nonbreeding fish becomes male.

Fourth: dwarf hawkfish. These are even more gender fluid. Hawkfish live in harems, with one dominant male mating with several females. When it comes to sex change, the size of the harem matters. Pay attention carefully now, because the plot to this is worse than a soap opera. If a male hawkfish takes on too many females, then one of the largest females will change sex, become male, and take over half of the harem. But, if that new male hawkfish loses a few females to other harems and is challenged by a larger male, then it goes back to being female. That way it doesn't lose precious energy fighting a losing battle. The ability to change sex in both directions maximizes an individual's ability to reproduce. So, gender-fluidity is the name of the game for many species!

Mistaken assumption #8: "No natural animal aborts its babies, does it?" Wrong. Female rodents can reabsorb a litter if they smell an unfamiliar male. If the litter is too far along for reabsorption, they will spontaneously abort the litter. This process is known as the Bruce effect, named after biologist Hilda M. Bruce. Wild horses, monkeys (geladas), and pipefish also spontaneously abort their broods when circumstances call for it.

Mistaken assumption #9: "So, it is clear that nature does not define sex roles, and it is clear that transsexuality and gender fluidity are real and found in nature, and spontaneous abortion does occur, but at least there are two sexes, right? At most two? Maybe one and a half or one, but two at most, right?" Wrong again. The organism with the most creative sex life that I know of is *Tetrahymena thermophila*. It has seven sexes. You heard me—seven.

This single-celled creature, which has been thoroughly studied by biologist Eduardo Orias, mostly reproduces without sex, dividing into two identical daughter cells. (That's Eve begetting Eve again.) But when food is scarce, the creature can opt for sexual reproduction, which—as I told you before—creates novel genetic combinations that may give daughter cells a better chance of surviving in a harsh environment.

Such tough conditions also rewarded the creatures when they developed more sexes—because it gave them more mating opportunities. That's because individuals of one sex can mate with individuals in any of the other six. If you only have two sexes, there's only a 50 percent chance that someone you meet will be of the right type. But with seven different sexes, a creature's chance of meeting Miss Right or Mr. Right increases to about 85 percent. Eighty-five percent is bigger than fifty percent, so seven sexes wins. *Tetrahymena thermophila* is the swingingest creature I know of.

I think I've done a pretty good job of destroying what is called the argument from nature in regard to gender roles or sexuality, or even abortion. There is no such thing as an "unnatural" gender role. Any time a religion—or anybody else—says that women are being "unnatural" if they support themselves, have men do some or all of the child rearing, or otherwise don't do what religious conservatives think they ought to do, it is clear that the religious conservatives are making things up. Any time a religion—or anybody else—says that non-heterosexual sex is wrong because it is unnatural, it is also clear that they are making things up. Even with abortion, the argument from nature fails. It's clear that we should not make assumptions about naturalness, or unnaturalness, of any given gender role, gender fluidity, transsexuality, or decisions about pregnancy. We cannot use the excuse of what is "natural" as an excuse for the bad treatment of women, or men, or anybody in the LGBTQ+ community, if by "natural" you mean anything that occurs in nature.

Women's Reproductive Systems Are Clearly Evolved, Because a Divine and "Intelligent" Designer Wouldn't Be This Incompetent

Now that I've discussed reproduction and gender roles in the rest of nature, let's move on specifically to women and examine the natural state of the human female reproductive system. In the days before modern medicine, giving birth frequently killed the woman, the baby, or both. In the 1700s, in England there was a one in one hundred chance of a woman dying, for every live birth.[3] In the United States in the early 1900s, six to nine women died for every thousand live births.[4] In places where modern medicine is not available, the situation is just as bad today. In 2002 in the Afghan province of Badakshan, fifty to eighty women died for every thousand live births.[5] In 2010 in Afghanistan, a woman had a one in thirty-four chance

---

3. Geoffrey Chamberlain "British Maternal Mortality in the 19th and Early 20th centuries," *Journal of the Royal Society of Medicine*, 99, no. 11 (November 2006), 559–63.

4. Centers for Disease Control and Prevention, "Achievements in Public Health, 1900–1999: Healthier Mothers and Babies," *Morbidity and Mortality Weekly Report* 48, no. 38 (October 1, 1999), 849–58.

5. Linda Bartlett et al., "Maternal Mortality in Afghanistan: Magnitude, Causes, Risk Factors and Preventability, Summary Findings," Afghan Ministry of Public Health, Centers for Disease Control and Prevention, and UNICEF, November 6,

of dying as a result of pregnancy over the course of her life.[6]

There is also the problem of fistula. In a prolonged labor, the tissue around the birth canal can get squeezed and deprived of blood for a long time. This can result in dead tissue. Unfortunately, the birth canal is not the only body system with a tube in that area. The tubes for the digestive system and the urinary system are right next to the birth canal and can get squeezed as well, also resulting in tissue death. The result is that when healing takes place, if it does, the dead tissue drops away and connections form between the birth canal and the rectum, or between the birth canal and the ureter. The result is that the woman dribbles feces uncontrollably from her birth canal. Or she dribbles urine uncontrollably from her birth canal. These connections are known as obstetric fistulas. The woman will probably eventually die from infections, kidney disease, or kidney failure, all of which are a direct result of obstetric fistulas. In the meantime, the woman will be uncontrollably filthy and may be rejected by her family and society.

Fistulas are a routine occurrence in areas where there isn't access to modern medicine. In the developed world, a labor that promises to be that prolonged will usually merit a cesarean section, which will prevent fistulas. Or if a fistula threatens to form after the birthing process, a doctor can intervene to prevent this during the healing period that follows birth. But this goes to show yet another way in which childbearing in the natural environment is difficult, dangerous, and even fatal. And if God designed this system, then God is a moron.

Babies, too, have a high mortality rate when modern medicine is not available. In 2011 in rural Bangladesh, seventeen out of a thousand babies died as a result of the birthing process alone.[7]

In short, women's reproductive systems don't work very well. In fact, these days, pregnant women and their doctors often avoid the birth canal altogether and do cesarean sections instead.[8] These are being done in

2002, afghana.com/Articles/maternalmortalityafghanistan.doc.

6. World Health Organization et al., "Lifetime Risk of Maternal Death (1 in: Rate Varies by Country)," Data, World Bank, 2015, http://data.worldbank.org/indicator/SH.MMR.RISK.

7. Abby Hafer, *The Not-so-Intelligent Designer* (Eugene, OR: Cascade Books, 2015), 51.

8. As of 2015, the rate of cesarean delivery was 32 percent in the United States. See Joyce A. Martin et al., "Births: Final Data for 2015," *National Vital Statistics*

ever-increasing numbers. Many times this is done in order to save the life of the woman, the baby, or both. Even when vaginal delivery does take place, the vagina is often sliced open so as to make it wider and make more room for the baby's head. This is to prevent the vagina from tearing, which, it is claimed, could be even more dangerous than this deliberate cut. This slicing is called an episiotomy, and it happens in about fourteen percent of all vaginal births.[9] If our reproductive systems worked well, then none of this would be necessary or even desirable.

Contrast these statistics about maternal mortality and health with the religious notion of intelligent design. Intelligent design says that an infallible supernatural being deliberately designed the human body. If intelligent design were true, childbirth would not be this dangerous. In fact, women's reproductive systems are a perfect argument *against* intelligent design. In other words, human women's reproductive systems are terrific evidence for evolution. Why? Because the quality standard for evolution is much lower.

The standard for intelligent design is "designed by an infallible creator." The standard for systems that evolve is "good enough to not cause death before reproduction, too much of the time." You can see the difference. With evolution, all that's required is that a species reproduces faster than it dies. If there is suffering and death, that does not matter to evolution, so long as dying does not outstrip breeding. So, many imperfect and even downright dangerous structures and systems can keep going because all that's required is that we breed faster than we die.

Understanding this means that we can understand that women's bodies are not "made" to give birth, as religious conservatives suggest. Understanding this means understanding that women should not be blamed for the pain and suffering that they endure during childbirth, nor should they be blamed for the pain and physical difficulties that they endure after giving birth. Understanding this means understanding that giving birth is painful, dangerous, and physically costly. Understanding this in turn also means understanding that contraception is a necessary part of keeping women alive and healthy.

Religious conservatives often do not accept evolution. Instead,

---

Reports 66, no. 1, January 5, 2017.

9. Alexander M. Friedman, et al., "Variation in and Factors Associated with Use of Episiotomy," *Journal of the American Medical Association* 313, no. 2 (January 13, 2015), 197–199.

they believe some variation on intelligent design. This includes our vice president, Mike Pence, who said the following on the floor of the US House of Representatives:

> I believe that God created the known universe, the earth and everything in it, including man, and I also believe that someday scientists will come to see that only the theory of intelligent design provides even a remotely rational explanation for the known universe.[10]

It should be noted that Mr. Pence's belief in the intelligent design of the human body did not prevent him and his wife from seeking fertility treatments when they had difficulty conceiving children, nor did it stop them from using modern medicine when she gave birth.

What's more, the difficulties involved in human childbirth and the traditional mortality levels for both women giving birth and for babies being born make the idea of an intelligent designer laughable. In addition, from a biological point of view, there are simple things that could have been done better, if only we had been designed, rather than evolved.

Let me explain. The basic design problem for human females is this: human beings walk upright while being very smart. These two attributes have opposing requirements. Walking upright favors people with narrow hips, which make walking much easier and more efficient. Great intelligence, on the other hand, requires large brains. Large brains require large heads. Those large heads have to fit through the female birth canal, and this favors large birth canals and wide hips. The result, in women, is an uneasy compromise. Women's hips are narrow enough that they can walk, because any woman who couldn't walk would die before she could reproduce, in the natural environment. Most women's hips are wide enough, on the other hand, that children can be born, most of the time. This compromise doesn't work very well. Gestation and giving birth are difficult, dangerous, and sometimes fatal. Remember—evolution doesn't care. Many people can die and suffer, just so long as a few more people manage to live.

However, if we had been designed, a good engineer could have come up with some simple fixes. First, we could give birth the way kangaroos

---

10. Speech given by Mike Pence, then a Republican congressman representing Indiana, at the US House of Representatives, July 11, 2002, C-SPAN video, 00:09:20, https://www.c-span.org/video/?171134-2/.

do. Kangaroos are bipeds like us! They give birth to tiny, embryo-like young that finish their gestation outside of the mother's body, in a nice comfy pouch, complete with a nipple for nursing. A large-headed baby could easily be born this way. Think of the benefits! We wouldn't have labor pains! We wouldn't have tissue death and fistula! No more episiotomies! No more cesarean sections! All this would be gone, if only we really had been designed rather than evolved!

Discerning biologists will also realize that if we had been designed from scratch, rather than evolved, there is no reason why we couldn't have been given extra limbs. If we had been built like the mythical centaurs, with four legs, two arms, and a head, then narrow hips would not be so necessary for walking. The four-limbed, one-headed bodies that we have are simply the basic tetrapod body map that has been with land vertebrates ever since lobe-finned fishes first crawled out of the water, some 340 million years ago. Our four-limbed bodies are not the result of planning—they are the result of our evolutionary history.

Of course, conservative religions also ignore the fact that women's bodies are hives of spontaneous abortions. I have already mentioned spontaneous abortions in other animals, but spontaneous abortion also happens routinely in humans. Where humans are concerned, the fact is that over thirty-one percent of all fertilized eggs do not result in live babies![11] I am not talking about human-induced abortions. I'm talking about spontaneous miscarriages. In fact, thirty-one percent is a conservative estimate, based on careful research.

What's more, about twenty-five percent of all fertilized eggs do not even manage to implant on the lining of the uterus, which is just the first step in a pregnancy, after fertilization.[12] This means that twenty-five percent of all fertilized eggs live for only about ten days and then fail to implant. Then they die and pass out of the body along with menstrual fluid. This means that every year millions of embryos come into existence and then die as an undifferentiated lump of cells. The remaining six percent of spontaneous abortions happen after implantation.

---

11. Allen J. Wilcox et al., "Incidence of Early Loss of Pregnancy," *New England Journal of Medicine* 319, no. 4 (July 28, 1988): 189–94.

12. Allen J. Wilcox, Donna Day Baird, and Clarice R. Weinberg, "Time of Implantation of the Conceptus and Loss of Pregnancy," *New England Journal of Medicine* 340, no. 23 (June 10, 1999): 1796–9.

What all this means is that for every one hundred live births, there were about forty-five spontaneous abortions.[13] This shows that our reproductive systems are far from perfect. It shows that gestation is frequently incomplete and often results in a naturally aborted fetus. It also means that if God gives life to each fetus at the moment when egg meets sperm as conservative Christians claim, then God subsequently kills millions and millions of little unborn babies, every year. God is by far the world's busiest abortionist!

This stands in stark contrast to the way that conservative Abrahamic religions view the world. They do not see their God as an abortionist, despite the evidence. They see their God as the giver of life. If fact, they see babies as gifts from God. Since babies are gifts from God, they see women as needing to cooperate with God and bear children whenever He wants them to. In other words, they see women as having one primary role in life: that of baby-birther. In fact, both ancient holy books and later doctrines are all adamant on this point.

I will illustrate this with the following quotations from religious texts. First, the Christian Bible:

> I permit no woman to teach or to have authority over a man; she is to keep silent. For Adam was formed first, then Eve; and Adam was not deceived, but the woman was deceived and became a transgressor. Yet she will be saved through childbearing, provided they continue in faith and love and holiness, with modesty. (1 Timothy 2:12–15)

Next, a longer section from Roman Catholic doctrine:

> The true practice of conjugal love, and the whole meaning of the family life which results from it, have this aim: that the couple be ready with stout hearts to cooperate with the love of the Creator and the Savior. Who through them will enlarge and enrich His own family day by day.[14]

---

13. Here's the math: 31 percent of all fertilized eggs wind up as spontaneous miscarriages. That's 31 out of 100. For every 100 fertilized eggs, 31 of them do not complete gestation. The other 69 do. Therefore, the ratio of spontaneous abortions to live births is 31 to 69, or 31/69. For every 100 babies born alive, there are (100 x 31/69) spontaneous abortions. That equals 44.9275 spontaneous abortions for every 100 live births. Rounding to the nearest integer gives us 45 spontaneous abortions for every 100 live births.

14. Pope Paul VI, "Gaudium et Spes (Pastoral Constitution on the Church in the Modern World)," Second Vatican Council, December 7, 1965, section 50, http://

This tells us that the point of sex is having babies, and the point of having babies is so that God can have as big a family as possible. Of course, the people who have to do the birthing are women. The doctrine continues: "Married Christians glorify the Creator and strive toward fulfillment in Christ when with a generous human and Christian sense of responsibility they acquit themselves of the duty to procreate." This tells us that people have a duty to procreate. This means that women have a duty to have babies. And: "Among the couples who fulfill their God-given task in this way, those merit special mention who with a gallant heart and with wise and common deliberation, undertake to bring up suitably even a relatively large family." This tells us that people are really, really good if they have large families. Which means that to be really, really good, women must give birth many times. Taken together, these statements that are doctrine in the Catholic Church tell us that sex should only be engaged in for the purpose of having babies, and that more babies are far better than fewer babies. Not one word is given regarding the problems and health hazards that women face in the process of gestating and giving birth.

Then there are Christian fundamentalists. Many Christian fundamentalist sects don't believe in using birth control. The Quiverfull movement best illustrates this, though many other fundamentalists act in similar ways for similar reasons. Here's what Kelly Swanson, a member of the Quiverfull movement, had to say: "We just started thinking, 'God is sovereign over life and death. God opens and closes the womb,' Kelly says. 'That's what his word says, so why we're trying to fiddle around and controlling ourselves, we need to stop doing that.'"[15] On the Quiverfull movement's own website, they are clear that they don't use birth control, and they use the Bible as their excuse. Here is their opening statement about themselves:

> We exalt Jesus Christ as Lord, and acknowledge His headship in all areas of our lives, including fertility. We exist to serve those believers who **trust**

---

www.usccb.org/issues-and-action/marriage-and-family/natural-family-planning/catholic-teaching/upload/Gaudium-et-Spes-NFP-Notes-on-Marriage.pdf.

15. Barbara Bradley Hagerty, "In Quiverfull Movement, Birth Control is Shunned," *Morning Edition*, NPR, March 25, 2009, http://www.npr.org/s.php?sId=102005062&m=1.

the Lord for family size, and to answer the questions of those **seeking truth** in this critical area of marriage.[16]

As to their reasoning for wanting large families, their excuse is the Bible, but their intent is political. They intend to outnumber other people, by breeding. Here is their foundational Bible quote:

> What does God say about children and Who creates Life. "Behold, children are a heritage from the Lord, the fruit of the womb is a reward. Like arrows in the hand of a warrior, so are the children of one's youth. Happy is the man who has his quiver full of them. They shall not be ashamed, But shall speak with their enemies in the gate." *Psalm 127:3–5*[17]

Here's their political agenda, as NPR reported from Kathryn Joyce, who has written a book on the subject:

> They speak about, "If everyone starts having eight children or 12 children, imagine in three generations what we'll be able to do," Joyce says. "We'll be able to take over both halls of Congress, we'll be able to reclaim sinful cities like San Francisco for the faithful, and we'll be able to wage very effective massive boycotts against companies that are going against God's will."[18]

This also means that children and parents are just tools. They are treated as such. Here's what they have to say about the demands of child rearing:

> In our own strength we will never have enough time, or patience for that matter, to deal with our children, be it two or ten. But Jesus has patience and we get our strength from Him. Sometimes we also tend to become tunnel-visioned on meeting our children's every whim under the guise of "needs" and feeling guilty if we cannot. We all desire to give each child our very best and plenty of time and love. But we have to face the reality that we cannot physically or mentally be all that they need. Only God can do that.[19]

---

16. "Homepage," Quiverfull.com, http://www.quiverfull.com/.

17. "Who Is in Control?," Quiverfull.com, www.quiverfull.com/birth_control/Who%20is%20in%20Control.doc.

18. Hagerty, "In Quiverfull Movement."

19. "Who Is in Control?," Quiverfull.com.

The above paragraph willfully ignores the fact that caring for two children is in reality very different from caring for ten. What's more, in these societies, women are the caregivers for children as well as the child bearers, and the physical and mental exhaustion caused by caring for children, especially large numbers of them, is pointedly ignored. This is most likely because the problems that women have are seen as unimportant. In fact, the quote above tells us that the men who run this church will take no responsibility at all for the problems created by their doctrine of maximal reproduction. Instead of offering real, substantive help for those raising lots of children, women are simply told that God will give their children what they need. As if God ever changed a diaper, cooked for a family, or went out and earned money.

Please note that the physical damage and suffering caused by child birthing is not even mentioned. I looked over their entire section on birth control and found nothing written about the physical problems of gestation and child bearing. And when it comes to the demands of childrearing, all that is said is that they must trust in God. As if God ever did any babysitting.

As to other Abrahamic religions, Jewish texts say the following on the subject of women and child bearing: "God blessed them and said to them, 'Be fruitful and multiply and fill the earth'" (Genesis 1:28), and after Noah's flood, the command is repeated: "And God blessed Noah and his sons and said to them, 'Be fruitful and multiply, and fill the earth'" (Genesis 9:1). So men are told to have children, but women's role in all this is not mentioned, even though they will be doing all that birthing. Some apologists claim that Jewish families are not required to be large, but their holy texts say otherwise.

First, we are told that the ultimate redemption will come more quickly if people have more children, because basically, there's a storehouse full of souls somewhere called a "guf," and redemption can't come until that storehouse is empty: "The son of David [Moshiach] will not come until there are no more souls in the guf" (Talmud: Yevamot 62a). In this code of law, people who do not fulfill the command to have children are considered to be analogous to murderers. Why? Because they are viewed as having depleted life and having minimized the amount of divine presence in the world. And this, evidently, is as hopelessly bad as murder is. If women don't have children, they might as well be murderers.

Islam also has a great deal to say on the subject of women and baby making: First, we are told that women and baby making should be used for the benefit of Muhammad, in the afterlife: "Marry the loving, child-bearing women for I shall have the largest numbers among the prophets on the day of Resurrection."[20] So according to this, if Muslims out-reproduce everybody else, then Muhammad gets to win a contest against the other prophets after everybody is dead—but living women are the ones who pay the price.

Next we are told that women, as baby makers, should be used for the benefit of men: "Your wives are a place of sowing of seed for you, so come to your place of cultivation however you wish and put forth [righteousness] for yourselves. And fear Allah and know that you will meet Him. And give good tidings to the believers" (Qur'an 2:223). And again, women are to be used for men's benefit: "Wealth and children are the adornment of the life of this world" (Qur'an 18:46). And finally, women are to be used as baby makers for political benefit:

> Undoubtedly the benefits of increasing the nation's offspring are obvious to everyone who thinks about the matter. Hence nations who understand this matter have been keen to encourage their people to increase their numbers and also to make their enemies reduce their numbers by means of specious arguments and sometimes by using means that lead to infertility and having few children, by means of drugs, contaminated food stuffs that reduce fertility and so on. This is one of the means of war used against the Muslim ummah by its enemies.[21]

In all these cases, we can see that the basic doctrine is not in doubt: Conservative Christianity, Judaism, and Islam all agree that women must justify their existence by giving birth, as often as men want them to. What's more, the exact babies that are birthed must be controlled by men. This is the point behind virginity cults, behind a father's permission being needed before a woman marries, and behind the far harsher penalties imposed on women who have sex outside of marriage than are imposed on men who have sex outside of marriage. Laws and traditions surrounding these

---

20. G. Hussein Rassool, *Cultural Competence in Caring for Muslim Patients* (London: Palgrave McMillan, 2014), 61.

21. Muhammad Saed Abdul-Rahman, *Islam: Questions and Answers; Jurisprudence and Islamic Rulings: Transactions, Part 2* (London: MSA Publication, 2014), 13.

dictates are both invented by and enforced by conservative Abrahamic religions.

Since women's primary "purpose" in life, according to conservative Abrahamic religions, is to bear and raise children, this means that women should jump at the chance to bear children. This is often extended to mean that women should only have sex for the purpose of creating children. Since women's bodies are seen as the perfect incubators for embryos, and since women are not supposed to have sex except in order to have children, no excuse may be given for wanting to end a pregnancy.

Creationism and intelligent design may try to make this sound nice by insisting that women's bodies are "designed" for gestation and birth, but as we have learned, nothing could be further from the truth. Ironically, even when they claim to extol motherhood, religions generally make light of the fact that giving birth can be very hard on women and babies. It is also both bizarre and contradictory that women's bodies are seen by Abrahamic religions as being so strong that they can hold up through any number of childbirths, yet they are so weak that women must always submit to men.

My point here is not to say that women should never want to bear children. My point is that women's ability to bear children has been hijacked by religion. In a rational world, childbearing should be a carefully considered decision involving the mother's health, the parents' ability to raise children, the community's willingness to support the family, and the parents' desire to have and raise children in the first place.

Instead, the Abrahamic religions made it into a command that women must follow. Everyone but women benefit from the formula that women must bear as many children as possible—God benefits, the Prophet benefits, political agendas benefit, and men benefit. But women are the ones left with the broken bodies, impaired health, exhaustion, responsibility for raising all those children, and complete dependence upon men. In addition, older children may not benefit from having a mother who is nearly always pregnant and tending to her newest infant.

It is clear that conservative Abrahamic religions want to tightly control female fertility. However, this desire for male control is in direct conflict with female sexuality. What's more, Abrahamic religions don't stop at trying to rigidly control women's childbearing—they are also horrified at female sexuality itself.

The Abrahamic Horror at Female Sexuality

In Abrahamic religions, women who have sex for reasons other than procreation are considered sinful. This is why these religions are so fixated on the idea that women should only have sex in order to give birth.

Think about the wide-ranging types of sexuality found in nature that I described earlier in this essay. Then contrast that with the attitude toward sex shown by conservative Abrahamic religions. In particular, contrast it with how Abrahamic religions look at women who have sex because it is good, healthy fun.

One simple way of understanding this is to look at religious attitudes to women masturbating. Masturbation will never result in an unintended pregnancy and therefore ought to be allowed, if religious sexual rules were really invented only in order to make sure that all children are born within a marriage. However, masturbating by oneself is clearly a case of women having sex strictly for their own pleasure, and it is uniformly forbidden in conservative Abrahamic religions.

Judaism

Judaism generally frowns upon female masturbation as "impure thoughts."[22]

Over the years, many Orthodox rabbis have denounced female masturbation as an illicit act that causes psychological harm and does damage to the marital union.[23]

Catholicism

"By masturbation is to be understood the deliberate stimulation of the genital organs in order to derive sexual pleasure. 'Both the Magisterium of the Church, in the course of a constant tradition, and the moral sense of the faithful have been in no doubt and have firmly maintained that masturbation is an intrinsically and gravely disordered action.'"[24]

---

22. Tracey R. Rich, "Kosher Sex," Judaism 101, http://www.jewfaq.org/sex.htm.

23. Cnaan Liphshiz, "Orthodox Slowly Lifting Taboo on Female Masturbation," *Times of Israel*, December 11, 2013, http://www.timesofisrael.com/orthodox-slowly-lifting-taboo-on-female-masturbation/.

24. "Part Three: Life in Christ," 2352, Catechism of the Catholic Church, http://www.vatican.va/archive/ccc_css/archive/catechism/p3s2c2a6.htm.

"The deliberate use of the sexual faculty, for whatever reason, outside of marriage is essentially contrary to its purpose." For her sexual pleasure is sought outside of "the sexual relationship which is demanded by the moral order and in which the total meaning of mutual self-giving and human procreation in the context of true love is achieved."[25]

Conservative Protestant Christian

If masturbation is done alone and accompanied by lust, then it is a sin.[26]

Islam

Masturbation in form of self-stimulation is forbidden in Shi'ah fiqh. While describing the believers, the Qur'an says, "The believers are...those who protect their sexual organs except from their spouses.... Therefore, whosoever seeks more beyond that [in sexual gratification], then they are the transgressors." (Qur'an 23:5–6)

The last sentence makes it very clear that any sexual gratification outside marriage is considered a transgression of the law of God. And this verse also implies that sex is an act in which two people must be involved. Once when Imam Ja'far as-Sadiq was asked about masturbation, he recited this very verse and mentioned masturbation as one of its examples. In another, the Imam was asked about masturbation; he said, "It is an indecent act."[27]

The short version is this: according to all conservative Abrahamic religions, a woman must never have sex purely for her own enjoyment. Conservative versions of the Abrahamic religions (Judaism, Christianity, and Islam) all treat women's sexuality as something that is dangerous and must be controlled by men, for the purposes of men's procreation, and sometimes, for men's pleasure.

But rules against women masturbating are just one easy example. In general, the idea of happy, responsible female sexuality, and especially promiscuity, is viewed with horror by traditional Abrahamic religions.

---

25. Ibid.

26. Marlena Graves, "Getting to the Root of Female Masturbation," *Christianity Today*, January 5, 2012, http://www.christianitytoday.com/women/2012/january/getting-to-root-of-female-masturbation.html.

27. Sayyid Muhammad Rizvi, *Marriage and Morals in Islam* (Qom, Iran: Ansariyan Publications, 2017), 39.

Getting back to Adam and Eve, the entire Genesis story is a way of illustrating the view that women's sexuality is a danger to men and to society, and it is abhorred by God. Throughout history, even a hint of female promiscuity could ruin lives and careers. This is the reason behind cults of virginity and the restrictive dress codes seen in conservative Abrahamic religions. It is also the reason for female genital mutilation, according to the United Nations:

> FGM is carried out as a way to control women's sexuality, which is sometimes said to be insatiable if parts of the genitalia, especially the clitoris, are not removed. It is thought to ensure virginity before marriage and fidelity afterward, and to increase male sexual pleasure.[28]

The idea that women having sex for their own enjoyment is bad continues to this day. In fact, punishing women for promiscuity both real and imagined also continues to this day, even in America. And it's worth noting that the treatment is not equal toward men. Famously, President Donald Trump tried to make a woman named Alicia Machado seem untrustworthy by saying that she had once made a sex tape.[29]

To that point, Ms. Machado's grievances against Mr. Trump were well documented. When she gained weight after being crowned Miss Universe, the pageant directors put her on a regimen of diet and exercise. Trump— who owned the Miss Universe pageant at the time—publicly humiliated Ms. Machado by inviting the press and their cameras to watch her sweat in a gym and pepper her with questions during her prescribed workout, while he, in a suit and tie, supervised. She further claimed that he referred to her as "Miss Piggy" because of her weight gain and as "Miss Housekeeping," which appears to have been an attempt at shaming her for being Latin American, since, in his racist estimation, all Latinas work in hotels, and since, in his snobbish estimation, housekeeping is an undignified occupation.

---

28. "Female Genital Mutilation (FGM) Frequently Asked Questions," United Nations Population Fund, January 2017, http://www.unfpa.org/resources/female-genital-mutilation-fgm-frequently-asked-questions.

29. Jose A. DelReal, "Trump Bashes 'Disgusting' Former Beauty Queen Alicia Machado, Accuses Her of Having 'Sex Tape,'" *Washington Post*, September 30, 2016, https://www.washingtonpost.com/news/post-politics/wp/2016/09/30/trump-falsely-cites-sex-tape-in-latest-attack-against-former-miss-universe/?utm_term=.e056d4a467d2.

The sex tape alleged by Mr. Trump had nothing to do with Ms. Machado's accusations against him. Trump's response to her accusations, however, was to try to make Ms. Machado seem untrustworthy, and he did this by alleging that she had made a sex tape. No sex tape of this type has ever been found. Mr. Trump himself, on the other hand, did appear in a soft-core pornography tape featuring Playboy Bunnies, but he didn't see this as making him appear to be any less trustworthy.[30] This is a clear case of a wealthy man using a woman's alleged sexual history as a way of gaining power over her, and claiming that she should not be trusted. He asserts that she is not a truthful individual, simply because she may have been sexually uninhibited in front of a camera.

The same thing happened at Fox News during Roger Ailes's time as CEO, from 1996 through 2016. Fox News employed numerous women and sometimes gave them positions of prominence. However, it has recently come out that the head of Fox News, Roger Ailes, routinely sexually harassed female employees and often insisted that if a woman wanted to succeed at Fox News, she had to give Mr. Ailes sexual favors. In one such instance with a woman named Laurie Luhn, he obtained favors in this way and made a videotape of her in a garter belt during their first encounter.[31] He then blackmailed her with: "I am going to put [the tape] in a safe-deposit box just so we understand each other." His reasoning was that if he ever released the tapes, her career would be ruined, but his career would not be. He used this threat to try to silence her. When Ms. Luhn indicated that she might tell the public about the problem of constant harassment at Fox News, Fox did all that it could to make her seem promiscuous, even alleging that she had had an affair with Lee Atwater. Because, evidently, if the woman was promiscuous, then she was automatically untruthful.

So powerful men wanting to control female sexuality is not relegated to the past. Women having sex for their own enjoyment is anathema to Abrahamic religions and to powerful male leaders everywhere. Women

---

30. David Moye, "Donald Trump Appeared in a Playboy Softcore Porn Video," *Huffington Post*, September 30, 2016, http://www.huffingtonpost.com/entry/donald-trump-playboy-porn_us_57eee2fbe4b0c2407cde0fd2.

31. Gabriel Sherman, "The Revenge of Roger's Angels: How Fox News Women Took Down the Most Powerful, and Predatory, Man in Media," *New York Magazine*, September 2, 2016, http://nymag.com/daily/intelligencer/2016/09/how-fox-news-women-took-down-roger-ailes.html.

who have had sex are shamed, especially if they are unmarried. Women who have an obvious sexuality are shamed. In general, powerful men want to control women's sexuality, and happy female promiscuity is seen as a threat to male control of women's bodies and fertility.

Back to the Problem of Being Male

This controlling behavior makes sense when you remember the problem of being male, which was discussed earlier. Remember, since a male's genes can only survive by contributing to somebody else's reproduction, males have to do something to make that reproduction possible. They have to find some way to convince a female to mate with them.

As we saw earlier, there are many approaches that have evolved over the millennia, and to some degree, human males use all four of the ones I listed: They show off, they give gifts, they trap females, and they have longer penises than most apes, which does appear to help with sperm competition. But human males have developed another approach not seen in the animal kingdom: they have invented religion.

The conservative Abrahamic religions combine the first three strategies for persuading women to mate with a given male, and in doing so they have created a package that puts men in charge. First, they show off, in that there is no big male who is bigger than God. Strut around with God on your side, and that'll impress the ladies. Second, they give gifts—what else is salvation, if not a gift? In fact, it is the best kind of gift, from the male point of view, since it requires no effort or giving on the part of the male. In fact, women are told that they are getting a gift, but what they are getting in reality is a set of rules that they must follow in order to achieve salvation in an afterlife that nobody sees. This brings us to strategy three: trapping females. The set of rules that conservative Abrahamic religions give to females basically requires them to be trapped. They must agree to submit to men, to mate only with a man who is their master, and to be dependent on men. This is a perfect recipe for trapping a female.

Once women agree to the basic premises of conservative Abrahamic religions, they are then forced into an authoritarian structure that benefits powerful men and disables women. Women are required to be baby makers who have no control over their own fertility, if they are to achieve salvation—that cheap gift. All power is concentrated in the hands of males, and the males have created authoritarian laws and traditions in order to keep themselves in power. Not surprisingly, this authoritarian strategy is on full display in all issues having to do with women and reproduction. Take, for example, the subject of abortion.

Abortion and Powerful Men

The authoritarian desire to control female fertility is highlighted by the fact that conservative Abrahamic religions love to oppose abortion. They don't just dislike abortion, or even abhor it. They appear to enjoy making public displays of how bad they think it is. Conservative Christians are particularly keen on public displays of opposing abortion. They give many excuses for opposing abortion. Among them are that babies are gifts from God. For instance, in 2012, Republican candidate for an Indiana US Senate seat Richard Mourdock stated that pregnancy, even from rape, is a gift from God: "I struggled with it myself for a long time, but I came to realize life is that gift from God. And I think even when life begins in that horrible situation of rape, that it is something that God intended to happen."[32]

They may also say that babies have souls given by God from the moment that they are conceived and therefore must be allowed to be born: "From the moment there is human life, then, at the moment of conception, there is a human soul, a human being, and a human person."[33] They also say, frequently, that life "begins" at conception. Ironically, the idea that life begins at conception appears to be the only time that conservative religious figures find themselves using science as a source of information and authority. Prior to the invention of the microscope and the scientist-published observations of eggs and sperm, and of the fusion of egg and sperm into a zygote, no one knew how fertilization actually worked. Prior to scientific investigation, conception was a nebulous idea that had something to do with sex, but nobody knew when, or why, or how it

---

32. Annie Groer, "Indiana GOP Senate Hopeful Richard Mourdock Says God 'Intended' Rape Pregnancies," *Washington Post*, October 24, 2012, https://www.washingtonpost.com/blogs/she-the-people/wp/2012/10/24/indiana-gop-senate-hopeful-richard-mourdock-says-god-intended-rape-pregnancies/?utm_term=.b1e8fa9d2f97.

33. Tim Staples, "A Person from the Moment of Conception," Catholic Answers, January 17, 2015, https://www.catholic.com/magazine/online-edition/a-person-from-the-moment-of-conception.

happened. The Bible and all other holy books are silent on the subject of egg meeting sperm.

Conservative Catholics and Protestants, who may not even agree on what God is, are nonetheless unanimous in their assertions that women should not have abortions. Judaism sometimes makes an exception for saving the life of the mother, and some Islamic scholars make exceptions for fetuses less than four months in gestation. But it is never suggested that the pregnant woman gets to make the final decision, if it contradicts what the men in her life want.

Conservative religious scholars argue it in many different ways and from different supposed viewpoints, but they all manage to come to the same foregone conclusion: women must not control their own reproductive systems. Why? Because the men say that God says so. This is bizarre considering the fact that there are no instructions by God in the Bible on the subject of abortion. There is also no factual description by God of what conception actually is. Furthermore, the biblical God is perfectly fine with killing newborn babies! Just take a look in the Old Testament: "Nevertheless, because by this deed you have utterly scorned the Lord, the child that is born to you shall die" (2 Samuel 12:14).

Mixed in with this, of course, is the attitude that giving birth is of no cost to the woman. Instead, the desire to control women's reproductive systems is often dressed up in a fake concern for women themselves. Consider the following excerpt from the "Manhattan Declaration: A Call of Christian Conscience": "We stand resolutely against the corrupt and degrading notion that it can somehow be in the best interests of women to submit to the deliberate killing of their unborn children."[34] Please note that the writers are talking about women in the United States in the twenty-first century. Please note the use of the words "to submit" in that quotation. The powerful male writers of this document are trying desperately to pretend that American women are being forced to have abortions by some nebulous or ghostly overlords. The reality is that women are the ones who are seeking abortions, and they are often prevented from doing what they think is best by self-righteous men who have more power than they do.

The religious writers of this declaration refuse to even contemplate the

---

34. "Manhattan Declaration: A Call of Christian Conscience," Catholic League, November 20, 2009, http://www.catholicleague.org/manhattan-declaration-a-call-of-christian-conscience/.

fact that women are independent thinkers who can figure out what they want and need for themselves. The religious writers of this document are also pretending to defend women. Aren't they sweet? This bizarre document would not be worthy of notice if it were not for the people who wrote it and signed it. They are some of the most powerful people in politics and religion, and they have used their power to control your lives.

The "Manhattan Declaration" was written and released in 2009 by Chuck Colson, Robert P. George, and Timothy George. Chuck Colson was a special counsel to President Richard Nixon. Timothy George is the dean of Beeson Divinity School. He has appeared on C-SPAN. He has written over twenty books. Robert P. George was an advisor to President George W. Bush, former Speaker of the House John Boehner, Senator Marco Rubio, Senator Ted Cruz, Governor Jeb Bush, Governor Mike Huckabee, and Dr. Ben Carson. He has had connections with the Supreme Court, with Congress, and within the White House, all at the highest levels. Religious men with connections like these could have used their power to substantively help women. They chose not to. Instead, they chose religious drivel as a cover-up for irresponsibility and oppression.

Since a responsible sexually active woman will want to bear only as many children as she wants to raise and thinks she can raise responsibly, using contraceptives is the responsible thing for her to do. It is understood that sometimes, contraceptives fail. For this reason, a responsible sexually active woman (and man) will see abortion as a necessary option in a birth control regimen. She may hope that she never needs to use this option, but as a responsible adult, she realizes that it may be necessary.

However, since conservative Abrahamic religions are distressed by female sexuality and horrified by female promiscuity, they oppose abortion. Since conservative Abrahamic religions want men to control women's fertility, they oppose abortion. These conservative religions don't care that their own God is the world's busiest abortionist. They only care about male control of women's fertility.

The idea that women would want to control their own fertility is horrifying to all conservative forms of the Abrahamic religions. The more liberal forms of these religions sometimes quietly accept that large families are not ideal and that control of fertility is a good thing, but these denominations are often considered to be the "light" forms of these religions, as though what they are doing is simply not as good or pure as what's being done by the more conservative faiths. The reality is that they are simply not as insane.

I will state it here: The idea that women should not control their fertility is ridiculous. It is also irresponsible. It is also cruel. Women's bodies are not made to have babies. They have evolved to be marginally adequate for it, and women live through giving birth often enough that the species has not died out. That's the only standard that women's reproductive systems meet, and it is not a high one. This means that many women find it difficult and even dangerous to give birth. When a woman finds it difficult to give birth, that is not her fault. Intimating anything otherwise is cruel. If a woman does not want to have children, she is still a woman and is as likely to be good as any other person.

"God Moves in Mysterious Ways"

The usual religious answer for an unwanted pregnancy, difficulties in childbirth, or problems of any sort is to say that we mortals are not capable of knowing God's plan. Here is Pastor Rick Warren on the subject:

> We ask questions like, "Why did that person walk out of my life? Why did he make a promise to me and then break it? Why did he hurt me? Why did I lose my job? Why did she die? Why did I get sick?"
>
> Friends, I've been studying the "why" question for years, and I'm going to give you my educated answer: I don't know. And I'm never going to know, because I'm not God. And neither are you! Some things we're just never going to understand until we get to the other side of death. Then it's all going to become very, very clear. Only God knows.[35]

So basically, Pastor Warren is saying that God works in mysterious ways and it's not up to us to try to figure out why God does what he does. It's also not given to us to know what God wants.

However, whenever anyone ever uses the argument that God works in mysterious ways (or any of the numerous ways of restating this), it means that they have just lost the debate about contraception, abortion, same-sex marriage, transgender rights, sexuality, evolution, and everything

---

35. Rick Warren, "God, Why Is This Happening to Me?" Pastor Rick's Daily Hope, April 10, 2017, http://pastorrick.com/devotional/english/god-why-is-this-happening-to-me1.

else. Here's why: as soon as anyone uses this argument, it means they are admitting they don't really know what God wants or what God intends. That's why it's mysterious.

If they don't know what God wants or intends, then they have no business telling others what God wants or intends. They shouldn't be telling other people not to get an abortion based on what God wants, because they've just admitted that they don't know what God wants. They also shouldn't be telling people not to marry someone who is their own sex based on what God wants, because they've just admitted that they don't know what God wants.

This extends to the writers of holy books. If God works in mysterious ways, then no one really knows what God wants or intends, including the writers of the so-called holy books. The writers of these books claim that the books were dictated by God. However, by the admission of religious people themselves, no one actually knows what God wants or intends, so no one can speak for God. These writers have no business telling other people that their book contains the word of God. They may think that it does, but they don't know it, and neither do their latter-day mouthpieces.

Did life begin with the first self-replicating molecule, or in the Garden of Eden? They don't know. Did sex begin as a means of genetic mixing, or as a divinely wrought system of male domination? They don't know. Are many forms of sexuality and gender natural, or only the one prescribed by these guys who don't know their God's plan? They don't know. Are women's reproductive systems evolved to be marginally adequate, or were they designed by an infallible designer? They have admitted that they don't know. What's more, they've admitted that they don't have any evidence, one way or the other. Unlike scientists. Scientists have evidence.

In short, if anyone ever says something resembling the idea that God works in mysterious ways, then they should immediately be stopped and told that if they don't know what God wants, then they shouldn't be forcing their ideas about what God wants onto other people. This includes all members of the clergy, all religious leaders, all judges who use religious reasoning, all politicians who use religious reasoning, all lobbyists for any religious position or organization, and all writers of holy books, all readers of holy books, and the writers of the Manhattan Declaration as well.

Let us start all conversations with them by reminding them that they don't actually know God's mind. Perhaps God approves of same-sex marriage and sent the same-sex marriage activists to correct a long, historical, human-made mistake. Perhaps God approves of abortion and gave us brains big enough to figure out how to do it so that we could take care of ourselves and our children in a responsible manner. Since I have already proven that God is the world's busiest abortionist, then maybe God approves of abortion.

If God works in mysterious ways, then no one really knows what God wants. Religious bullies should stop pretending that they do know. Since the religious bullies won't stop trying to bully others, it's up to the rest of us to tell them—and the rest of the world—that their arguments make no sense and that their arguments have no business showing up in an adult conversation, much less in an adult legislature or courtroom.

Nonsupernatural Morality Is Better Morality

Let's also not let conservative religious types be the only ones who talk about morality, as if they are the only ones who care about it. From now on, let's insist that all people must justify their actions and morals without referring to the supernatural, including referring to so-called holy books. Since no one really knows what God thinks anyway, let's leave God out of it. Let us loudly and proudly proclaim that we adhere to a morality that is not based on the supernatural. And let's loudly and proudly proclaim the obvious: that a nonsupernatural moral code is a *better* moral code.

13

A Creative Departure

Gretta Vosper

We do not need magic to change the world. We carry all
the power we need inside ourselves already. We have the power
to imagine better.

—J.K. Rowling[1]

It is almost as though I am an interloper in two worlds. Or some sort of shade that moves between them, never really fully seen or captured in either, my ideas, my work, my vision compromised by their limited embodiments. How easy it would be to explain, to engage, to interact if there were hundreds of communities, leaders, and individuals doing what it is I do. But there are yet a handful, and we remain outside both circles—the church one, built of tradition, stone, and thick, dogmatic doors; the other, the reality-based one, circumscribed by reason and the too-easy caricatures of atheism it refuses to be.

I, an atheist, live and work in the church, leading a congregation in Canada's largest Protestant denomination, the United Church of Canada

---

1. http://www.npr.org/templates/story/story.php?storyId=91232541

(UCCan). Ordained in 1993, I have led my current congregation, West Hill United Church, for over twenty years. There, the congregation and I have created a theologically barrier-free community of faith, if you will, which strives to meet the varied needs of a committed and passionate group of people, many of whom travel significant distances to be together. And most who call West Hill their home would not be in church at all if it weren't for the extraordinary work that we do.

Recently, however, the United Church has found me unsuitable for leadership because I refused to affirm belief in a Trinitarian God.

Meet My Church

The United Church of Canada was formed in 1925. The country's Methodists, Congregationalists, and about half its Presbyterians began negotiating their way toward one another in the early years of the century when the country was a mere fifty years old. The vision was huge: to become Canada's own church, a denomination that would build a Christian nation as the country established its stature in the world.

The UCCan was born in the turbulent times of the social gospel movement, a new interpretation of Christianity that dragged the Kingdom of God out of the heavens, the site of its otherworldly lore, and down to the streets of an increasingly stratified industrial society. In the challenge and complicity of human life and relationships, attending to the needs of the sick, alleviating the pains of the poor, and unsettling the comfortable assumptions of the rich became more than just good things to do; they became the focal elements of the gospel mandate. The United Church of Canada wasn't just about evangelizing a nation; it was about challenging a nation to see and understand that the building of a great nation required a foundation of justice and compassion. The Jesus story embraced and shared by the United Church was the social gospel story of a man who lived and died for the love of his people; living that out in the modern world would, it was believed, bring about the Kingdom of God on earth, or, at least, in Canada.

For many decades, the UCCan built on that promise and worked alongside the nation in creating a society of compassion and understanding. It was the first denomination in Canada to ordain women, to allow divorced clergy to remain in the pulpit, to openly discuss abortion and assert that a woman has the right to decide what happens to her body. Being and sharing the love we read in the gospel stories of Jesus was what United Church members worked to do. That passion brought us to the celebration of LGBTQ+ leaders decades before some denominations even began discussing the issue openly. It has challenged our communities to stand in solidarity with peoples across the nation and around the world when their rights have been threatened, denied, or abused. We have risked choosing a just compassion over both law and doctrine on many occasions and at great cost.

Church Was Everything Normal to Me

I was born into the United Church of Canada. The limestone edifice I was baptized in as an infant and grew to call my home was a hop, skip, and tumble out my backyard gate. Too often last in the doors, as we entered the massive portal to a majestic and mysterious world, my family received the same warm welcome as did families in thousands of churches across the country. Quietly ushered to our seats, footsteps muffled by the elegantly understated carpeting, the family slipped into a gently curved pew, four kids first, Mom next, Dad patient beside the usher until we were all seated and he, too, could take his place. I could find that pew with my eyes closed if I had to, so worn was the path that took me there.

Hundreds joined us as we rose to sing the opening hymn, the choir processing from a side entrance, mortarboards on their heads and followed by the clergy. The singing was uplifted by the tremendous skill and artistry of master organists, plying the keys of a majestic pipe organ. It was bliss realized. The opening music always powerful and vaulted to the ceiling through two stories of harmony, the action of singing was rapturous, the connection with others, palpable. Of course, I've since learned about the scientific exploration and the oxytocin explanation of such rapture, the strength of the bond that group singing creates perhaps used by militaries around the world as a proven way to create the powerful bond soldiers need in times of war. The experience, mundane as it ultimately may have been, nevertheless fixed in me the sense that there was something greater than just me, something powerful and filled with meaning and purpose. I experienced it every Sunday morning and reveled in it. Here, the world was okay. Here, we were one.

As Churches Go, Radically Inclusive Isn't Normal

A peculiar reality about my upbringing in the UCCan is that I attended Sunday school through the precise years that the New Curriculum was in use.[2] Published in 1964, much of it was written by theological professors who introduced a Christianity that emerges as the result of a critical perspective. Under that curriculum, Sunday school taught me the stories of Jesus, but not the traditional belief that Jesus was the source of exclusive salvation. It taught me about God, but not of a supernatural Father who lived in the sky, some great arbiter of a wrathful justice; God was love, the exact opposite. It taught me to be a Christian, but not one defined by judgment and doctrinal assertions; rather, I learned to be a Christian exemplified by the lives of those around me who brought justice issues to the fore, sometimes through great struggle and at personal cost. The stories of my Sunday school helped me figure out how to be a good kid, not to think of myself as better than anyone else because of some superior relationship with Jesus or God. Jesus was the only person against whom I was taught to judge myself—not because he was my judge, because he was my example.

The basic premise underlying the scholarship of the New Curriculum became clearer much later, in both my undergraduate religious studies courses and in my theological training: God was an idea, perhaps even our best-ever idea. But it was still just an idea. When I was an adolescent, we talked about God as a verb. It was a very sixties thing, of course, but it laid the groundwork for the expansion of understanding and the clarification of language that has brought me to the place I am today. And it remains with me as the definition of how I live.

A Ministry Interrupted

I did my ministry internship in Kingston, Ontario, with one of the bravest ministers I've ever met. The Reverend Doug Paterson was not liked by

2. The New Curriculum was mandated by the United Church of Canada in 1952. It sought to bring contemporary scholarship into the Sunday school and adult study in congregations. It was completed and published in 1964 to the vehement opposition of the Baptist Church, previously a partner with the UCCan in religious publication enterprises, which was alarmed by its progressive and contemporary content. Because of the heavy preparation demands, however, the curriculum was not a favorite with Sunday school teachers. It was only published until 1971.

everyone, but to me, he was disliked for all the right reasons. He was outspoken, opinionated, impatient for justice, and he refused to assume anything, seeking instead to educate himself about whatever it was he needed to know. Before he served as my supervisor, he sought a feminist reading list from Shelley Finson, probably the most radical feminist the United Church had at the time, and Paterson refused to flinch in his pursuit of understanding. I couldn't have had a better mentor.

After five years in ministry in downtown Toronto, I was called to West Hill United Church, a fifty-year-old congregation in the city of Scarborough, soon to become Toronto's most easterly suburb. As my family and I drove out to my first service, I was sure that I was going to wake up and find my new church had been but a dream and that I was still in my old church, a place of much struggle and pain. But I didn't wake up. It wasn't a dream. We fell in love, and my ministry began.

Inheriting a rigid Sunday service in which form had become highly ritualized, I began the work of creating a more accessible, intimate leadership style. The congregation was educated, professional, and eager to engage. We pulled ourselves out of a devastating deficit in the first couple of years and set our plans for a vibrant future.

In 2001, I hit a critical point in my ministry, though, and it has been a defining one. I suppose it is what David Friedrich Strauss, as he explored the edges and tolerance of Christianity in the middle of the nineteenth century, identified as the twin problems of hypocrisy and offense. I felt I could no longer speak using terms for which I had a logical and reasoned definition that did not presuppose a supernatural realm, power, or being but which continued to be heard to describe those exact things. If I did not explain exactly what I meant by *God*, believed about Jesus, and thought was the essence of Christianity in clear terms that could not be misunderstood, I would be perpetuating a hypocrisy that compromised the very values I tried to live. At the same time, I recognized that in doing so, I would offend the many who may have believed that in all our years together, I had been reinforcing their belief in a benevolent, intercessory divine being called God. I was in Strauss's crosshairs, an uncomfortable place to be.

It was the age-old dilemma: Now that you see there's a problem and you're part of it, what are you going to do about it? I couldn't un-know that the language I used allowed people in the pews to comfortably retain a pre-Copernican worldview, the fantastic constructs of a supernatural realm, a divine being, and the book he'd benevolently shared with us. And I couldn't not know that giving up that language, one that had comforted me as much as it had comforted my parishioners, was going to be like shedding skin.

So I shed the skin. Strauss would have been proud. Or rolled over in his grave. I'm not sure which.

Obviously, choosing to avoid the use of theological language or the accoutrements of ecclesial leadership while leading a church is a decision not to be taken lightly. Fortunately, I was spared the weeks of "Should I? Shouldn't I?" by the events of one Sunday morning when I spontaneously, and to the surprise of both myself and my congregation, preached a sermon in which I completely deconstructed God.

After that, the rest was pretty straightforward. With my church's board—the support of which most clergy in my situation would not enjoy—we took a step into the unknown and began this amazing journey. My congregation, many of whom had studied contemporary Christian scholarship in book studies for many years, were intrigued; some wondered what had taken us so long. They were ready to move to language that expressed what we wanted to express without relying on archaic ecclesial terms to convey the meaning. We could share what we meant without complicating it. And that meant it wasn't exclusive at all. So we began to shift, first introducing slight changes to song lyrics, then to the way we responded to prayer, to the elements of baptism and communion, and on through the liturgy. Ultimately, everything we said matched everything we meant. We had created the first truly post-theistic church in the United Church of Canada, and quite possibly, anywhere.

That's a pretty good reason to stay in the church. We labored carefully, lovingly, and persistently to create this new form of community, and we did it at a significant cost. Many people we deeply loved found the journey too much for them. But those who left had their pick of communities to go to. Those who were slipping into the pews at West Hill for the first time were coming because they had nowhere else they could go. The safe space we created for them was something many of them had not known for years.

Why Me?

Being the first to do something often comes with the obligation to share what you've done with others who are intrigued or want to follow you.

That's what explorers do: they chart the course, often not realizing their role until much later. I knew the work we'd undertaken was important and those elsewhere who might also want to do it would need tools and not a few warnings. The bleeding edge is called that for a reason. With each step, the terrain is new and one needs to take note, gather bearings, and decide the next step. Sometimes those steps are ill chosen or the illumination one needs to make the right choice comes too late. We made mistakes. We bled. Sometimes profusely. Were we to make the same journey today, it wouldn't be the same journey. We are, through pain, much wiser.

I suspect there are reasons I am the person who had the privilege of leading the brave people of West Hill into this uncharted wilderness and work alongside them to get as far as we have come. It could have to do with where I am in my family's birth order (second children have recently been found to be "troublemakers") or the teacher who praised me for reading aloud in first grade even though I'd just had a tooth pulled and my mouth was full of bloody gauze. There is probably an astrological chart out there that could be construed to have predicted all this. And someone once told me I must have been burned at the stake in a previous lifetime. Whether that meant I'm looking for payback or wanting to relive the experience— figuratively, of course—she never said. Who will ever really know? But I have a strong conviction that the major catalyst of the moment was my gender. Like so many women who have made significant changes in the world, I can do what I do because as a woman, I am primed to see the faults, limitations, and blind spots that exist, even in this progressive denomination. And even the most progressive denomination in Christendom has its blind spots.

Think about it. Women haven't had a particularly good time of it in the church. Since the embellishment (such a lovely word for "bullshit") of an unbroken hymen, we've been doomed to the rack, stretched between the impossibility of veneration and the convenience of condemnation. Who better to address Christianity's lamentable practices than women?

Nietzsche explored the conundrum of stable societies in *Human, All Too Human*.[3] Those who conform to all the privileges and niceties of culture invariably reject those who do not. In a strange sort of way, the privilege of rejection heightens the senses of those outside the circle's influence. We have time to consider things more deeply. We see better. And once we've

---

3. Friedrich Nietzsche, *Human, All Too Human: A Book for Free Spirits*, trans. Alexander Harvey (Chicago: Charles H. Kerr, 1908).

removed our culturally attuned lenses, what we see when looking at the church is a "hierarchical, self-preserving, bigoted, chauvinist [institution] dulled by successive generations of leaders whose circumcised intellect prevented them from exploring beyond their own reiterated dogma and canonical laws."[4] Once you see it, those scales, you know…they don't just fall; they crash.[5]

Progressive communities are always looking for ways to be, well, progressive. Once liberal churches got over the whole biblical-prohibition-of-women-in-leadership thing and started ordaining women, it was hard to stop.[6] Most liberal denominations, and a few conservative ones, have followed suit. But those who have been part of an excluded group who find their way inside a power structure sometimes enjoy just basking in their newfound insiderness. There has been much ire raised within feminist circles about women who step into patriarchal church roles and assume the same stature and presumption of their male colleagues. Assimilation, however, is only one possibility.

When you've come from the outside and made your way in, carrying either your own personal history with you or the history of your people, you're more open to the idea of wrecking the joint. Not only do women know that power structures are expendable—after all, we've survived millennia outside of them—we have witnessed firsthand the damage perpetrated by the exact structures of which we are now invited to be a part. If we see injustice perpetrated by the system, we are more likely to cooperate with the victims than we are those still wanting to work the privileges of the system.

In the eighteenth century, just as women were celebrating their admission to the intellectual circles men enjoyed, Mary Wollstonecraft was sharp in her critique of the urge to belong. She challenged women to refuse

---

4. Gretta Vosper, *With or Without God: Why the Way We Live Is More Important than What We Believe* (Toronto: HarperCollins, 2008), 11.

5. Acts 9:18.

6. The retired Bishop of Edinburgh, Richard Holloway, claimed that the ordination of women—which he supported—was the first dropped stitch in the whole biblical inerrancy doctrine. If one thing was wrong, who was to say it wasn't all wrong? See "Anglo-Catholic Bishops in Great Britain Challenge Opposition to Women's Ordination," October 26, 1989, Episcopal News Service, Archives of the Episcopal Church, https://www.episcopalarchives.org/cgi-bin/ENS/ENSpress_release.pl?pr_number=89202.

to simply become part of the discourse of the day but rather to responsibly mold and invigorate it in ways only women could do. Sometimes, we are slow on the uptake. But change is a patient ally. She'll grant you time to rally your resources, build your networks, garner the courage to break ranks. She has truth on her side; she can wait until you are ready.

When I reached that critical point in my ministry, when I realized I could no longer lead in the classic, privileged, UCCan way with a smug superiority over all the other denominations that weren't as progressive as we were, all the social preparation for revolt that is hatched in women by the obstacles they meet in life broke out. I was ready to make change happen.

Power Rarely Chooses to Give Itself Up

Since breaking with the ranks and working to open ourselves to a different, previously excluded demographic, West Hill and I have welcomed questions from others in our own denomination and around the world. The curious have engaged, asked for details, and copied and appreciated resources created in this innovative crucible where almost everything "churchy" has turned to ash and everything worthy of the human community has emerged, pure and beautiful. While we've been fairly isolated in our work, a reality created mostly by the sheer magnitude of the responsibility, we have welcomed those seeking to engage, wanting to observe, and even those who arrive at our doors in judgment. Our task was not to criticize and tear down, though that was what many experienced our work to be; rather it was to create, to invite, to realize clarity in our common quest.

Despite our openness, neither my congregation nor I were asked to share who we are or the details of our work with our denomination. Isolated invitations from congregations across the country have allowed me to share our story from place to place. But the denomination did not engage, did not send a delegation, did not inquire as to what we were doing. As the years went by and we moved inexorably forward, the denomination and our own presbytery were seemingly uninterested in what we were learning, the demographic we were serving, or the challenge we were proposing. While we appeared regularly in the denomination's magazine, *The United Church Observer*,[7] and every Sunday welcomed visitors from across

---

7. *The United Church Observer* operates independently of the United Church of

the country and around the world, the wider church ignored us. It was a phenomenon of a congregation transforming itself in order to bring people otherwise excluded from church into community while the denomination closed churches at the rate of one a week—and it was lost to them. Blind spot.

Uninterested, that is, until individuals unfamiliar with the United Church or West Hill asked church leaders questions about what we were up to and how an atheist could be a minister in a Christian church. Without engaging to understand, the institution suddenly realized it had no answer. Embarrassed by a sudden flurry of media attention, it fell back on what it knew rather than leaning forward, curious about what it didn't. And what every institution knows is process. Create a process and the details will work themselves out. How patriarchally perfect is that?

Fifteen years after beginning the project that has become the extraordinary community I serve, my denomination, confused and irritated by criticism from conservatives both within and beyond its membership, decided to create a process to deal with me. I'm still trying to figure out why I was so taken by surprise. Perhaps it was because I believed my church to have become resilient, responsive, and ready to risk a radical inclusivity. Perhaps I thought eighty years of female leadership had had such an effect on it. I seem to have been wrong. No matter how progressive institutions may be, sadly, they have their limits.

Of course, a process to deal with an atheist minister didn't exist. The only way a minister in the United Church of Canada can be disciplined is if he or she is ineffective or refuses to comply with the directives of its overseeing body. Clearly, that wouldn't work; I passed both tests. So Toronto Conference, newly responsible for the oversight of clergy, a responsibility that had previously been held closer to home by my presbytery, decided they needed a process. They reached out to the general secretary, the denomination's highest paid executive, and asked for a way to deal with "a female minister who calls herself an atheist." No pretense necessary.

The general secretary, whose mandate is limited to the interpretation of polity, sought to clarify. And she did so with aplomb, arguing that a minister who was not in ongoing affirmation of her ordination questions was unsuitable. Further, an individual who is unsuitable for ministry

---

Canada. A small percentage of its budget is received from the UCCan, but its editorial board is not answerable to the denomination.

cannot be effective as a minister. With that interpretation of polity, she launched a new order in the United Church and brought me within the requirements for review. My theological beliefs made me unsuitable for ministry even though the denomination had actually taught me what it is I believe. Remember, it wasn't my beliefs that changed; it was how I felt compelled to lead with them.

With a newly minted disciplinary process in hand, the Toronto Conference in which my congregation is situated undertook to discern my effectiveness as a minister based on my theological compliance with orthodox doctrinal beliefs, a requirement we had never previously mandated. Eighteen months later, I was deemed unsuitable for ministry in the United Church of Canada, though still permitted to remain active until the time of a further hearing, scheduled fifteen months down the road from that finding. The expectation is that I will have my credentials stripped as a result of that hearing. And that, my friends, may just be the most classic response threatened power ever makes to something it doesn't understand.

So here's the thing. Just between you and me, it may actually be time to leave. And for oh so many reasons.

Bye-Bye, Daddy

One of the aspects of my disciplinary process that many outside the United Church of Canada fail to understand is that while I've been found to be unsuitable for ministry for not literally believing in a Trinitarian God, two-thirds of clergy in the UCCan don't believe in a traditional understanding of god either. When they get up in pulpits on Sunday mornings or sit down with study groups midweek, the god they talk about isn't the Father part of the Trinity or the Trinity at all. In fact, only 1 percent of those who responded to the somewhat badly prepared and discriminately shared survey created by a colleague of mine went out of their way to declare belief in a Trinitarian God.[8] In contrast, over half of clergy who responded indicated that they believe in a panentheistic god. That term wasn't even really legitimate in the decade I went to theological college but was popularized by Roman Catholic theologian Matthew Fox, whose unorthodox views got him silenced by the Vatican and ultimately expelled

---

8. Richard Bott, "UCCan Ministers and God/God Survey," Richard Bott Consulting, http://richardbott.com/2016/uccan-ministers-and-godgod-survey/.

from his church. A panentheistic god is a god that exists in all of the known and unknown world, interpenetrating it but also transcending it. Yeah, I have difficulty getting my head around it too. 'Splaining the oblique, vague, and often self-negating definitions of that idea of god on a Sunday morning can be tricky.

What being a panentheist means for most, however, is that there is no big daddy god answering prayers or even interested in what humans really get up to from day to day. Which is, of course, confusing because the traditional idea of god is theistic, meaning that it is a being and it answers prayers, while a panentheistic god is not really a being although it contains the suffix—*theistic* so could be construed to answer prayers. Panentheism can, like god, be stretched to mean anything, really, but what it mostly means is that people can still use the word *god* and talk about the god called God no matter what they really believe.

Many of those most critical of my leadership don't believe in a traditional god either. Some people fancy up their views with contemporary theological language that makes them feel smarter, often self-identifying as "highly evolved." A Facebook comment by a progressive Christian who very likely has a highly evolved understanding of god, in response to an invitation to comment on a reporter's question about Christianity indicates the level of hostility and arrogance those with highly evolved understandings of god have with respect to those who don't: "I would ask what [the reporter] means by 'Christianity.' If I think she has a clue, I might [tell her]...." There is no patience on the part of many of those who "know" for those left behind in the literalistic Christianity they eschew. Those who believe in god—but not the big daddy god—look down on others they think haven't a clue about what god, according to a highly evolved believer, really is. They also dismiss atheists who, they believe, also haven't got a clue about god because atheists too often rail against the dangers of the traditional god called God in which, of course, those highly evolved believers don't believe.

While I might agree that there are more highly evolved ideas about god, the trouble is that the language is still relatively the same. If you sat in a Sunday service by a "highly evolved" minister, if you were really looking for a different understanding of god, you might find it. If you weren't on the lookout, you would likely find yourself ensconced within traditional language. The progressive theology, the panentheism of the minister, exists almost exclusively in his or her head; it is often not transferred into the rest of the service because the language used in the service remains the same as it has for decades and decades. I strongly disagree that those highly evolved ideas should be given the same name as that highly evolved god's clueless younger brother. Can't we come up with our own label and leave the one that 99.9999 percent of the world's population who have a different clue about what *god* means keep theirs? That's what we were trying to do at West Hill. Ah, but no. To do that would mean a church has to own up to the fact that it doesn't really believe in the god called God at all.

Shall We Stay for the Fireworks?

One of the skills of a very fine woman is knowing when to leave a party. Those who leave too early miss the opportunity to shine while others are fading, and those who stay too long, well, not to put too fine a point on it, but they fade. So knowing exactly when to leave is crucial. After all, an entrance isn't everything. Sometimes, it's the exit that leaves the most powerful impression. And death throes can be so maudlin if they aren't properly choreographed. It takes more than a brilliant soprano to pull one off well. No, leaving on time is everything, even if it means missing the fireworks.

It *is* time to go. The clock has long since struck midnight, and the party is well past its prime. Tattered decorations of a once-vibrant soiree are scattered around the room, the fizzed-out pomp of former glories. Already, the crowd is embarrassingly thin and anyone passing by might catch a glimpse of revelers absorbed in the drama of their own stories, oblivious to whether anyone found their message significant or not. The party's fading, and fast. Time to get out of here before the whole thing is just a bad memory or even worse, a morning after.

Unfortunately, I can't abandon the party quite yet, but you certainly can. Go on. Get out of here. You aren't mixed up in a legal battle, the result of which may leave all your colleagues, several of whom you truly love, dreadfully worse off than they were before you opened your mouth. The ruling created to instigate proceedings against me threatens all clergy in the United Church, most of whom were ordained or commissioned when a diversity of belief was welcome and credentials could only be stripped for reasons of ineptitude, criminal activity, or insubordination. Before I leave,

I want to make sure that my legacy is somewhat less than a disciplinary protocol. Or something more. It seems I have to stay for the fireworks whether I like it or not.

The Detritus of Aftermath

The institutional church is in catastrophic decline, shored up temporarily by the current rise in its popularity in Asia, Africa, and Latin America. Here in North America, Roman Catholicism and evangelical Christianity are also experiencing that brief bump as religious communities stand in as cultural homelands for immigrants.

For mainline, liberal denominations whose predominantly white, European membership isn't featured in current immigration trends, the decline is quietly hailed as a privileged state of grace. Disturbing talk of the superior commitment and theological purity of the "righteous remnant" was already swirling through theological corridors a quarter of a century ago when I first trod those hallowed halls. It has become a more persistent whisper and a troubling characteristic of overly pompous clergy these last few years. Spiritual practices are more pervasive, reinterpreted ritual more creative, the language of devotion more intense. Those who remain consider themselves more worthy than those who don't have the stomach for true belief—of a decidedly liberal and highly evolved sort, that is. And this in the relatively rational branch of the dysfunctional Christian family!

A few months before the American 2016 election through which four out of five white evangelicals helped vote Donald Trump into power, Robert P. Jones, chief executive officer of the Public Religion Research Institute, published a powerful tale of the pending apocalypse in American Christianity, *The End of White Christian America*.[9] In it, Jones describes a decline that, against most popular assumptions, breaches the evangelical-liberal divide. He explores the very real crisis currently felt across the board by white Christians. Fewer than half of Americans are both white and Christian, and that number keeps dropping. At the same time, a quarter of Americans identify as religiously unaffiliated, and that number keeps growing. And while it isn't true that most white evangelical Christian voters were stimulated to vote for Trump because of threats to

---

9. Robert P. Jones, *The End of White Christian America* (New York: Simon and Schuster, 2016).

religious freedom, their desire to influence the Supreme Court, or Hillary Clinton's record on abortion, the erroneous belief that they are backsliding economically—which spurred them to turn out in droves in their illusory quest to "Make America Great Again"—has an element of truth in it.[10] They *are* disappearing as America's most powerful voters, and they *will* lose their hold on the economic reins of the country.

On this side of the border, United Church of Canada congregations are closing at the rate of approximately one per week. Not long ago, an article exploring the unprecedented amalgamation of four congregations into one in Edmonton, Alberta, reported that same city's Roman Catholic diocese was adding thirteen churches to meet the demand of new immigrants. Clearly, immigrants are interested in neither the more conservative theology the UCCan edged into in order to attract them nor the intercultural ministry initiative it has championed to encourage their welcome. At least, not in Edmonton.

Congregations in my area of Toronto, Canada's largest city, have dwindled or disappeared altogether. When I first began my ministry here two decades ago, there were twenty-three congregations; thirteen remain. Several of them survive only because of amalgamations or the closure of neighboring churches. Between 2010 and 2014, all but two of them suffered significant losses representing almost a quarter of their membership over those four years.

Such losses aren't a surprise when you consider the average age of those in United Church pews on Sunday mornings. Some congregations have few if any gainfully employed members remaining; most of their participants are retirees, and not recent retirees either. We should have been concerned twenty-five years ago when we started seeing the pews empty out between December and March every year as snowbirds headed to the sunny south. Instead, we just planned around it, oblivious to the disaster it presaged. With the average age of UCCan members in Scarborough likely in the very high seventies if not the early eighties (we don't keep those statistics, unfortunately), it doesn't take much to imagine what precipitous decline really looks like. When most of your donors are a decade or less

---

10. Myriam Renaud, "Myths Debunked: Why Did White Evangelical Christians Vote for Trump?," The Martin Marty Center for the Advanced Study of Religion, University of Chicago Divinity School, January 19, 2017, https://divinity.uchicago. edu/sightings/myths-debunked-why-did-white-evangelical-christians-vote-trump.

away from being unable to participate, one way or another, it means it's a decade or less between now and the total collapse of the United Church in my neighborhood.

It Isn't All Demographics

When it comes to the crash and burn of Christianity, the predictable disappearance of an elderly demographic isn't the reason. The absence of the youngest three generations is more like it. Even then, presence and absence aren't the only impact; it's what created those two opposites that is significant: bonding. For one generation, lifelong and powerful relationships were forged. For the rest there is only that vacuum, a multigenerational failure to bond.

We don't usually consider the presence of the elderly in our churches very remarkable, but it is. Mainline churches don't scare the hell out of their members or promise them God-given prosperity, so fear or greed don't bring people in the door every week. Nor does pre-Copernican theology, much as atheists might like to think. The generation that gathers in liberal churches week after week does it because they love one another and have loved one another for decades. They were the parents of young children decades ago. They brought their kids to Sunday school every week; they ran the women's groups, baked cookies and cakes, took church finances seriously, and wouldn't dream of missing a congregational meeting. Church was often the center of their social world and the relationships that developed in those times—when men ran the boards and finance committees and women volunteered for everything else, many of them stay-at-home moms—those relationships have survived everything that's happened since. They bonded with one another *because of church*. And because of the bonds forged there, they make church a priority in their lives. It's where they connect, continue to make sense of life, offer their love to the community and the world, and so continue to weave meaningful lives. While it may look like church is the important thing, it isn't; what is important is one another. Atheists usually don't understand that community is what good church is really about. They aren't alone; church leaders don't usually get that, either.

I know, it sounds almost ridiculous to suggest that the most important thing a church does is create and nurture relationships. After all, isn't the purpose of church more fundamental and cosmically more important than bonding? Isn't it to teach the Gospel of Jesus, or fill you with the fear of God? Or, at the very least, get us to love our neighbor? For some in the church, at least one of those covers it, and for those outside, at least one is a very good reason to avoid it altogether. But if a church can't build deep and abiding bonds between and among its members, while it might be able to scare the hell out of them, it will have little opportunity to do anything else. The church I've loved, the one that does remarkable social justice work and creates safe space for complex diversities to gather, that church is the one that has lost the most—and that is because it has failed to create those bonds.

Not Feeling the Love

Beginning with the mobility of the boomer generation and their dislocation from the churches of their youth, liberal churches began to die. If boomers were bonded to the liberal church, all our churches would be stuffed to the rafters because they would have sought church out no matter where they found themselves. After all, they were the generation that filled church basements to overflowing and built the excitement of new, now-often-empty, Christian education wings. Despite all the effort poured into their childhood and youth, for the most part, they are absent in droves, if absence can be calculated in droves. I believe the single most important factor in their disappearance is that, despite the joys of childhood church camps and preteen flirtations over youth group hot chocolates at the skating rink, their early bonds did not last through to adulthood, and the churches of their early adult years failed to engage boomers as they had their parents.

While, like me, many have been instilled with the sense of something powerful and meaningful by the resonant tones of rooms full of voices uplifted in song, the adult spaces into which boomers graduated, often at a distance from their childhood home, failed to nourish them. Boomers were the first generation to demand reason in church, but most services didn't provide them a place where its insistent pressure was welcomed, embraced, and turned toward the work of creating meaning in increasingly complex lives. Uprooted and mobile, few were willing to abide church language and the belief system it represented, both of which were so far from anything happening in the real world, they made no sense. The church, in all its arrogance and doctrinal prowess, refused to consider the possibility that its own language and ecclesial prejudices were the reason boomers fled. Few boomers were willing to discomfit themselves with fourteenth-century theological terms and referents in their efforts to build new relationships. And besides, no one had even noticed, let alone told them, that relationships were the most important thing about church. So they went a few times, maybe even for a decade or more while the kids moved through Sunday school, but by the time they'd reached their late thirties or mid-forties, it simply didn't matter. Any bonds they had created at church were mirrored or more comfortably nourished elsewhere, or, as with too many, never really formed at all. At least not in the same way as those their parents forged through the hilarity of church basement talent shows and the chatter that surrounds a sink full of soapy dishwater.

I'm not just running through all this to explain why no one is in church. It is because I want you to get a very strong sense of the church's almost complete lack of interest in understanding its own importance for civil society. It hasn't sought to understanding what creates good community, healthy congregations, and the importance of thickening the web that holds us to one another. Most congregational-development or church-building books are about bringing people in. But they don't share any reason for doing so beyond strengthening the church itself (or the classic doing-it-for-God reasons). The evidence of the gift church has been to society, and the impact of our squandering that gift, was right in front of us if we'd been interested in examining it.

But the church is so wrapped up in its survival—proved through the careful preservation of its traditions, resources, stories, liturgies, language, and perhaps even justice ministries—that, while it sees it's hemorrhaging, it hasn't yet assessed the true cost of its demise. It feels good about producing citizens who are more likely to volunteer, donate, take food to a neighbor, and vote but doesn't take any responsibility for abdicating the three generations who are less likely to do those crucial things or the creation of a society that will be decidedly less friendly, welcoming, safe. Church leaders do not see the demise of the liberal church as a problem to anyone but them, and that is a tragically myopic perspective. By misunderstanding that its single most important activity was creating community and nourishing well-being as a result, the church has failed us all.

When was the last time you chose to sit in front of your computer in your pajamas on a Sunday morning instead of spending it doing something you love with your absolute best friends? If you are with them on Sunday morning, you'll be having breakfast at your favorite place, cheering on your team from the sidelines, spreading towels on the beach, rounding the bend on a trail with your running group, or out with your binoculars pointing out birds to the only people in your world who really understand such an obsession. People want to spend time with people who make them feel great, and the church wants them to give that up for its Sunday morning program instead of working to make sure they can have both. In the vibrant churches of the 1950s and '60s, it was a package deal; no one gave one up for the other.

All the heightened well-being that religious folk experience comes from the relationships they have in the community.[11] But just going to church Sunday mornings isn't going to do it for you; it's the times you get together midweek whether you made it there on Sunday or not that create the kind of bonds that last a lifetime. People flourish when those connections are many and strong.

Outta Here

So what is the impact of this failure by the church to realize the crucial importance of creating relationships? Beyond the ongoing demise of the institution, the greatest losses, I believe, are to the individual and to the community. There are innumerable ways to have fun with friends, and I encourage the development of even more. Playing and training together, being part of a team, creating something beautiful, or doing community work with friends is always a good thing. But our communities are also fracturing into greater isolation, a pervasive lack of trust, and the rise of personal entertainment that doesn't involve or include building relationships. These are very real threats to our security and our lives. During the 1995 heat wave in Chicago in which 739 people died, the single most significant cause of death in addition to the heat was isolation and the absence of shared community space.[12]

---

11. Chaeyoon Lim and Robert D. Putnam, "Religion, Social Networks, and Life Satisfaction," *American Sociological Review* 75, no. 6, (December 13, 2010): 914–933.

12. Eric Klinenberg, "Dying Alone: An Interview with Eric Klinenberg, Author of *Heat Wave: A Social Autopsy of Disaster in Chicago*," University of Chicago Press, 2002, accessed August 27, 2017, http://www.press.uchicago.edu/Misc/

When whole generations grow up stressed by increasingly complex demands and expectations, provided with ever more fantastical ideals toward which they are driven by multimedia campaigns, whether they are mobile and totally disconnected from their roots or entangled in dysfunctional social systems they cannot escape, culture works contrary to its normal function. Rather than bringing people together, it seems to drive them apart. Perhaps, in our multicultural and pluralistic world, that's to be expected. And it is easy to just go with it. Bringing people together is a difficult thing especially when it is around meaning, relationship, or values.

Activity that does bring people together is often focused on entertainment. I mentioned community work a couple of paragraphs ago, but the number of people volunteering is dropping and, in the United States in 2014, at a sliver over 25 percent, was at its lowest point in a decade.[13] Much of what we do both together and alone, if it isn't work related, is about entertainment of some sort, be it art classes and yoga or video games and bottle bars. Talk at such gatherings, if there is talk at all, rarely turns toward the intimacy of fear, the universality of loss, the examination of perspective-shaking truths, or our exquisite and repetitive vulnerability to beauty. In other words, it rarely breaches the mundane to spill over into the realm of the poetic, or all those places where we keep and protect those things we might consider essential to our humanity.

If we are to experience the fullness of our humanity and lean into the challenging work of creating a sustainable future, we need those conversations. Badly. Yet even if we went looking for them, there aren't many places open to them. Much of the population, prone to opining on whatever the latest outrage, be it political or the personal life of some superstar, may not even have the skills to engage in such conversations. Outside of some really good religious communities and facilitated self-help groups, conversations on the far side of the politically and socially acceptable don't have many outlets. They can't compete with 140 characters of immediate release or the easy diversions we are so prone to habituate.

Often trained religious leaders aren't great at facilitating such conversations either. At least once a week, however, in thousands of pulpits,

Chicago/443213in.html.

13. Anna Bernasek, "Volunteering in America is on the Decline," *Newsweek*, September 23, 2014, http://www.newsweek.com/2014/10/03/volunteering-america-decline-272675.html.

their opportunity to engage people at these deep and crucial levels arises. Whether it is taken up with diligence or shared with enough people to make a difference is dependent upon the speaker and those seated before the podium. I expect there is a great deal of waste happening out there on both counts.

If we are going to address the growing rifts in our communities, we will need to create new organizations or communities. West Hill and I thought we were modeling that in the transition we undertook within the United Church. But while the UCCan may be the most progressive denomination on the planet, it has proven itself to be nothing but a church steeped in its increasingly irrelevant theology, performing the rituals that appease none but the righteous remnant who do not understand what they have lost.

Whither Next?

I'm passionate about community. I'm passionate about defending the planet for future generations. I'm passionate about creating positive change in both individual lives and in the world. And I've always been passionate about what I used to call *God*—the work of discerning and creating right relationship with ourselves, others, and the planet; work that fosters and nurtures incredible power, courage, and strength in all those party to it, religious or otherwise. When I entered the ministry, all those things were priorities for me, as I expect they are for many of you. Leadership in the progressive church that was the United Church of Canada provided me the opportunity to create safe space in which that work, often work of transformation, could take place. I am proud of what I have done in the church.

In February 2016, without leaving our denomination, my congregation joined the Oasis Network, a growing affiliation of secular communities that are coming together to do just that sort of work outside of traditional religious institutions.[14] A year later, just as two others opened in Wichita,

---

14. The Oasis Network was founded when Kansas City Oasis launched under Helen Austen's leadership in 2014 using the model established by Mike Aus at Houston Oasis in 2012. There are now nine Oasis communities in four US states and two in Toronto, Canada, including West Hill. The Oasis Network receives requests from individuals around the world. Its planning process is straightforward and, to date, has bred only success. See the Oasis Network's website, http://www. peoplearemoreimportant.org.

Kansas, and Austin, Texas, we launched Toronto Oasis, a secular community in the heart of the city. We welcomed a full house in a blinding blizzard. It was amazing.

Most of us on the leadership team of Oasis Network have roots in religious groups, Muslim or Christian. We know what religious community does for people because we've felt it. We also know it has nothing to do with doctrine or dogma or whatever you want to call religious belief. It has everything to do with the quality of the relationships you build and the poetry that emerges when people begin to love whole groups of one another. We will keep building these communities, adding them to the many informal gatherings created through online networks of people looking for the same thing outside of religion.

Don't Leave to Get Away from Something; Leave to Create Something Better

Religions have built their empires on basic human needs, longings, and values. When those secondary, religious structures fall away, we are left with what we started with: those same unmet needs, longings, and values. They emerge with an urgency that demands much but anticipates no prescribed solutions. In addressing what religion once addressed, we are forced to engage, seek and articulate common values, establish limits, press for the diversity of inclusion, and so, so, so much more. It is captivating and fulfilling work, and because it is a human instinct to find solace, to seek solutions, to reach toward one another rather than away, those who recognize what is happening are drawn to it. We are empathic beings, and we work best when we are close to one another, feeling our way along the responses that ripple through community.

There are very good reasons for women to leave religion, many of which have already been shared in greater detail in the other essays of this book and will come forth in the commentary and projects that will develop over the coming years. But the only reason I want to write about why we should leave is so I can write about what we can do next. Freed from what religion has been—much of it terribly, terribly wrong and much of that wrong aimed at women—we can and should take what is worthy with us to use beyond religion's dreadful edifices for the creation of something beautiful. Women are creators. It's what we do. We can do this.

The basic human needs, longings, and values with which religion entangled its roots and from which it drew its suffocating strength, are now ours to address. Many of us who have been engaged with religion all our lives know them well: our need to see ourselves reflected in a community to which we belong and in the eyes of those who love us; our responsibility to hand our hard-won truths down to our children and future generations; our urgent need for an ever-responsive, ever-evolving moral framework through which we can negotiate life in the complexity of all our relationships—personal, communal, global, and planetary; our desire for approval, recognition, conviction when we fall short of our ideals, and edification when we soar; our yearning to experience the balm of forgiveness, whether swift or long awaited; our longing to get over our self-satisfactions and absorptions and be awed by our interconnectedness in the magnificence of life; and our aspiration to become poetry. I call these the off-label benefits of religion only because religion is the place we have known them best. But they are fundamental to our humanity. They always have been.

Too many have walked away from religion and ignored the primal nature of these needs, longings, and values. We cannot, in the crises we have created among us and for future generations, walk away without them now. And so, as women, we can take on the responsibility of aligning ourselves with organizations that hold the potential for offering these in community, as well as the responsibility of providing them leadership or support, or we can create those communities ourselves. The Oasis Network is one such organization. It is at the beginning of the work, has eleven communities in five states and two countries with inquiries coming all the time from around the world. If there is one near you, find it and help strengthen it. If there isn't one, be in touch and learn how to be part of bringing one to your community.

It won't be easy. In fact, it's something like the biblical creation story. We can all make little clay figures out of mud, but the ability to breathe life into them, we are to understand, is not ours. Whoever wrote that tale knew how difficult creation is, any creation. A bunch of people in a room aren't going to intuitively manage the list of fundamentals I've noted above, let alone the many others I haven't. But women have the capacity for it in ways that I think are a challenge for men who have been socialized in Western culture. We excel in empathy. We know how to set another place at the table. We intuitively lean toward those in pain, who are suffering, who grieve. We know those things intimately. And so we can create spaces that allow them to be present because we are not afraid; our own vulnerability welcomes vulnerability.

At the same time, the experience of our own pain has given us enormous capacity for joy, laughter, and the full, rich experience of contentment. We can break a frozen silence with a smile as quickly as a child can because we never lose that wonder even though we too often seal it away to survive. And we can turn a smile to a laugh in a blink, knowing that laughter *at* impoverishes but laughter *with* makes us rich. We recognize beauty with a swiftness cultivated of necessity in our multitask-filled lives. We point to it because we are naturally compelled to share it, to ease tensions, to soften spaces so curiosity and engagement may unfold. It softens our own irritability and invites a mindful attentiveness, no matter how brief. We hold, we carry, we create. We love, we live, we create. We celebrate, we acknowledge, we create.

So by all means, leave. As you do, take a look around. Choose what it is you want to take with you. Match it with your own skills. And then create. Leave to create. Apply yourself to creating whatever it is that comes after church, after religion, that we all need to heal the divisions religion has riven between us. Be bold. Be brave. Be its creators. And make it beautiful.

Acknowledgments

I would like to profusely thank the women who agreed to write the essays contained in this anthology. Each of them took their individual subject very seriously and did a great amount of research in its preparation. I am honored to have been able to put these essays together in a serious volume that addresses the issue of the cultural barrier that religion poses to women who desire to be considered equal to men in our world today. A special thanks to Alexis Record who did the final proofreading!

Ali Shaw from Indigo: Editing, Design, and More worked assiduously with the authors to hone their message and to assure that references were correctly labeled and accurate. Each of the authors expressed their pleasure in working with Ali.

A special thanks to my family, in particular my husband, Ron Garst, and our son, Sam Garst, who listened to me throughout the process. Sam provided valuable marketing advice as well. My sister, Kathleen Schwartz, proofread the entire manuscript. Our mother, an English teacher, would have been proud!

Kurt Volkan at Pitchstone Publishing has been generous in his acceptance of my work, and I appreciate the opportunity to work with him once again.

About the Editor

Karen L. Garst is editor of *Women Beyond Belief: Discovering Life Without Religion* and writes for *Faithless Feminist*. She has a bachelor's degree and a master's degree in French and obtained her PhD in Curriculum and Instruction from the University of Wisconsin, Madison. She served as field representative of the Oregon Federation of Teachers for a number of years and later served as the executive director of the Oregon Community College Association and the executive director of the Oregon State Bar. She lives in Oregon.